ARISTOTLE'S "POETICS"
AND ENGLISH LITERATURE

GEMINI BOOKS
PATTERNS OF LITERARY CRITICISM

General Editors

MARSHALL McLUHAN
R. J. SCHOECK
ERNEST SIRLUCK

ARISTOTLE'S "POETICS" AND ENGLISH LITERATURE
A Collection of Critical Essays

Edited and with an Introduction by
ELDER OLSON

The University of Toronto Press

This book is also available in a clothbound edition from
THE UNIVERSITY OF CHICAGO PRESS

THE UNIVERSITY OF TORONTO PRESS, TORONTO 5, CANADA
The University of Chicago Press, Chicago & London

PREFACE

The present volume is not intended as a collection of references to Aristotle's *Poetics* or of incidental employments of his doctrines. That function has been served, very ably indeed, by Professor Marvin T. Herrick's *The Poetics of Aristotle in England*. Instead, for reasons that I hope the Introduction will make clear, I was interested in works which exhibited some philosophical affinity with the *Poetics*, in the sense that they were concerned with concepts and problems of an Aristotelian order. These seem to me to represent an important, and hitherto almost neglected, aspect of Aristotle's influence.

I should like to express my gratitude to the authors and publishers who have kindly permitted me to use the copyrighted essays which appear in this book, and to certain friends and colleagues: Professor Ernest Sirluck, the General Editor of this series, whose sympathy and enthusiasm meant so much to me, and Professors Fredson Bowers, Bernard Weinberg, and Richard McKeon, all of whom gave me invaluable advice. My debt to Professor McKeon I can hardly assess. After nearly thirty years of friendship and discussion, I cannot be certain what is his and what is mine in my interpretation of the *Poetics*. If I have ever said anything of value about the work, I should gladly see it attributed to him, rather than cheat him of one particle of his due.

CONTENTS

CONTENTS

INTRODUCTION

The *Poetics* of Aristotle is the oldest extant treatise on the art of poetry and has been more variously interpreted and more extensively discussed than any other document of literary criticism. One might reasonably be led to suppose for it, therefore, a history of early and continued influence, if not dominance. Yet there is no evidence that in antiquity the work was widely known or regarded as particularly important. Afterward it seems to have remained unknown, except to its Greek commentators, until almost the close of the Middle Ages, when a few knew it and to little effect: and the regnant kinds of ancient and medieval criticism were far from Aristotelian in principles, methods, tendencies, and even general concern. The *Poetics* was the last of Aristotle's works to be accorded special prominence and authority, and it achieved such status long after the reputation of Aristotle the philosopher had declined. Even in Italy, where it had its earliest significant effect, it can hardly be said to have become fundamental for literary criticism much before Robortello's commentary of 1548, and it did not become so in France and England until the seventeenth century. Its influence waned in France about the time of the quarrel over *The Cid*, and in England, about the mid-eighteenth century. It was still to be frequently edited, translated, cited, even commented upon; but its maximal authority was at an end.

Even in a generous view, thus, the period of its primacy in European criticism spans only some two hundred years. At no time was its authority such as to be unrivaled or unchallenged. The very notion of the *Poetics* as possessing special authority was relatively late in developing. To its early commentators the *Poetics* did not appear a revolutionary document or even one significantly at variance with established doctrine; they conceived of it not as threatening, but as illuminating, clarifying, and in fact substantiating such doctrine; and such importance as they accorded it was as a part of that doctrine. Its doctrines were, accordingly, blended into the general synthesis which had survived antiquity and the Middle Ages—a synthesis of elements gathered from Plato, Horace, Cicero, Quintilian, Diomedes, Euanthius, and Donatus, to name no more; and its original role in that synthesis was not a principal but a subordinate one. What Aristotle himself might have meant was, to the first interpreters of the *Poetics*, of less concern than the light he could shed on the meaning of others—of Horace in particular. Thus, from the beginning, the *Poetics* was fitted into a context from which, even in the period of its greatest authority, it was not to escape: when it ceased to be a commentary upon Horace's the *Ars Poetica*, the *Ars Poetica* became a commentary upon it.[1] From the beginning too it was regarded as an arrangement of dicta rather than as a scientific treatise resulting from the application of a particular philosophic method to a particular subject matter; in consequence, statements could be interpreted beyond Aristotle's meaning to produce doctrines such as that of the three unities, and inferences which Aristotle would not have sanctioned could be drawn to provide such theories as those of moral purgation, or to raise problems that Aristotle would have thought irrelevant to poetics, such as whether purgation was allopathic or homeopathic. More importantly, Aristotelian doctrines, isolated from their supporting arguments, could be reordered in sequences which frequently converted premise into conclusion, or conclusion into premise, or both into a mere succession of dicta; and defense as well as attack turned on such arguments as learning or ingenuity might provide, quite independently of their relevance to Aristotelian principles and method. The numerous debates over the important doctrine of the priority of plot, for example, seldom if ever attempted to discern whether the Aristotelian *mythos* might be something distinct from the Roman *fabula*, and as seldom had reference to the proofs which Aristotle supplies. The doctrine of Catharsis could be, and was, glossed by reference to the *Politics* without consideration of possible differences between poetic and political problems, and without reference to any other statement of Aristotle. The doctrine of imitation might

---

[1] See Marvin T. Herrick, *The Fusion of Horatian and Aristotelian Literary Criticism* ("Illinois Studies in Language and Literature," Vol. XXXII, No. 1 [Urbana, Ill.: University of Illinois Press, 1946]), esp. pp. 106–7; Bernard Weinberg, *A History of Literary Criticism in the Italian Renaissance* (2 vols.; Chicago: University of Chicago Press, 1961), I, Part I, iv.

be confirmed by observing that Plato had held it also, without reflection on the possibility that the same word might have been used for very different concepts.[2] Moreover, the cryptic succinctness of Aristotle's style invited commentary, as the corrupt condition of the texts demanded it; and it was only natural, in view of the difficulties that both presented, that in general Aristotle should have been confused with his commentators and that notions of the Aristotelian poetic should have been drawn from the latter rather than from the former. It is notable, for instance, that when Dryden's Eugenius ascribes to Aristotle the division of a play into the four parts of *protasis*, *epitasis*, *catastasis*, and *castastrophe*—a division stemming from Donatus and found in Scaliger but not in Aristotle—not one of the other interlocutors of *An Essay of Dramatic Poesy* offers the slightest objection.

Aristotelian poetic theory has been, and continues to be, associated with neoclassicism. While neoclassical criticism comprehends a far greater variety of doctrines and methods than is generally supposed, certain important characteristics can be claimed for it as a whole. These, however, do not identify it with, but distinguish it from, the poetic of Aristotle. Neoclassical poetic at its most "Aristotelian" is distinct from the Aristotelian in, for example, the conception of poetic form, of the constitutive parts, of their interrelation, and of the unity and whole into which they enter; of poetic species and their status in theory, of the methods of their determination and definition, and of the status of propositions which treat of them; and finally, of the ends or functions of poetry.

Full establishment of the fact of these differences would require lengthy discussion; perhaps it will suffice to indicate simply the lines of argument which would be entailed. At what appears, superficially at least, to be its closest approximation to Aristotle, neoclassical poetic is Horatian. The theory which Horace expounds in the *Ars Poetica* is a manifest effect of the Roman view of rhetoric as the master art of which all other literary arts were subdivisions, or on which they at least depended for their fullest development. Consequently, the general principles of rhetoric could be made specific to provide

[2] See Richard McKeon, "Literary Criticism and the Concept of Imitation in Antiquity," in *Critics and Criticism: Ancient and Modern*, ed. R. S. Crane (Chicago: University of Chicago Press, 1952), pp. 147–75.

those of a given art, such as history or the arts of poetry; and indeed, if one removes from the *Ars Poetica* the terms and distinctions which specify it to the poetic arts, the broad outlines of Roman rhetorical theory become perfectly patent. What is envisioned here is a particular rhetorical situation in which the poet, like the orator, proposes the production of a certain effect upon his audience by means of his poem, as by an oration. The same general problems obtain as in rhetoric: the natural and acquired faculties of the poet and their relation to what he proposes, the kinds of subject matter and the kinds of style appropriate to them, the conditions upon which an audience will believe and respond emotionally to what is set before it, etc., all have their obvious parallels in rhetoric. The aspect of poetry as an imitative art is secondary to its aspect as an instrument productive of certain effects; and the poetic arts are distinguished, not in terms of their differences as forms of imitation, but in terms of the special characteristics of subject matter and style (*res et verba*) which set them apart from each other and from other forms of persuasive discourse. Given the determining influences of "nature" and custom, what the work should be can be stated as the "logical product" of what the powers of the poet permit and of what the audience demands, in relation to subject, style, and the relation between these.

In this rhetorician's-view of poetry, the problems which would be relevant to poetry as imitation[3] undergo certain trans-

[3] For the discrimination of the Aristotelian senses of "imitation" from the Horatian see J. W. H. Atkins, *Literary Criticism in Antiquity* (Cambridge: Cambridge University Press, 1934), II, 75, 79; McKeon, *op. cit.*, pp. 173–74; Herrick, *op. cit.*, pp. 28–29.

The primary senses of "imitation" in Horace are those of *copying* (as in *Ars Poetica* l. 33 *mollis imitabitur aere capillos*), *modeling upon an author or work* (*A.P.* ll. 134–35 *nec desilies imitator in artum / unde pedem proferre pudor vetet, aut operis lex*), and *modeling upon life and manners* (*A.P.* ll. 317–18 *respicere exemplar vitae morumque iubebo / doctum imitatorem et vivas hinc ducere voces*. Horace's infrequent use of the term would in itself indicate that the concept of imitation was not of central importance to him, and the passages which use the term treat of what are, in the epistle, relatively minor matters.

Aristotle has often been charged with obscurity or even inconsistency in his use of the term μίμησις, among other terms (cf., e.g., Gerald F. Else, *Aristotle's Poetics: The Argument* [Cambridge, Mass.: Harvard University Press, 1957], p. 2.) J. M. Gray, "Aristotle's Poetics and Elder Olson," *Comparative Literature*, XV (1963), 168–70. It is curious that these charges should be brought against a philosopher who, well aware of the fundamental reason for verbal ambiguity (cf. *De Sophist. Elench.* i. 165ᵃ 11–13), took unusual measures to

formations. Aristotle's anlysis of imitation in terms of its four causes—the means, object, manner, and power (*dynamis*) of imitation—is not relevant because imitation itself is not here the

---

make his meaning plain. (There are no measures one may take against being *misread*.)

There is no ambiguity in Aristotle's use of the word *mimesis* and its derivative expressions. For his uses of the word, it is clear that mimesis admits of degree, that someone or something may be *more or less* imitative (cf. *mimetikotaton* "most imitative," *Poetics* 4. 1448[b] 7). That either particulars or universals may be imitated is clear from these considerations: (1) man is not the only imitative animal, but the *most* imitative; if other animals imitate, they must imitate particulars, since they have no grasp of universals (*Metaphysics* iii. 1. 980[b] 25 ff.); imitation is therefore possible of the particular; (2) it is also possible of the universal, since in fact comedy shifted from imitation of the particular to that of the universal (*Poetics* 4. 1449[b] 8–9). Moreover, the dramatic method is more imitative than the narrative (*Poetics* 24. 1460[a] 6–8).

Imitation of the *particular* is, of course, *copying;* but tragedy and comedy are not "copies," since they imitate not the particular but the universal. Clearly imitating means "behaving like" or "making a likeness"; the dramatic manner is more imitative than the narrative in that it affords more possibility of likeness. Since poetic imitation is of the universal, likeness involves necessity and probability; for bare possibility, the merely incidental, comes through the particular only.

Man enjoys imitating and witnessing imitations because he learns thereby, and learning is natural, and what is natural is pleasant. He learns through likeness; it is through likeness that memory becomes experience (*Metaphysics* i. 1. 980[b] 27 ff.) and by likeness that the universals with which science and art are conversant arise out of experience (981[a] 5 ff.). The pleasure involved in the recognition of likeness explains our pleasure in simile and metaphor also; for these involve perception of a likeness hitherto unobserved, and the analogical metaphor is the most effective, since it goes beyond specific or generic likeness (*Rhetoric* iii. 10. 1410[b]; 10. 1411[b] 21). A cognitive pleasure is thus clearly present here, as *basic;* here Aristotle differs sharply from Plato, for whom imitations imply deception and falsification in such degree as they are removed from the Idea. Of course this basic pleasure must not be supposed to account for all the pleasure we receive from art.

It should be evident, thus, that Twining and others are incorrect in identifying imitation with fiction or, for that matter, with impersonation. The former is rather a Platonic notion; the latter is much too narrow. It should be evident, too, that *imitation is by no means restricted to art* for Aristotle; for some animals obviously participate in it, and animal mimicry can hardly be called art. It is only when imitation involves *making*—that is, of a product over and above the activity entailed—that imitation borders on art; and even then it is strictly so only when made in accordance with right principle. If not all imitation is art, neither is all art imitation, as is indicated by *Poetics* 4. 1447[a] 14–15 ἡπλείστη. This point has been observed by Rostagni, among others: "L'Auletica e la Citaristica (non tutte, ma ἡπλείστη, 'la maggior parte') . . . " Augusto Rostagni, *Aristotle Poetica* (2d ed.; Turin, 1945), p. 4, n.

central concept. Irrelevant also, consequently, are his differentiation of the various arts, his method of defining a given art such as that of tragedy, the derivation of the qualitative parts of plot, character, thought, and the rest, together with the whole sequel. Plot (*mythos*) becomes *fabula;*[4] character becomes personage;[5] thought, since it is properly a matter of rhetoric, is not affected, but the object of imitation, from which these three parts derive, becomes simply the subject matter (*res*) of discourse. In this collapsing of qualitative parts, the hierarchy in which plot as form determines character, which in turn determines thought, which in turn determines diction, is replaced by the primacy of subject as determining diction and meter. Questions of probability resolve into questions of credibility, involving consistency and decorum; questions of unity and wholeness resolve into questions of the unity and wholeness of the discourse or of its subject. The specific *dynamis* of a species such as tragedy is transformed into the general end of all poetry: instruction and delight. From the Aristotelian point of view, the discovery of common attributes of things having the same matter (in this instance, words) is no guarantee that the attributes are essential or that there is similarity of essence, and in the absence of the formal principles of imitation, species of poetry can be described only in terms of accidental determinations of their matter, for example, by conventions. Given

[4] *Mythos* must by all means be kept distinct from *fabula*. Mythos is the form or soul (psyche) of the tragedy; *fabula* is the *matter handled*. The Horatian reverses the Aristotelian conception.

[5] Aristotle's term for personages of the drama is *prattontes Ethos* character in his sense, is manifested (moral) choice, that is *proairesis*. A drama without personages would be impossible, but a drama without *proairesis* is perfectly possible. Every action, says Aristotle (*Rhetoric* i. 10. 1369ª 5 ff.), is due to one or another of seven causes: "chance, nature, compulsion, habit, reasoning, passion, or desire." But choice is much narrower: it is the deliberate desire of things in our power, and deliberation (*boule*), which is a kind of reasoning about our own actions (i.e., ones we can initiate) as means to an end in matters which, though governed by rules that obtain for the most part, are uncertain in their result (*Nicomachean Ethics* iii. 3). Since habit, reasoning, passion, and desire fall under voluntary action, it is clear that not even all voluntary action involves character in Aristotle's sense, so that a tragedy "without character" is simply one which involves actions manifesting no *proairesis*. It is obvious that this meaning is very different from any modern sense of the term *character;* yet confusion on this point has led to much futile discussion, including the many debates over whether character or plot is prior.

what is, in this view, a basic confusion of convention with principle, there is nothing surprising in the fact that Horatian critics should subsequently have treated conventional forms (genres) as if they were "real" species, reduced the latter to their conventional elements, and, in their accounts of the parts of drama, confounded the qualitative parts which depend upon principle with the quantitative parts which depend upon convention. Moreover, as conventions are a kind of custom, and as custom everywhere lays claim to the sanction of nature, propositions descriptive of poetic genres could readily be elevated into precepts of poetic practice and laws or rules of poetic form which seemed to have their foundation in nature itself. In addition, the injunctions to follow Homer and other ancients tended both to perpetuate convention and to confirm the opinion that Homer and nature and the rule were one.

Allowing for individual variation, we may say that the neoclassical critics, at their most Aristotelian, remain committed to the Horatian view of poetry. The numerous and enthusiastic eulogies of Aristotle, together with the numerous citations of his doctrines and appeals to his authority, should not mislead us. Neither poetry nor imitation is conceived as Aristotle would have conceived these, when poetry is said to imitate nature, general nature, *la belle nature*, human nature, characters or manners, passions and humors, changes of fortune, even ideas. Aristotle's conception of poetic species is hardly involved when catalogues of these include pastoral, which is merely a set of conventions that may be employed in various different species;[6] epigram, which is a form not of poetry but of discourse; to say nothing of iambics, satire, elegy, and the rest. Moreover, *unity*, *whole*, *part* are relative terms, and in address to a correlative so

---

[6] See, e.g., Mia I. Gerhardt, *La Pastorale* (Assen, 1950), pp. 21–22: ". . . qu'est-ce que le genre pastoral?—Le mot *genre*, dans cette combinaison, prend une acception à la fois plus libre et plus restreinte que son acception de *genus* au sens d'Aristote. Là, c'est la forme qui décide: genre épique, genre dramatique. Dans des expressions comme *genre pastoral*, *genre picaresque* cependant, le mot genre indique l'ensemble de toutes les oeuvres, quelle que soit leur forme, qui traitent d'une certaine manière de bergers, de *picaros*. (Une acception plus restreinte encore se trouve dans une expression comme *genre burlesque*, où ce n'est ni la forme, ni le fond qui constitue le genre, mais le procédé.) C'est donc le fond qui détermine si une oeuvre—poème, roman, pièce de théâtre—appartient au genre pastoral. . . ."

different, shift their significances accordingly. Indeed, while neoclassical critics speak often enough of "part," "whole," "imitation," it is precisely the concept of a poetic imitation as an organic whole which is missing in their criticism. In Addison's papers on *Paradise Lost*, for example, each of the four "parts" of the epic—fable, characters, sentiments, and language—is in effect co-ordinate with the other, for each is referred to such criteria as "greatness" or "magnificence" or "sublimity" without consideration of its organic interrelation with the others. To treat a work thus is not to treat it as a whole but as a total, and the "parts" function merely as topics.

Aristotle's view, on the contrary, is that the products of the poetic arts are *synola* or *concreta*—composites of form and matter—the principles of whose organic unity must be found in the fact that their existence is due, not to nature, but to art. They have natural bases; but their existence, like that of the virtues, is neither by nature nor contrary to nature. Man imitates instinctively, and he has also an instinct for tune and rhythm; but while these instincts must be taken into account, they cannot be made wholly to explain the specific forms of imitation which happened ($\tau v \gamma \chi \acute{a} v o v \sigma v$) to develop out of them. The history of the development of such forms also cannot explain them, although it affords important indications of what they are. What they are is imitations—likenesses—of human actions. Likeness presupposes a similarity of form, in some sense, between things different in number, species, or genus, and poems are generically different from what they imitate; therefore there is a difference of matter; and that matter is made to assume a given *form*, somehow, to some end. If so, they are to be defined—that is, their "nature" is to be stated—in terms of in what the imitation takes place (means), of what is imitated (object), how it is imitated (manner), and that for the sake of which it is imitated (the end). These are the principles or causes of the imitation's being what it is: respectively, the material, formal, efficient, and final causes of its being. Since the imitation is an artificial thing, it can have no natural genus or differentia, and consequently cannot be defined in terms of these; but since means, object, and manner, when adequately differentiated, represent the materials ordered, and the end represents that to which they were ordered—that which is actualized out of them—these can serve respectively as genus and differentia, or potency and actuality, or matter and form, of the definition of any given kind of imitation.[7]

Such definition, stating what an object of art is as an artificial whole in terms of its intrinsic principles, is at a far remove from the conventionally established forms of Horace[8] or the quasi-natural forms of Boileau. In these, the universal, the class or kind, is sovereign; the individual poem *must* have such and such characteristics because it belongs to a certain species, as an individual oak must have certain characteristics because it belongs to the species "oak." This is in effect an equation of art with nature. For Aristotle, on the contrary, it is the individual that is sovereign in art; the class of fabricated things has its characteristics because the individuals which belong to it have them. Nor are the forms "settled" or static; indeed, it is impossible on poetic grounds to ascertain whether a given kind has reached its fullest development.[9]

Furthermore, such a conception of art does not lead to rules or laws. What is right or wrong in art, on this view, is right or wrong because it is so in the individual instance, although causes may be found for success or failure and although critical discussion may be conducted in terms of universals. In this respect, the case of poetics is comparable to that of ethics: the ethical "mean relative to us"—that is, the mean relative to the condition of the individual—has its analogue in "the things which are to be observed" in poetics, in the making or the examining of an individual poem.

In tracing the development of a form of art, Aristotle clearly distinguishes between the artistic or intrinsic and the non-artistic or extrinsic causes which have influenced that development; and he maintains this distinction just as clearly in his discussion of criteria. Ethical or political criteria, for example,

---

[7] See below p. 181 (Olson).

[8] See Atkins, *op. cit.*, II, 82–83, where the Horatian kinds are discussed. See also Max Kommerell, *Lessing und Aristoteles* (Frankfurt a.M., 1940), p. 55: "Keineswegs aber darf man die den Bau der Tragödie betreffende Belehrung in ihrem ganzen Umfang so auffassen, dass dem Aristoteles als Hauptzweck vorgeschwebt hätte, den Dichtern der Zukunft zu sagen, wie sie die Arbeit angreifen müssten. Eine Poetik in diesem Sinn ist die Poetik des Aristoteles nicht, auch wenn im einzelnen bedeutende Winke dieser Art gegeben werden, und darum ist sie schon im Thema der Horazischen Epistola ad Pisones unähnlich."

[9] *Poetics* 4. 1449ª 6–8.

may indeed be applied to poems; but they must not be confused with the criteria proper to the poetic art. Just as tragedy is not a thing existing by nature, what is imitated is different from the imitation of it: plot is not action but action imitated, and character and thought are not what they are in life, but what they are as imitated in a poem. Artistic judgment, consequently, must depend, not on the nature of the thing imitated, but on the nature of the imitation.[10]

On this comparison, only the most superficial resemblances can be found between the poetic theory of Aristotle and the theories advanced by neoclassical critics; in all essential respects one is more likely to find antithesis than agreement betwen them; and critics who ignored or dismissed Aristotle have sometimes been closer to him in spirit than those who professed to base their discussion upon his doctrines. Indeed, leaving these superficialities aside, it is hardly too extreme to say that the general development of neoclassical criticism would have remained much the same had the *Poetics* never figured in it.

If we deny that the period in which the *Poetics* was supposedly most influential was "Aristotelian," what measure of influence may we attribute to the *Poetics?* That depends, I think, on how we conceive of the treatise. The *Poetics* is in the first place a mass of words which may be translated into other words, according to our conception of their meaning. In this view the *Poetics* offers a critical vocabulary, and that vocabulary has been influential indeed, even for the expression of concepts which had no relation to Aristotle's. Second, it is a statement of doctrines which, even in the wildest vagaries of interpretation, have proved to have a curious seminal power—a power, that is, of stimulating fresh insight, speculation, and theory; and in this respect it has been very influential also. Third, even if all its doctrines are disavowed, it raises problems which are persistent ones for those who attempt to contemplate the object of art in itself; and in this respect it has had great influence also. But if we regard it as a treatise adumbrating the foundations of a given productive science—involving a given philosophic method which may be used not only to interpret the statements of the *Poetics* but also to develop that science

---

[10] *Poetics* 25. 1460^b 22 ff.

further and make it commensurate with the continuous developments of art—then, seen in this light, it can hardly be said to have had influence at all, for the methodological interpretation and extension of the *Poetics* is very recent.

Yet, curiously enough, this last is the very respect in which the *Poetics* ought to be most influential, and in which it should have its greatest value. That value is still to be realized, and can be realized only when critics and theorists have managed to disembarrass themselves of what may at best be called a certain philosophical naïveté—the naïveté which has led many to suppose the *Poetics* meaningless because they could not interpret it, erroneous because they did not grasp its concepts and doctrines, fallacious because they did not follow its arguments, obsolete because it differs from the trend of thought in their own day, or unfruitful because it answers questions other than those they chose to raise. Perhaps that naïveté will disappear only when we have abandoned the supposition that lies at its root: the supposition that a single philosophical or critical system can embody all possible truths and must be adopted to the exclusion of all others. That supposition abandoned, the *Poetics* of Aristotle, like his philosophy, will appear only as one among many possible systems; but the meaning assigned to it will be its own, and the influence it has, such as will be proper to it.

Probably this is at best a vision of the distant future. Meanwhile, the essays in this volume testify that the *Poetics* has been and continues to be regarded as, in some way, close to the mysteries of art.

The intention in making this collection is not that of tracing the fortunes of the *Poetics* in the hands of its interpreters, but of illustrating its influence upon the literary criticism of men writing in English. It is perhaps impossible, however, to do the latter without in some degree doing the former; for the *Poetics* fared according to what its interpreters made of it, and what they made of it determined its influence. There is some irony in the fact that as the *Poetics* declined in authority, it gained as a critical document. The more responsible editions and translations began after that decline, a phenomenon due not to the veneration of Aristotle but to the spread of the study of Greek.

ELDER OLSON

The first noteworthy translation into English was that of Henry James Pye, in 1788.[11] The following year, the translation of Thomas Twining was published, a work which Pye himself recognizes, in the Preface to his amended edition of 1792, as "of distinguished excellence . . . which, had it appeared earlier, would probably have precluded any attempt of mine on the same subject." Until 1798, those who had only English were dependent chiefly on Rymer's translation of Rapin's *Reflections* (1674), the English version of Dacier (1705), and an anonymous translation in 1775, of which Pye observes that it "is in general as much beneath criticism as it is above comprehension." Twining's translation was to reign until the publication of Samuel Henry Butcher's (1895), which perhaps has been superseded by the version of Ingram Bywater (1905). Among editions of the Greek text itself, those of Butcher and Bywater remain valuable. These editors and translators approach Aristotle, not as devoted proponents of his theory, but simply as scholars.

Interest in the *Poetics*, thus, gradually shifted from a concern with doctrinal disputation or synthesis to a concern with what Aristotle actually said, as indispensable preliminary to a concern with what he may have meant. It shifted, too, in another direction, the direction of what may be called philosophic inquiry. That inquiry took the form of an investigation of problems that Aristotle would have found relevant to poetics: questions of the senses in which the arts might be said to be imitative, of distinctions between the arts in terms of their media or means and the possibilities resulting from simple or combined uses of the means, of the nature and kinds of poetic form and the criteria appropriate to them, of differences be-

[11] Pye's remark (Preface, p. x) is of interest here: "Strange prejudices have been entertained with regard to this celebrated treatise of Aristotle, especially in this country, where for want of any tolerable translation of it into English, it has either been confined to the cabinet of the learned, or seen through the medium of French criticism. To read the works which have appeared in this country, either censuring our dramatic poets for deviating from the rules of Aristotle, or apologizing for Shakespeare on the same account from his original and eccentric genius, a person unacquainted with the work itself would be led to imagine, that the three celebrated dramatic unities, as explained by Dacier and his countrymen, and the bloodless action, and unempassioned declamation of the French theatre, were explicitly enjoined and enforced by the rules of the Stagirite."

tween critical methods and the relation of critical to philosophic method. Such inquiry, whether or not Aristotelian in
principles, method, or conclusions, would doubtless have been
far more congenial to the philosopher than would the reasser-
tion and reinterpretations of his supposed doctrines; and it is
such inquiry that this collection is intended chiefly to represent.

Thus while James Harris, the author of *Hermes*, is committed to the doctrine of "rules" in neoclassical fashion, his
second treatise, "A Discourse on Music, Painting, and Poetry"
(1744), anticipates Lessing's *Laokoon* (1766) in its investigation of the nature of the different media, and consequent powers and limitations, of the several arts. The treatise is Aristotelian in intention at least: it is clearly distinct, on the one hand,
from the mere parrotings of doctrine into which Anglo-French
classicism had degenerated and, on the other, from the qualitative criticism, with its problems of beauty, genius, taste, etc.,
which was in the process of developing. The plan of the treatise
is simple. After an initial distinction between the arts which
relate to human necessity, or mere existence, and those which
relate to elegance, or "well-being" as opposed to "mere being,"
Harris states his design: "to treat of Music, Painting, and Poetry, to consider in what they *agree,* and in what they *differ;*
and which upon the whole, is more excellent than the other
two." These arts use only the senses of seeing and hearing;
hence they can imitate only through the media of the objects
proper to these senses, namely, motion, sound, color, and figure.
The subject imitated, however, may be "foreign to [a given]
sense, and beyond the power of its perception": painting, for
instance, though its sensible media are color and figure, may
have as subjects "motions, sounds, moral affections, and actions;
none of which are either colors or figures, but which however
are all capable of being imitated thro' them."

The arts in question agree in that they are all imitative; they
differ as they imitate by different media. Painting imitates by
color and figure, music and poetry—insofar as words are considered to be no more than mere sounds—by sound and motion.
Painting and music utilize media which are natural; but
poetry—since words are more than mere sounds, having meaning by "compact" or convention—uses a medium which is "for
the greatest part" artificial. Upon this distinction everything

hangs; for inferior to painting and music as poetry may be in its natural media, its actual superiority becomes evident once the powers of its artificial medium—powers resulting from the assignment of meaning by compact or convention—are considered.

Influential as his work was in his own day, Harris has had far less than his due from the generality of latter-day critics. There is however probably more sound and original thought manifested in this little work than in the combined works of most of Harris' detractors; and this treatise deserves to be remembered as an important investigation of the problem of how imitation is possible in the arts concerned.

Henry James Pye was, as observed above, the author of the first noteworthy translation of the *Poetics* into English; he was also a poet—indeed, he became poet laureate; his interest for us today, however, lies rather in the commentary which he appended, "broken . . . into notes," to the 1792 edition of his translation. The chief intention of his commentary, as he remarks, "is as an illustration of the rules, and the examples confirming those rules, which are found in Aristotle's remarks on dramatic and epic poetry, from similar passages in the modern, and more especially in the English poets." Pye is by no means a thoroughgoing Aristotelian; he feels, indeed, that Aristotle would have changed some of his views had it been possible for him to know Shakespeare, as well as the possibilities of spectacle in the modern theater. No great perceiver of subtleties or difficulties, Pye is a man of sound common sense, and his illustrations from Richardson, Fielding, and Sheridan, among others—illustrations highly interesting in themselves —exhibit him as examining candidly and sensibly the degree to which Aristotelian doctrines retained validity for the literature of his day. The notes to chapter xv of his translation of the *Poetics*, given here in their entirety, illustrate the quality of the commentary as a whole. The fact that Pye commits once more the time-honored mistake of interpreting the Aristotelian *ethos* as dramatic character in the modern sense does not seriously detract from his value.

Of the two dissertations which Thomas Twining prefixed to his translation of the *Poetics*, the first, "On Poetry Considered as an Imitative Art," is the more relevant to the purpose of this volume, and is alone reproduced here. It amounts to a careful investigation into the sense in which poetry may properly be called imitative; and in it Twining answers, for once and for all, not merely those of his precursors who had echoed the doctrine of poetic imitation without due reflection, or who, like Le Bossu, had extended it beyond its proper meaning, but also those who have since sought to deny the imitative aspect of poetry. He distinguishes four different senses of the term: "Poetry can justly be considered as *imitative*, only by *sound*, *description*, by *fiction*, or by *personation*." He denies that all poetry is imitation, except in some sense which "will make it true of *all Speech*," and remarks that he is unaware (and it is not ignorance that speaks here) of any instance in which Aristotle asserts *all* poetry to be imitative. Twining argues, first, that for Aristotle imitation signifies fiction, whether in the narrative or dramatic (personative) manner and, second, that Aristotle considered dramatic poetry "as *peculiarly* imitative, above all other species." He is able thus to resolve the apparent inconsistency between Aristotle's statement, in chapter iii, that "the poet may imitate, etc., in his own person throughout, without change," and the later assertion, in chapter xxiv, that the poet should speak as little as possible in his own person, for he is not *then* the imitator. Doubtless it may be objected that there is rather more to the question of imitation than Twining perceives, but his essay remains one of the most thoughtful on the question.

The excerpt from Thomas Taylor's Introduction to his translation of the *Rhetoric, Poetic, and Nicomachean Ethics* (1811) is perhaps a slight thing; but its presence here is justified by its representing a tendency which has become all too common among recent commentators: that of bringing Aristotle into the camp of Plato, to be judged favorably or unfavorably by Platonic standards. "Tom Taylor the Platonist" is far more respectful toward Aristotle than is the later (and greater) Platonist of the same surname; that he Platonizes his author is most strikingly indicated by his apparent supposition that "the loss sustained by the want of the 2nd and 3rd books of the Poetic" is compensated by the survival of the account of the species of poetry by the Neoplatonist Proclus, whom he translated also. (We may remember that for Dryden, Horace had done a similar office.) Since the somewhat lengthy account by Proclus exhibits no perceptible relation to Aristotle, it seemed expedient to omit it here, together with the remainder of the Introduction, which treats of the *Ethics*. Taylor seems to have set great store by his explanation of catharsis, which he gives in the form of a note to chapter vi: the note is reprinted here, following the excerpt. The text is taken from the edition of 1818.

The nineteenth century was, in England at least, no great stronghold of Aristotelianism. One may find many sporadic references and citations, and of these a good number contain expressions of enthusiasm. But one fact is clear: in the view of most critics, the *Poetics* had become a repository of insights, perceptions, observations, to be interpreted ad libitum and picked over for occasional nuggets of profundity. Matthew Arnold's construction of *philosophoteron kai spoudaioteron* into the doctrine of "high seriousness" is one among a thousand examples. Apart from pieces of classical scholarship, however, whole essays are rare. Practically, one has to choose between Newman's essay—originally a review of *The Theatre of the Greeks*, for the very short-lived *London Review*—and Arnold's Preface to the 1853 edition of his poems, or the Preface to *Merope* (1858). Newman's essay was chosen as less familiar and, in certain respects, of more interest.

Newman's essay has as little to do with the *Poetics* as the original review had to do with the work it reviewed. His first concern is to overset the doctrine of the primacy of plot. Aristotle had formed "the beau idéal of a tragedy on scientific principles," but the actual beauty of Greek tragedy is as "a matter of fact" not due to plot but to character and language. His second concern is "to question even the sufficiency of the rules of Aristotle for the production of dramas of the highest order." This interesting end is accomplished by a comparison of the *Agamemnon*, the *Oedipus* (*Tyrannus*), and the *Bacchae*. It turns out that, on Aristotle's principle, "the inferior poem may . . . be the better tragedy." But compensation is at hand: "we will try to compensate for our rudeness, by illustrating his general doctrine of the nature of poetry, which we hold to be most true and philosophical." This "most true and philosophical" doctrine is unfortunately one which Aristotle never held: "Poetry, according to Aristotle, is a representation of the ideal." Cardinal Newman permitted the reprinting of this essay (composed in 1828) as late as 1871, and evidently never saw fit to withdraw it in the remaining nineteen years of his life. The text reprinted here is that of the 1895 edition.

If we pass over the work of Butcher and Bywater, important as it is, as still readily accessible, as well as many incidental approbations or eulogies of Aristotle, the second of Sir Arthur Quiller-Couch's Cambridge lectures on *First Aid in Criticizing* looms relatively large. For Sir Arthur, the *Poetics* is "Elementary." But if it is elementary, it is also seminal. The history of the *Poetics* as he sets it forth in his second section may not be absolutely accurate, but it has its points. His remark, too, that no critic can "disregard or get away" from "this little, unshapely book" was abundantly disproved before he made it, and has been disproved superabundantly since he made it. He is, of course, facetious; but there is more than a humorous point to his remarks about the history of the *Poetics*, and the "three good reasons" why a critic cannot avoid it or get away from it. The lecture moves on to the discussion of subjects irrelevant here; consequently, the latter portion has been omitted.

The remaining essays in this volume are by Americans. This is not strange; it was in the United States, rather than England, that the *Poetics* came to be seen in new and different lights, implying new possibilities of use and treatment and opening new areas of controversy. The question of why there should have been a resurgence of interest in Aristotle must await the historian. A reason often alleged is that it developed as a reaction against the New Criticism; but such an explanation is entirely superficial and probably false. In the first place, the interest in Aristotle was shared by certain of the leading New Critics themselves—notably John Crowe Ransom and Allen Tate—to say nothing of others who are frequently grouped with them, such as Kenneth Burke, Francis Fergusson, and R. P. Blackmur. Some of them, indeed, were early in the field. In the second place, the controversies which sprang up between the New Critics and the "Neoaristotelians" of the University of Chicago—it is the latter group alone that could be said to have *reacted*—had their origin in the fact that both groups claimed to deal with the literary work "in itself"; in a word, there was a greater possibility of disagreement between them, precisely because they were attempting to deal with the same subject, than existed between them and the more remote schools of Humanists, New Humanists, Marxists, Freudians, and the rest.

At any rate, the Aristotelian essays which conclude this

volume can scarcely be claimed to belong to a single school; and the Aristotle who is resurgent here seems not to be a single Aristotle. The late Maxwell Anderson and John Gassner both come to Aristotelian conceptions of catharsis and recognition as solutions to practical problems—the one as a practicing playwright, the other as a critic, and both as men of immense knowledge and experience of the theater. They are manifestly less concerned with their solutions as "Aristotelian" than as useful and true. Kenneth Burke, who over the years has built up, through a series of books and essays, one of the most impressive critical theories of this century, finds the work not only of Aristotle himself but also of the "Neoaristotelians" to be relevant to his own. In the present essay he investigates the problem of the intrinsic in art with great dialectical skill, and in a manner which not merely gives intimations of his own system but which exhibits his fresh interpretation of Aristotle as well.

The poet, playwright, and critic Francis Fergusson has used Aristotelian conceptions fruitfully in much of his work. The present selection formed the Appendix to his well-known *The Idea of a Theater;* it offers perhaps the clearest illustration of his use of Aristotle, particularly in connection with such cardinal concepts as those of plot, action, catharsis, imitation, matter, and form. Professor Reuben Brower confronts the problem of utilizing Aristotle without sacrificing valuable critical achievements of the twentieth century, and asks two basic questions: "What can a contemporary critical reader 'do' with the Aristotelian account of dramatic structure? And how can he translate it to his advantage?" Professor Brower's essay reflects a feeling, crescent as twentieth-century criticism developed, that the Aristotelian analysis might, if blended tactfully with modern theory, result in a criticism more adequate than either—a point very similar to that of R. P. Blackmur in "The Lion and the Honeycomb." This is the modern equivalent, perhaps, of the older device of supplementing Aristotle with Horace, or Horace with Aristotle. Its consequence would clearly be a syncretism, in its perfected form a single comprehensive method which would blink none of the literary aspects, at least, of the work under examination. The positions of Francis Fergusson and Kenneth Burke seem to tend also in the direction of syncretism: for Fergusson, the *Poetics* must be supplemented by a sense of "the shifting perspectives of history" which constitute "the idea of the theater"; for Burke, it must be supplemented by the "dramatistic perspective."

The three final selections—all by members of the "Chicago Aristotelians"—are based upon a quite opposite view. The authors are not "Aristotelians" (they were first so named by Burke in the essay included here) although they would certainly defend the Aristotelian approach; and they do not see the solution of critical problems in a fusion or syncretism of Aristotelian with any other method of criticism. On the contrary, they posit a plurality of valid critical—as well as philosophic—methods, and seek to differentiate as sharply as possible not merely these, but also even the diverse methods which Aristotle himself utilizes in the different sciences. For them, consequently, the *Poetics* lays the foundation of principles which may be developed, *by Aristotelian method*, to deal with forms of literature which have evolved since Aristotle's time, in relation, however, only to such questions as are, in the Aristotelian conception, poetic. More broadly, they would recognize that, still within the system of Aristotle, problems other than poetic—for instance, moral, political, rhetorical—might be posed and solved. But they would insist, also, that a single critical or philosophical system could not exhaust all conceivable questions about art or existence, and that consequently certain questions are best pursued by methods other than the Aristotelian. The pluralism of these critics has often been questioned on the ground that they have disapproved of the critical method of Empson or Brooks; but a commitment to pluralism—to, that is, the view that there is *more than one* valid critical or philosophic system—by no means entails the necessity of approving *every* system. Nor does it entail, as some have thought, the necessity of actively working in every such system, although as a matter of fact members of the Aristotelian group have produced studies in Platonic, Longinian, Humeian, and other methods.

The essay by the editor suggests the pluralistic view in its very title. Like Brower's study, it was one of a series of papers on the *Poetics* given at Columbia University in 1951, under the auspices of the English Institute. Weinberg's essay sketches briefly the transformation of Aristotle into pseudo-Aristotle, a phenomenon which he investigates far more fully in his massive *History of Literary Criticism in the Italian Renaissance.*

Finally, McKeon's study, printed here for the first time, sets forth the Aristotelian conceptions of rhetoric, poetic, and art, together with the workings of his method, in a manner which not only illuminates these but also sheds much light on the confusions to which these have given rise. It was McKeon whose researches into critical and philosophic methodology both established the basis and determined the direction of critical pluralism. In the opinion of the present editor, this was more than a triumph of philosophic exegetics; it was a Copernican revolution in philosophy itself, for its radical investigation of the very bases of critical and philosophic method set the principles, methods, and conclusions of the different systems in clear relation, and made unnecessary, for those who grasped its implications, the adoption of dogmatic, skeptical, or eclectic positions. It was McKeon, too, who established the conception of Aristotle which has proved so illuminating and so fruitful for many of his colleagues.

I

JAMES HARRIS

A Discourse on Music, Painting, and Poetry

CHAPTER I

Introduction.—Design and Distribution of the Whole.—Preparation for the following Chapters.

All Arts have this in common, that *they respect Human Life.* Some contribute to its *Necessities,* as Medicine and Agriculture; others to its *Elegance,* as Music, Painting, and Poetry.

Now, with respect to these two different *Species,* the *necessary* Arts seem to have been *prior in time;* if it be probable, that Men consulted how *to live* and *to support themselves,* before they began to deliberate how *to render Life agreeable.* Nor is this indeed unconfirmed by Fact, there being no Nation known so barbarous and ignorant, as where the Rudiments of these *necessary* Arts are not in some degree cultivated. And hence possibly they may appear to be the *more excellent and worthy,* as having claim to a *Preference,* derived from their *Seniority.*

The Arts however of *Elegance* cannot be said to want Pretentions, if it be true, that Nature framed us for *something more than mere Existence.* Nay, farther,[1] if *Well-being* be clearly preferable to *Mere-being,* and this without it be but a thing contemptible, they may have reason perhaps to aspire even to a *Superiority.* But enough of this, to come to our Purpose.

2. The Design of this Discourse is to treat of Music, Painting, and Poetry; to consider in what they *agree,* and in what they *differ;* and which upon the whole, is more excellent than the other two.

Reprinted from *The Works of James Harris, Esq., with an account of his life and character by his son the Earl of Malmesbury* (5 vols.; London, 1803), I, 47–103.

[1] οὐ τό ζῆν περί πλείστου ποιητέον, ἀλλά τὸ εὖ ζῆν.

Plato, *Crito*

In entering upon this Inquiry, it is first to be observed, that the Mind is made conscious of the *natural World* and its Affections, and of other *Minds* and their Affections, by the several *Organs of the Senses.*[2] By the *same Organs*, these Arts exhibit to the Mind *Imitations*, and imitate either Parts or Affections of this *natural World*, or else the Passions, Energies, and other Affections of *Minds*. There is this Difference however between these *Arts* and *Nature;* that Nature passes to the Percipient thro' *all* the Senses; whereas these Arts use *only two* of them, that of Seeing and that of Hearing. And hence it is that the *sensible Objects* or *Media*, thro' which[3] they imitate, can be *such only*, as these two Senses are framed capable of perceiving; and these Media are *Motion, Sound, Colour*, and *Figure*.

Painting, having the *Eye* for its *Organ*, cannot be conceived to imitate, but thro' the Media of *visible* Objects. And farther, its Mode of imitating being always *motionless*, there must be subtracted from these the Medium of *Motion*. It remains then, that *Colour* and *Figure* are the only Media, thro' which Painting imitates.

Music, passing to the Mind thro' the *Organ* of the *Ear*, can imitate only by *Sounds and Motions*.

Poetry, having the *Ear* also for its *Organ*, as far as *Words* are considered to be no more than *mere Sounds*, can go no farther in Imitating, than may be performed by *Sound* and *Motion*. But then, as *these its Sounds stand by*[4] *Compact for the various Ideas with which the Mind is fraught*, it is enabled by this means to imitate, *as far as Language can express;* and that it is evident will, in a manner, include all things.

---

[2] To explain some future Observations, it will be proper here to remark, that the Mind *from these Materials thus brought together, and from its own Operations on them and in consequence of them, becomes fraught with* Ideas—and that many Minds *so fraught, by a sort of* Compact *assigning to each* Idea *some* Sound *to be its* Mark *or* Symbol, *were the first* Inventors *and* Founders *of* Language. See *Hermes*, Lib. iii. cap. 3. 4.

[3] To prevent Confusion it must be observed, that in all these Arts there is a Difference between the *sensible Media, thro' which they imitate*, and the *Subjects imitated*. The sensible Media, thro' which they imitate, must be always *relative to that Sense, by which the particular Art applies to the Mind*; but the Subject imitated may be *foreign to that Sense, and beyond the Power of its Perception*. Painting, for instance, (as is shewn in this Chapter) has *no sensible Media, thro' which it operates, except* Colour *and* Figure: But as to *Subjects*, it may have Motions, Sounds, moral Affections and Actions; *none of which* are either *Colours* or *Figures*, but which however are *all capable of being imitated thro'* them. See Chapter the Second, Notes 3, 4, 5.

[4] *See Note 2 above.*

Now from hence may be seen, how these Arts *agree*, and how they *differ*.

They *agree*, by being *all* Mimetic, or Imitative.

They *differ*, as they imitate by *different Media;* Painting by *Figure* and *Colour;* Music, by *Sound* and *Motion;* Painting and Music, by *Media which are Natural;* Poetry, for the greatest Part, by a *Medium which is Artificial.*[5]

As to that Art, which upon the whole is *most excellent of the three;* it must be observed, that among these various *Media* of imitating, some will naturally be *more* accurate, some *less;* some will *best* imitate one Subject; some, another. Again, among the Number of *Subjects* there will be naturally also a Difference, as to *Merit* and *Demerit.* There will be some *sublime*, and some *low;* some *copious*, and some *short;* some *pathetic*, and others *void of Passion;* some formed to *instruct*, and others *not capable* of it.

Now, from these *two* Circumstances; that is to say, from the *Accuracy of the Imitation*, and the *Merit of the Subject imitated*, the Question concerning *which Art is most excellent*, must be tried and determined.

This however cannot be done, without a *Detail of Particulars*, that so there may be formed, on every part, just and accurate *Comparisons.*

To begin therefore with Painting.

CHAPTER II

On the Subjects which Painting imitates.—On the Subjects which Music imitates.—Comparison of Music with Painting.

The fittest Subjects for Painting, are all such Things, and Incidents,[1] *as are peculiarly characterised by* Figure *and* Colour.

---

[5] A Figure painted, or a Composition of Musical Sounds have always a *natural Relation to that, of which they are intended to be the Resemblance.* But a Description in Words has rarely any such *natural Relation to the several Ideas, of which those Words are the Symbols. None* therefore understand the *Description,* but *those who speak the Language.* On the contrary, Musical and Picture-Imitations are *intelligible to all Men.*

Why it is said that Poetry is *not universally*, but *only for the greater part* artificial, see below, Chapter the Third, where what *Natural Force* it has, is examined and estimated.

[1] P. 2.

Of this kind are the whole Mass of *Things inanimate and vegetable;*[2] such as Flowers, Fruits, Buildings, Landskips—The various Tribes of *Animal Figures;* such as Birds, Beasts, Herds, Flocks; The *Motions* and *Sounds*[3] *peculiar* to each Animal Species, when accompanied with *Configurations,* which are *obvious* and *remarkable;* The *Human Body* in all its *Appearances* (as Male, Female; Young, Old; Handsome, Ugly;) and in all its *Attitudes,* (as Laying, Sitting, Standing, etc.)—The *Natural Sounds*[4] *peculiar* to the *Human* Species, (such as Crying, Laughing, Hollowing, etc.); All *Energies, Passions,* and *Affections,*[5] of the *Soul,* being in any degree *more intense* or *violent* than ordinary; All *Actions and Events,*[6] whose *Integrity* or *Wholeness* depends upon a *short and self-evident* Succession of Incidents; Or if the Succession be extended, then *such Actions*[7]

[2] The Reason is, that *these* things are almost *wholly* known to us by their *Colour* and *Figure.* Besides, they are as *motionless,* for the most part, in *Nature* as in the *Imitation.*

[3] Instances of this kind are the Flying of Birds, the Galloping of Horses, the Roaring of Lions, the Crowing of Cocks. And the Reason is, that though to paint Motion or Sound be *impossible,* yet the Motions and Sounds here mentioned having an *immediate and natural Connection with a certain visible* Configuration *of the Parts,* the Mind, from a Prospect of this *Configuration, conceives insensibly that which is concomitant;* and hence it is that, by a sort of *Fallacy,* the Sounds and Motions *appear to be painted also.* On the contrary, not so in *such* Motions, as the Swimming of many kinds of Fish; or in *such* Sounds, as the Purring of a Cat; because *here* is no such *special Configuration* to be perceived.—*Homer* in his Shield describing the Picture of a Bull seized by two Lions, says of the Bull—ὁ δὲ μακρὰ μεμυκὼς "Ελκετο—*He, bellowing loudly, was drag'd along.* Where *Eustathius,* in commenting on this Bellowing, says, ὡς ἐδήλου τῷ σχήματι, *as he* (the Bull) *made manifest* (in the Picture) *by his Figure or Attitude.* Eustathius, *Commentarii ad Homeri Iliadem,* Σ. Ed. Rom. p. 1224. See Demetrius Phalereus *De Stylo* II. 76.

[4] The Reason is of the *same* kind, as that given in the Note immediately preceding; and by the *same* Rule, the Observation must be confined to *natural Sounds* only. In *Language,* few of the Speakers know the *Configurations,* which attend it.

[5] The Reason is still of the *same* kind, *viz.* from their *Visible* Effects on the Body. They naturally produce either to the *Countenance* a particular *Redness* or *Paleness;* or a particular *Modification of its Muscles;* or else to the *Limbs,* a particular *Attitude.* Now all these Effects are *solely referable* to Colour and Figure, the two grand sensible Media, *peculiar* to Painting. See *Raphael's* Cartoons of St. *Paul* at *Athens,* and of his striking the Sorcerer *Elymas* blind: See also the Crucifixion of *Polycrates,* and the Sufferings of the Consul *Regulus,* both by *Salvator Rosa.*

[6] For of *necessity* every Picture is a *Punctum Temporis or* Instant.

[7] Such, for instance, as a Storm at Sea; whose *Incidents of Vision* may be nearly all included in foaming Waves, a dark Sky, Ships out of their erect

at least, whose *Incidents are all along, during that Succession, similar;* All *Actions* which being qualified as *above*, open themselves into a *large* Variety of Circumstances, *concurring all in the same Point of Time*;[8] All *Actions* which are *known*, and known *universally*,[9] rather than Actions *newly invented* or *known but to few*.

And thus much as to the Subjects of Painting.

In Music, the fittest Subjects of Imitation are all such Things and Incidents, *as are most eminently characterised by* Motion *and* Sound.[10]

Posture, and Men hanging upon the Ropes; Or as a Battle; which from Beginning to End presents nothing else, than Blood, Fire, Smoak, and Disorder. Now *such Events* may be well imitated *all at once*; for how long soever they last, they are but *Repetitions of the same*—*Nicias*, the Painter, recommended much the same Subjects, *viz.* a Sea-fight or a Land-battle of Cavalry. His reasons too are much the same with those mentioned in Note 8. He concludes with a Maxim, (little regarded by his Succesors, however important,) that the Subject itself is as much a Part of the Painter's Art, as the Poet's Fable is a Part of Poetry. See Demetrius Phalereus *De Stylo* II. 76.

[8] For Painting is not bounded in Extension, as it is in Duration. Besides, it seems true in *every Species of Composition*, that, as far as *Perplexity* and *Confusion* may be avoided, and the *Wholeness* of the Piece may be preserved *clear and intelligible*; the more ample the *Magnitude*, and the greater the *Variety*, the greater also, in proportion, the *Beauty* and *Perfection*. Noble instances of this are the Pictures, above-mentioned in Note 5. See *Aristot. Poet.* cap. 7. Ὁ δὲ καθ' αὑτὴν τὴν φύσιν τοῦ πράγματος ὅρος, ἀεὶ μὲν, etc. See also *Characteristics*, V. I. p. 143. and *Bossu*, B. 1. cap. 16. *L'Achille d'Homére est si grand*, etc.

[9] The Reason is, that a Picture being (as has been said) but a *Point* or *Instant*, in a Story *well known* the Spectator's Memory will supply the *previous* and the *subsequent*. But this cannot be done, *where such Knowledge is wanting*. And therefore it may be justly questioned, whether the most celebrated Subjects, borrowed by Painting from History, would have been any of them intelligible *thro' the Medium of Painting only*, supposing History to have been silent, and to have given *no additional Information*.

It may be here added, that *Horace*, conformably to this Reasoning, recommends even to *Poetic* Imitation a *known* Story, before an *unknown*.

—*Tuque*
Rectius Iliacum carmen *deducis in actus,*
Quam si proferres ignota, indictaque primus.

Art. Poet. v. 128.

And indeed as *the being understood to others*, either Hearers or Spectators, seems to be a *common Requisite* to all *Mimetic* Arts whatever; (for to those, who understand them not, they are in Fact no Mimetic Arts) it follows, that *Perspicuity* must be *Essential* to them *all*; and that no prudent Artist would neglect, if it were possible, any just Advantage to obtain this End. Now there can be no Advantage greater, than the *Notoriety of the Subject imitated*.

[10] P. 2.

Motion may be either *slow* or *swift*, *even* or *uneven*, *broken* or *continuous*. Sound may be either *soft* or *loud*, *high* or *low*. Wherever therefore any of these Species of *Motion* or *Sound* may be found in an *eminent* (not a *moderate* or *mean*) *degree*, there will be room for Musical Imitation.

Thus, in the *Natural* or *Inanimate World*, Music may imitate the Glidings, Murmurings, Tossings, Roarings, and other *Accidents of Water*, as perceived in Fountains, Cataracts, Rivers, Seas, etc.—The same of Thunder—the same of Winds, as well as the stormy as the gentle. In the *Animal World*, it may imitate the *Voice* of some Animals, but *chiefly* that of singing Birds—It may also *faintly copy* some of their *Motions*. In the *Human Kind*, it can also imitate some *Motions*[11] and *Sounds*[12]; and of Sounds those *most perfectly*, which are expressive of *Grief* and *Anguish*.[13]

And thus much as to the Subjects, which Music imitates.

It remains then, that we *compare these two* Arts together. And here indeed, as to *Musical Imitation in general*, it must be confessed that—as it can, from its Genius, imitate *only* Sounds and Motions—as there are not *many* Motions either in the *Animal* or in the *Inanimate* World, which are *exclusively peculiar* even to any *Species* and scarcely any to an *Individual*—as there are no *Natural* Sounds, which characterise at least *lower than a Species* (for the *Natural* Sounds of *Individuals* are in every Species the *same*)—farther, as Music does but *imperfectly* imitate even these Sounds and Motions[14]—On the contrary, as Figures, Postures of Figures, and Colours characterise not only *every sensible Species*, but even *every Individual;* and for the most part also *the various*[15] *Energies* and *Passions* of every Individual—and farther, as Painting is able, *with the*

---

[11] As the *Walk* of the Giant *Polypheme*, in the Pastoral of *Acis* and *Galatea*.— *See what ample Strides he takes*, etc.

[12] As the *Shouts* of a Multitude, in the Coronation Anthem of, *God save the King*, etc.

[13] The Reason is, that *this Species* of Musical Imitation *most nearly* approaches *Nature*. For *Grief*, in most Animals, declares itself by *Sounds*, which are not unlike to *long Notes in the Chromatic System*. Of this kind is the Chorus of *Baal*'s Priests in the Oratorio of *Deborah, Doleful Tidings, how ye wound*, etc.

[14] The Reason is from the *Dissimilitude* between the Sounds and Motions of *Nature*, and those of *Music*. *Musical Sounds* are all produced from *Even* Vibration, most *Natural* from *Uneven; Musical Motions* are chiefly *Definite* in their Measure, most *Natural* are *Indefinite*.

[15] *See Note 5 of this Chapter.*

highest Accuracy and Exactness, to imitate all these Colours and Figures; and while Musical Imitation pretends *at most* to no more, than the raising of Ideas *similar*, itself aspires to raise Ideas *the very same*—in a word, as Painting, in respect of *its Subjects*, is equal to the *noblest* Part of Imitation, *the Imitating regular Actions consisting of a Whole and Parts;* and of *such* Imitation, Music is *utterly incapable* —from all this it must be confessed, that Musical Imitation is greatly below that of Painting, and that *at best* it is but an imperfect thing.

As to the *Efficacy* therefore of Music, it must be derived from *another* Source, which must be left for the present, to be considered of hereafter.[16]

There remains to be mentioned Imitation by Poetry.

CHAPTER III

On the Subjects which Poetry imitates, but imitates only thro' natural Media, or mere Sounds.—Comparison of Poetry in this Capacity, first with Painting, then with Music.

Poetic Imitation *includes every thing in it, which is performed either by* Picture-Imitation or Musical; for its *Materials* are *Words*, and Words are *Symbols by Compact of all Ideas*.[1]

Farther as *Words*, beside their being *Symbols* by Compact, are also *Sounds variously distinguished* by their Aptness to be *rapidly* or *slowly* pronounced, and by the respective Prevalence of *Mutes, Liquids*, or *Vowels* in their Composition; it will follow that, beside their *Compact-Relation*, they will have likewise a *Natural Relation* to all such Things, between which and themselves there is any *Natural Resemblance*. Thus, for instance, there is *Natural* Resemblance between all sorts of *harsh* and *grating* Sounds. There is therefore (exclusive of its Signification) a *Natural* Relation between the Sound of a vile Hautboy, and of that Verse in *Virgil*,[2]

> *Stridenti miserum stipulâ disperdere Carmen.*

or of that other in *Milton*.[3]

> *Grate on their Scrannel Pipes of wretched Straw.*

[16] Ch. VI. [1] *See Note 2, Chap*. I.

[2] *Eclogue* 3. ver. 27. [3] In his *Lycidas*.

So also between the *smooth swift* Gliding of a River, and of that Verse in *Horace*,[4]

—*at ille*

Labitur, & labetur in omne volubilis aevum.

And thus in part even *Poetic* Imitation has its Foundation in *Nature*. But then this Imitation goes not far: and taken without the *Meaning* derived to the Sounds from *Compact*, is but little intelligible, however perfect and elaborate.

If therefore Poetry be *compared* with Painting, in respect of this its *merely Natural and Inartificial* Resemblance, it may be justly said that—In as much as of *this sort* of Resemblance, Poetry (like Music) has no other Sources, than *those two* of *Sound* and *Motion*—in as much as it often wants these Sources *themselves* (for Numbers of Words neither *have*, nor *can have* any Resemblance to those *Ideas*, of which they are the *Symbols*)—in as much as *Natural* Sounds and Motions, which Poetry thus imitates, are themselves but *loose* and *indefinite Accidents* of those *Subjects*,[5] to which they belong, and consequently do but *loosely* and *indefinitely* characterise them—lastly, in as much as *Poetic* Sounds and Motions do but *faintly* resemble those of *Nature*, which are *themselves* confessed to be so *imperfect* and *vague*—From all this it will follow (as it has *already* followed of Music) that—Poetic Imitation founded in mere Natural Resemblance is much inferior to that of Painting, and *at best* but very *imperfect*.

As to the Preference, which such Poetic Imitation may claim before Musical, or Musical Imitation before that; the Merits on each Side may appear perhaps *equal*. They both fetch their Imitations from *Sound* and *Motion*.[6] Now Music seems to imitate *Nature* better as to *Motion*, and Poetry as to *Sound*. The Reason is, that in *Motions*[7] Music has a *greater Variety;* and in *Sounds*, those of *Poetry* approach nearer to *Nature*.[8]

---

[4] *Epistle* 2, l. 1, ver. 42, 43.   [5] Pp. 6, 7.   [6] P. 2.

[7] Music has no less than *five different Lengths of Notes* in ordinary use, reckoning from the Semi-brief to the Semi-quaver; all which may be *infinitely compounded*, even in any *one* Time, or Measure. Poetry, on the other hand, has but *two Lengths* or *Quantities*, a *long* Syllable and a *short*, (which is its Half) and *all the Variety of Verse* arises from such Feet and Metres, as these *two Species* of Syllables, *by being compounded*, can be made produce.

[8] Musical Sounds are produced by *even* Vibrations, which *scarcely any Natural* Sounds are—on the contrary, *Words* are the Product of *uneven* Vibration, and

If therefore in *Sound* the *one* have the Preference, in *Motion* the *other*, and the *Merit* of Sound and Motion be supposed nearly *equal;* it will follow, that the Merit of the two Imitations will be nearly equal also.

CHAPTER IV

On the Subjects which Poetry imitates, not by mere Sounds or natural Media, but by Words significant; the Subjects at the same time being such, to which the Genius of each of the other two Arts is most perfectly adapted.—Its Comparison in these Subjects, first with Painting, then with Music.

The *Mimetic* Art of Poetry has been hitherto considered, as fetching its Imitation from mere *Natural* Resemblance. In this it has been shewn much *inferior* to Painting, and nearly *equal* to Music.

It remains to be considered, what its Merits are, when it imitates not by mere *Natural* Sound, but by Sound *significant;* by Words, the *compact Symbols* of all kinds of Ideas. From hence depends its genuine Force. And here, as it is able to find Sounds expressive of *every* Idea, so is there *no Subject* either of Picture-Imitation, or Musical, to which it does not aspire; all Things and Incidents whatever being, in a manner, to be described by Words.

Whether *therefore* Poetry, *in this its proper sphere, be equal to the Imitation of the other two* Arts, is the question at present, which comes in order to be discussed.

Now as *Subjects* are *infinite*, and the other two Arts are *not equally adapted* to imitate *all;* it is proposed, first to *compare* Poetry *with them in such* Subjects, *to which they are most perfectly adapted.*

To begin therefore with Painting. A Subject, in which the Power of this Art may be *most fully* exerted, (whether it be taken from the *Inanimate*, or the *Animal*, or the *Moral* World) must be a Subject, *which is principally and eminently characterised by certain Colours, Figures, and Postures of Figures —whose Comprehension depends not on a Succession of*

---

so are *most Natural* Sounds—Add to this, that *Words* are far more *numerous,* than *Musical Sounds.* So that Poetry, as to imitation by *Sound,* seems to exceed Music, not only in *nearness of Resemblance,* but even in *Variety* also.

Events; or at least, if on a Succession, on a short and self-evident one—which admits a large Variety of such Circumstances, as all concur in the same individual Point of Time, and relate all to one principal Action.

As to such a Subject therefore—In as much as Poetry is forced to pass thro' the Medium of *Compact,* while Painting applies immediately thro' the Medium of *Nature;* the one being understood to all, the other to the Speakers of a certain Language[1] only—in as much as *Natural* Operations must needs be more *affecting,* than *Artificial*—in as much as Painting helps *our own rude* Ideas by *its own,* which are *consummate and* wrought up to the Perfection of Art; while Poetry can raise *no other*[2] than what every Mind is furnished with *before*—in as much as Painting shews all the *minute and various concurrent Circumstances* of the Event in the *same* individual Point of Time, as they appear in *Nature;* while Poetry is forced to *want* this Circumstance of Intelligibility, by being ever obliged to enter into some degree of *Detail*—in as much as this Detail creates often the Dilemma of either becoming *tedious,* to be *clear;* or if *not tedious,* then *obscure*—lastly, in as much as all Imitations more *similar,* more *immediate,* and more *intelligible,* are preferable to those which are *less* so; and for the Reasons above, the Imitations of *Poetry* are less *similar,* less *immediate,* and less *intelligible* than those of *Painting;* from all this it will follow, that—in all Subjects where Painting can fully exert itself, the Imitations of Painting are superior to those of Poetry, and Consequently in all such Subjects that Painting has the Preference.

And now to compare Poetry with Music, allowing to *Music*

---

[1] *Note* 5 p. 3.

[2] When we read in Milton of Eve, that
> *Grace was in all her Steps, Heav'n in her Eye,*
> *In ev'ry Gesture Dignity and Love;*

we have an Image *not* of that Eve, which Milton conceived, but of *such an* Eve *only,* as every one, *by his own proper Genius,* is able to represent, from reflecting on those *Ideas,* which he has annexed to these several *Sounds.* The greater Part, in the mean time, have never perhaps bestowed one accurate Thought upon what *Grace, Heaven, Love,* and *Dignity* mean; or ever enriched the Mind with Ideas of Beauty, or asked *whence* they are to be acquired, and by what *Proportions* they are *constituted.* On the contrary, when we view Eve as painted by an *able Painter,* we labour under no such Difficulty; because we have exhibited before us the *better Conceptions of an* Artist, the *genuine Ideas* of perhaps a Titian or a Raphael.

the same Advantage of a *well-adapted* Subject, which has already been allowed to *Painting* in the Comparison just preceding. What such a Subject is, has already been described.[3] And as to *Preference*, it must be confessed, that—In as much as Musical Imitations, tho' *Natural*, aspire not to raise the *same* Ideas, but only Ideas[4] *similar* and analogous; while Poetic Imitation, tho' *Artificial*, raises Ideas the very *same*—in as much as the *Definite* and *Certain* is ever preferable to the *Indefinite* and *Uncertain;* and that more especially in *Imitations*, where the principal Delight[5] is *in recognizing the Thing imitated—it* will follow *from hence* that—even in Subjects the best adapted to Musical Imitation, the Imitation of Poetry will be still more excellent.

CHAPTER V

On the Subjects which Poetry imitates by Words significant,
being at the same time Subjects not adapted to the Genius of

---

[3] *See Chap.* II. [4] Pp. 6, 7.

[5] That there is an eminent Delight in *this very* Recognition *itself*, abstract from any thing pleasing in *the Subject recognized*, is evident from hence—that, in all the Mimetic Arts, we can be *highly charmed* with *Imitations*, at whose *Originals* in Nature we are *shocked* and *terrified*. Such, for instance, as Dead Bodies, Wild Beasts, and the like.

The Cause, assigned for this, seems to be of the following kind. We have a Joy, not only in the *Sanity* and *Perfection*, but also *in the just and natural Energies* of our several *Limbs* and *Faculties*. And hence, among others, the *Joy* in Reasoning; as being *the Energy of that principal Faculty*, *our* Intellect *or* Understanding. This Joy extends, not only to the Wise, but to the Multitude. For all Men have an *Aversion to Ignorance and Error*, and in some degree, however moderate, are glad to *learn* and to *inform* themselves.

Hence therefore the *Delight*, arising from these *Imitations*; as we are enabled, in each of them, to *exercise the* Reasoning Faculty; and, by *comparing* the *Copy* with the *Archetype* in our Minds, to infer that this is such a thing; and, that, another; a Fact remarkable among Children, even in their first and earliest Days.

Τό τε γὰρ μιμεῖσθαι σύμφυτον τοῖς ἀνθρώποις ἐκ παίδων ἐστὶ καὶ τούτῳ διαφέρουσι τῶν ἄλλων ζῴων ὅτι μιμητικώτατόν ἐστι καὶ τὰς μαθήσεις ποιεῖται διὰ μιμήσεως τὰς πρώτας, καὶ τὸ χαίρειν τοῖς μιμήμασι πάντας. Σημεῖον δὲ τούτου τὸ συμβαῖνον ἐπὶ τῶν ἔργων. Ἅ γὰρ αὐτὰ λυπηρῶς ὁρῶμεν, τούτων τὰς εἰκόνας τὰς μάλιστα ἠκριβωμένας χαίρομεν θεωροῦντες οιον θηρίων τε μορφὰς τῶν ἀτιμοτάτων καὶ νεκρῶν. Ἀίτιον δὲ καὶ τοῦτο, ὅτι μανθάνειν οὐ μόνον τοῖς φιλοσόφοις ἥδιστον ἀλλὰ καὶ τοῖς αλλοις ὁμοίως, ἀλλ' ἐπὶ βραχὺ κοινωνοῦσιν αὐτοῦ. Διὰ γὰρ τοῦτο χαίρουσι τὰς εἰκόνας ὁρῶντες, ὅτι συμβαίνει θεωροῦντας μανθάνειν καὶ συλλογίζεσθαι τί ἕκαστον, οἶον ὅτι οὗτος ἐκεῖνος.

either of the other Arts.—The Nature of those Subjects.—The Abilities of Poetry to imitate them.—Comparison of Poetry in these Subjects, first with Painting, then with Music.

The Mimetic Art of Poetry has now been considered in *two* Views—First, as imitating by *mere natural* Media: and in this it has been placed *on a level* with Music, but *much inferior* to Painting. It has been since considered as imitating thro' *Sounds significant by Compact,* and that in *such* Subjects respectively, where Painting and Music have the *fullest Power* to exert themselves. *Here* to Painting it has been held *inferior,* but to Music it has been *preferred.*

It remains to be considered—what *other Subjects* Poetry has left, to which the Genius of the other two Arts is less *perfectly adapted*—How far Poetry is *able* to imitate them—and whether from the *Perfection* of its Imitation, and the *Nature* of the Subjects themselves, it ought to be called no more than *equal* to its Sister Arts; or whether, on the whole, it should not rather be called *superior.*

To begin, in the first place, by comparing it with Painting.

The *Subjects of Poetry,* to which the Genius of *Painting* is *not adapted,* are—all Actions, whose *Whole*[1] is of so *lengthened* a Duration, that *no Point of Time,* in any part of that Whole, can be given *fit for Painting;* neither in its *Beginning,* which will teach what is *Subsequent;* nor in its *End,* which will teach what is *Previous;* nor in its *Middle,* which will declare both the *Previous* and the *Subsequent.* Also all Subjects so framed, as to lay open the *internal Constitution of Man,* and give us an Insight into *Characters, Manners, Passions,* and *Sentiments.*[2]

---

[1] For a just and accurate Description of *Wholeness* and *Unity,* see *Arist. Poet.* Ch. 7 and 8, and *Bossu,* his best Interpreter, in his *Treatise on the Epic Poem.* II. 9, 10, 11.

[2] For a Description of Character, see below, Note 6 of this Chapter.

As for Manners, it may be said in general, that a *certain System of them* makes a *Character;* and that as these Systems, by being *differently compounded,* make each a *different* Character, so it is that *one* Man *truly differs* from *another.*

Passions are obvious; *Pity, Fear, Anger,* etc.

Sentiments are discoverable in all those Things, which are the *proper Business and End of* Speech *or* Discourse. The chief Branches of this *End* are to *Assert* and *Prove;* to *Solve* and *Refute;* to express or excite *Passions;* to *amplify* Incidents, and to *diminish* them. It is in these things therefore, that we must look for *Sentiment.* See *Arist. Poet.* c. 19.—ἔστι δὲ κατὰ τὴν διάνοιαν ταῦτα ὅσα ὑπὸ τοῦ λόγου δεῖ παρασκευασθῆναι. Μέρη δε τούτων τό τε ἀποδεικνύναι καὶ τὸ λύειν καὶ τὸ πάθη παρασκευάζειν,—καὶ ἔτι μέγεθος καὶ μικρότητα.

The *Merit* of these Subjects is obvious. They must necessarily of all be the most *affecting;* the most *improving;* and such of which the Mind has the *strongest Comprehension*.

For as to the *affecting Part*—if it be true, that all *Events* more or less *affect* us, as the *Subjects*, which they respect, are more or less nearly *related* to us; then surely those *Events* must needs be *most affecting*, to whose *Subjects* we are of all the *most intimately related*. Now such is the Relation, which we bear to *Mankind;* and Men and Human Actions are the Subjects, here proposed for Imitation.

As to *Improvement*—there can be none surely (to *Man* at least) so great, as that which is derived from a just and decent Representation of *Human Manners*, and *Sentiments*. For what can more contribute to give us that *Master-Knowledge*,[3] without which, *all other* Knowledge will prove of little or no Utility.

As to our *Comprehension*—there is nothing certainly, of which we have so *strong* Ideas, as of that which happens in the

[3] ΓΝΩΘΙ ΣΑΥΤΟΝ. But farther, besides obtaining this *moral Science* from the Contemplation of Human Life; an End *common* both to Epic, Tragic, and Comic Poetry: there is a *peculiar* End to *Tragedy*, that of eradicating the Passions of *Pity* and *Fear*. Ἔστιν οὖν τραγῳδία μίμησις πράξεως σπουδαίας—δι' ἐλέου καὶ φόβου περαίνουσα τὴν τῶν τοιούτων παθημάτων κάθαρσιν. Arist. Poet. c. 6. Tragedy *is the Imitation of an Action important and perfect, thro'* Pity *and* Fear *working the* Purgation *of such-like Passions*.

There are none, it is evident, so devoid of these two *Passions*, as those *perpetually conversant*, where the *Occasions* of them are most *frequent;* such, for instance, as the *Military* Men, the Professors of *Medicine*, *Chirurgery*, and the like. Their Minds, by this Intercourse, become as it were *callous;* gaining an *Apathy* by *Experience*, which no *Theory* can ever teach them.

Now that, which is wrought in *these* Men by the *real Disasters of Life*, may be supposed wrought in others by the *Fictions of Tragedy;* yet with this happy Circumstance in favour of Tragedy, that, without the Disasters being *real*, it can obtain the *same* End.

It must however, for all this, be confessed, that an Effect of this kind cannot reasonably be expected, except among Nations, like the *Athenians* of old, who lived in a perpetual Attendance upon these Theatrical Representations. For it is not a *single* or *occasional* Application to these Passions, but a *constant* and *uninterrupted*, by which alone they may be lessened or removed.

It would be improper to conclude this Note, without observing, that the Philosopher in this place by Pity means not Philanthropy, *Natural Affection, a Readiness to relieve others in their Calamities and Distress;* but, by *Pity*, he means that Senseless Effeminate Consternation, *which seizes weak Minds, on the sudden Prospect of any thing disastrous;* which, in its more violent Effects, is seen in *Shriekings, Swoonings*, etc., a Passion, so far from laudable, or from operating to the Good of others, that it is certain to deprive the Party, who labours under its Influence, of all Capacity *to do the least good Office*.

Moral or *Human* World. For as to the *Internal Part*, or *Active Principle* of the *Vegetable*, we know it but *obscurely*; because there we can discover neither *Passion*, nor *Sensation*. In the *Animal* World indeed this *Principle* is more seen, and that from the *Passions* and *Sensations* which *there* declare themselves. Yet all still rests upon the mere Evidence of *Sense*; upon the Force only of *external* and *unassisted Experience*. But in the *Moral* or *Human* World, as we have a Medium of *Knowledge* far more *accurate* than this; so from hence it is, that we can comprehend *accordingly*.

With regard therefore to the various *Events* which happen *here*, and the various *Causes*, by which they are produced—in other Words, of all Characters, Manners, Human Passions, and Sentiments; besides the Evidence of *Sense*, we have the *highest Evidence additional*, in having an express *Consciousness* of something *similar within*; of something *homogeneous* in the Recesses of our own *Minds*; in that, which constitutes to each of us *his true and real Self*.

These therefore being the Subjects, *not adapted to the Genius of Painting*, it comes next to be considered, *how far Poetry can imitate them*.

And here, that it has *Abilities* clearly *equal*, cannot be doubted; as it has *that* for the *Medium* of its Imitation, through which *Nature* declares herself in the *same* Subjects. For the *Sentiments* in *real Life* are only known by Men's *Discourse*.[4] And the *Characters, Manners*, and *Passions* of Men being the *Prompters* to what they *say*; it must needs follow, that their *Discourse* will be a *constant Specimen* of those *Characters, Manners*, and *Passions*.

> *Format enim Natura prius nos intus ad omnem*
> *Fortunarum habitum; juvat, aut impellit ad iram:*
> *Post* effert Animi Motus, Interprete Lingua.[5]

Not only therefore *Language* is an *adequate Medium* of Imitation, but in *Sentiments* it is the *only* Medium; and in *Manners* and *Passions* there is no other, which can exhibit them to us after that *clear, precise*, and *definite Way*, as they in *Nature* stand allotted to the various sorts of Men, and are found to constitute the *several Characters* of each.[6]

---

[4] P. 12, *Note* 2.   [5] *Hor. de Arte Poet.* vers. 108.

[6] It is true indeed that (besides what is done by *Poetry*) there is some Idea of *Character*, which even *Painting* can communicate. Thus there is no doubt, but

To *compare* therefore *Poetry*, in *these Subjects*, with Painting—In as much as no Subjects of Painting[7] are *wholly superior* to Poetry; while the Subjects, here described, *far exceed the Power* of Painting—in as much as they are of *all* Subjects the most *affecting*, and *improving*, and such[8] of which we have the *strongest Comprehension*—further, in as much as Poetry can *most accurately* imitate[9] them—in as much as, besides all Imitation, there is a *Charm* in Poetry, arising from its very *Numbers*[10]; whereas Painting has Pretence to no Charm, except that of Imitation only—lastly, (which will soon be shewn[11]) in as much as Poetry is able to *associate Music*, as a most powerful Ally; of which Assistance, Painting is utterly

---

that such a *Countenance* may be found by *Painters* for *Aeneas*, as would convey upon view a *mild, humane*, and yet a *brave* Disposition. But then this Idea would be *vague* and *general*. It would be concluded, only in the gross, that the Hero was *Good*. As to that System of Qualities *peculiar to Aeneas* only, and which alone *properly constitutes his true and real Character*, this would still remain a Secret, and be no way discoverable. For how deduce it from the mere *Lineaments* of a Countenance? Or, if it were deducible, how few Spectators would there be found so sagacious? It is here, therefore, that Recourse must be had, not to *Painting*, but to *Poetry*. So *accurate* a Conception of Character can be gathered only from a *Succession of various, and yet consistent Actions;* a Succession, *enabling us to conjecture*, what the Person of the Drama will do in the *future*, from what already he has done in the *past*. Now to such an Imitation, Poetry only is *equal;* because it is not *bounded, like Painting*, to *short*, and as it were, *instant* Events, but may imitate Subjects of *any Duration whatever*. See *Arist. Poet.* cap. 6. Ἔστιν δὲ ἦθος μὲν τὸ τοιοῦτον ὃ δηλοῖ τὴν προαίρεσιν ὁποιά τις ἐν οἷς οὐκ ἔστι δῆλον ἢ προαιρεῖται ἢ φεύγει ὁ λέγων. See also the ingenious and learned Bossu, *Traité du poeme épique* Book 4. ch. 4.

[7] Pp. 2, 3, 9, 10.   [8] Pp. 13 ff.   [9] Pp. 14 ff.

[10] That there is a *Charm* in *Poetry*, arising from its *Numbers* only, may be made evident from the five or six first Lines of the *Paradise Lost;* where, without any Pomp of Phrase, Sublimity of Sentiment, or the *least Degree of Imitation*, every Reader must find himself to be sensibly delighted; and that, only from the graceful and simple *Cadence* of the *Numbers*, and that artful *Variation* of the *Caesura* or *Pause*, so essential to the Harmony of every good Poem.

An *English Heroic* Verse consists of ten *Semipeds*, or Half-feet. Now in the Lines above-mentioned the *Pauses* are varied upon *different* Semipeds in the Order, which follows; as may be seen by any, who will be at the Pains to examine.

Paradise Lost, Book I.

Verse			Semiped
1			7
2			6
3	has its Pause		6
4	fall upon		5
5			3
6			4

[11] *Chap.* VI.

incapable; from all this it may be fairly concluded, that—Poetry *is not only Equal, but that it is in fact* far Superior to its Sister Art of Painting.

But if it exceed *Painting* in *Subjects,* to which Painting is *not adapted;* no doubt *will it exceed* Music in *Subjects* to Music *not adapted.* For *here* it has been *preferred,*[12] even in those Subjects, which have been held *adapted the best of all.*

Poetry is therefore, on the whole much superior to either of the other Mimetic Arts; *it having been shewn to be equally excellent* in the Accuracy[13] of its Imitation; *and to imitate* Subjects, which far surpass, as well in[14] Utility, as in Dignity.[15]

CHAPTER VI

On Music considered not as an Imitation, but as deriving its Efficacy from another Source.—On its joint Operation by this means with Poetry. —An Objection to Music solved. —The Advantage arising to it, as well as to Poetry, from their being united.—Conclusion.

In the above Discourse, Music has been mentioned as an *Ally*[1] to Poetry. It has also been said to derive its *Efficacy*[2] from *another Source,* than *Imitation.* It remains, therefore, that these things be explained.

Now, in order to this, it is first to be observed, that there are various *Affections,* which may be raised by the Power of *Music.* There are Sounds to make us *chearful,* or *sad; martial,* or *tender;* and so of almost every other Affection, which we feel.

It is also further observable, that there is a *reciprocal Operation* between our *Affections,* and our *Ideas; so* that, by a sort of *natural Sympathy,* certain *Ideas* necessarily tend to raise in us certain *Affections;* and those *Affections,* by a sort of Counter-Operation, to raise the *same Ideas.* Thus *Ideas* derived from Funerals, Tortures, Murders, and the like, naturally generate the Affection of *Melancholy.* And when, by any *Physical*

---

[12] *Ch.* IV.   [13] P. 14.   [14] P. 13.
[15] *See* pp. 12, 13 *and* p. 5, *Note* 8. *See also* p. 3.
[1] P. 15.   P. 7.

Causes, that *Affection* happens to prevail, it as naturally generates the same *doleful Ideas.*

And hence it is, that *Ideas,* derived from *external* Causes, have at *different* times, upon the *same* Person, so *different* an Effect. If they happen to suit the Affections, which *prevail within,* then is their Impression *most sensible,* and their Effect *most lasting.* If the contrary be true, then is the Effect contrary. Thus, for instance, a Funeral will much more affect the same Man, if he see it when melancholy, than if he see it when chearful.

Now this being premised, it will follow, that whatever happens to be the *Affection* or *Disposition* of Mind, which ought naturally to result from the Genius of any *Poem,* the *same* probably it will be in the Power of some Species of *Music* to excite. But whenever the *proper Affection* prevails, it has been allowed that then *all kindred Ideas,* derived from external Causes, make the *most sensible Impression.* The Ideas therefore of Poetry must needs make the most sensible Impression, when the Affections,[2] peculiar to them, are already excited by the Music. For here a *double Force is made co-operate to one End.* A Poet, *thus assisted,* finds not an Audience in a Temper, averse to the Genius of his Poem, or perhaps at best under a cool *Indifference;* but by the Preludes, the Symphonies, and *concurrent Operation* of the Music in all its Parts, rouzed into *those very Affections,* which he would most desire.

An Audience, so disposed, not only embrace with Pleasure the Ideas of the Poet, when exhibited; but, in a manner, even *anticipate* them in their several Imaginations. The Superstitious have not a more previous Tendency to be frightened at the sight of Spectres, or a Lover to fall into Raptures at the fight of his Mistress; than a Mind, thus tempered by the Power of Music, to enjoy all Ideas, which are suitable to that Temper.

And hence the *genuine* Charm of Music, and the *Wonders* which it works, thro' its great Professors.[3] A Power, which

---

[2] Quintilian elegantly, and exactly apposite to this Reasoning, says of *Music* —*Namque et voce et modulatione grandia elatè, jucunda dulciter, moderata leniter canit, totâque arte* consentit cum eorum, quae dicuntur, Affectibus. *Institutio Oratoria.* l. 1. cap. 10.

[3] Such, above all, is *George Frederick Handel;* whose Genius, having been cultivated by continued Exercise, and being itself far the sublimest and most universal now known, has justly placed him without an Equal, or a Second. This transient Testimony could not be denied so excellent an Artist, from

consists not in Imitations, and the raising *Ideas*[4]; but in the raising *Affections*, to which Ideas may correspond. There are few to be found so insensible, I may even say so inhumane, as when good Poetry is justly set to Music, not in some degree to feel the Force of so *amiable an Union*. But to the Muses Friends it is a Force *irresistible*, and penetrates into the deepest Recesses of the Soul.

> — *Pectus inaniter angit,*
> *Irritat, mulcet, falsis terroribus implet.*[5]

Now this is *that Source*, from whence Music was said formerly *to derive its greatest Efficacy*.[6] And here indeed, not in Imitation, ought it to be chiefly cultivated. On this account also it has been called a *powerful Ally*[7] to Poetry. And farther, it is by the help of this Reasoning, that the *Objection* is solved, which is raised against the *Singing of Poetry* (as in Opera's, Oratorio's, etc.) from the want of *Probability* and *Resemblance to Nature*. To one indeed, who has no musical Ear, this Objection may have Weight. It may even perplex a Lover of Music, if it happen to surprise him in his Hours of *Indifference*. But when he is feeling the Charm of Poetry *so accompanied*, let him be angry (if he can) with that which serves only to interest him *more feelingly* in the Subject, and support him in a *stronger* and *more earnest* Attention; which enforces, by its Aid, the several Ideas of the Poem, and gives them to his Imagination with unusual Strength and Grandeur. He cannot surely but confess, that he is a *Gainer in the Exchange*, when he *barters* the want of a single Probability, that of *Pronunciation* (a thing merely arbitrary and every where different) for a *noble Heightening of Affections* which are suitable to the Occasion, and enable him to enter into the Subject with double *Energy* and *Enjoyment*.

From what has been said it is evident, that these two Arts can never be so powerful *singly*, as when they are *properly united*. For *Poetry*, when alone, must be necessarily forced to *waste*

---

whom this Treatise has borrowed such eminent Examples, to justify its Assertions in what it has offered concerning Music.

[4] For the *narrow* Extent and *little* Efficacy of Music, considered as a Mimetic or Imitative Art, see Ch. II.

[5] Horace *Epistle* 1. l. 2. vers. 211.

[6] P. 6.   [7] P. 15.

many of its richest *Ideas*, in the mere raising of Affections, when, to have been properly relished, it should have *found* those Affections in their highest Energy. And *Music*, when alone, can only raise *Affections*, which soon *languish* and *decay*, if not maintained and fed by the nutritive Images of Poetry. Yet must it be remembered, in this Union, that *Poetry* ever have the *Precedence;* its *utility*,[8] as well as *Dignity*, being by far the more considerable.

And thus much, for the present, as to Music, Painting, and Poetry,[9] the Circumstances, in which they *agree*, and in which they *differ;* and the Preference, due to one of them above the other two.

[8] Ch. V. p. 12.   [9] P. 1.

19

II

HENRY JAMES PYE

From A Commentary on the Poetic of Aristotle
Notes to Chapter XV

NOTE I

In forming the manners four things are to be attended to.
The first and most essential is, that they should be good.

Before I enter on the particular passage which is the more
immediate subject of this note, I cannot avoid remarking the
superiority of the dramatic writer, from which we may draw
our examples, to any that the author of the *Poetic* could have
recourse to. In regard to fable, as Shakespeare was seldom an
original inventor, so he was not scrupulously nice in his choice;
and as to his arrangement of those subjects which he took for
the ground-work of his dramas so as to produce the best tragic
effect, his most sanguine admirers must allow that he has seldom
studied it much in the general conduct of the fable, though he
has frequently done it in particular parts; and wherever he has
done it, he is, as in every other respect, inimitable.

But in painting manners, he stands alone and unrivaled: to use
the words of the author[1] of the essay on the dramatic character
of Sir John Falstaff:

The reader must be sensible of something in the composition of
Shakespear's characters, which renders them essentially different
from those drawn by other writers. The characters of every drama
must indeed be grouped; but in the groups of other poets, the parts
which are not seen do not in fact exist. But there is a certain round-

Reprinted from *A Commentary Illustrating the Poetic of Aristotle* (London, 1792),
pp. 307–37. Notes I–V only are reprinted here.

[1] [Maurice Morgann, *An Essay on the Dramatic Character of Falstaff*, 1777.
1820; 1825; ed. W. A. Gill, 1912. ED.]

20

ness and integrity in the forms of Shakespear, which give them an independence as well as a relation, insomuch that we often meet with passages which, though perfectly felt, cannot be sufficiently explained in words, without unfolding the whole character of the speaker.

See Note on the Essay, page 58, of which I have only quoted a small part, the whole note is well worth the perusal of every admirer of Shakespeare, as placing his superiority in the delineation of manners in the clearest light. Indeed, to recommend that original and convincing piece of criticism partially is doing it injustice, since every part of it is replete with elegance of taste and accurate and impartial judgement.

In regard to the Analysis of the character of Falstaff; though I first took the book up on the recommendation of a friend, it was with the strongest prejudice against what I thought an indefensible paradox; yet every word led to conviction; and I laid it down with the firmest assurance, that the author was perfectly in the right. I have since recommended the perusal of it to several of my friends, who have all opened it with the same prejudice, and shut it with the same conviction. That the perusal of the book will not be equally convincing to all I can easily believe. For, to use the words of the author:

How many sorts of men are there whom no evidence can persuade! How many, who ignorant of Shakespear, or forgetful of the text, may as well read heathen Greek or the laws of the land as this unfortunate commentary! How many who, proud and pedantic, hate all novelty and damn it without mercy under one compendious word paradox![2] How many more who, not deriving their opinions from the sovereignty of reason, hold at the will of some superior lord, to whom accident or inclination has attached them, and who, true to their vassalage, are resolute not to surrender, without express permission, their base and ill-gotten possessions.

We have another writer also, Henry Fielding, who in his comic epopees, is a most accurate delineator of manners. However there is one distinction between him and Shakespeare, which, though perhaps it gives his pictures a more striking

---

[2] The author of the Dramatic Miscellany seems to have been a critic of this description. He says he cannot think the author serious in his hypothesis. One of the proofs (and he says it is unquestionable) is Falstaff giving an additional wound to Percy. I confess I think with the author of the Essay, it is rather indecent than cowardly.

effect, renders them not equal in real merit to those of our great dramatic poet. Shakespeare paints for all ages and all countries; while the portraits of Fielding are generally drawn from local and national circumstances.[3]

To return to the particular object of the note. The meaning of the word *good*, as the first essential of tragic manners, has been a cause of much difference of opinion among the translators and commentators of the *Poetic*. If we consider χρηστὰ here in its usual and obvious sense of morally good, the passage is neither reconcilable with Aristotle's definition of the proper tragic character in chapter XIII, nor with the practice of all the serious epic and dramatic writers, ancient and modern. To still greater impropriety shall we be driven, if we take up the opinion, originally I believe started by Bossu, and since followed by Dacier, Harris, and Metastasio; that Aristotle by χρηστὰ meant manners well marked. So strongly expressed, as to shew clearly what the character is, whether good or bad. For such a quality, so far from being distinguished from the other three requisites, is essential to them all. Since, whether a character is to be drawn good, or proper, or like, or uniform, it certainly ought to be well drawn, and strongly marked. In short, this is removing the epithet from the character of the manners represented, to that of the mode of representing them, and is nearly equivalent with a person who in laying down rules for composing a good poem, should begin with saying, that the first and most essential rule was, that the poem should be good.

But I think Aristotle has sufficiently explained his meaning in several parts of this treatise, and especially in the beginning of the second chapter, where he points out the difference as to manners of the objects of tragic and comic imitation; the first of

[3] Dr. Johnson says, "There is all the difference in the world between the characters of Fielding and those of Richardson. Characters of manners are very entertaining; but they are to be understood, by a more superficial observer, than characters of nature, where a man must dive into the recesses of the human heart." Boswell's *Life of Johnson*, Vol. I., p. 299. This I think would be a very just distinction between the manners of Fielding and Shakespeare, but I cannot allow it between Fielding and Richardson. His characters can never be drawn naturally which are drawn contrary to his own intention. Richardson certainly meant Clarissa for a perfect character. And yet Dr. Johnson says of her in another place, that "there always appears something in her conduct that she prefers to truth"; and he adds, "that Fielding's *Amelia* is the most perfect heroine of a novel." Mrs. Piozzi's Letters. In Boswell's *Life* Vol. I., p. 342, Johnson says he read *Amelia* through without stopping.

which only he is now treating of particularly. The same idea is, I conceive, kept up with regard to tragic action; viz. that it should be important, in the sixth chapter,[4] and in the thirteenth as to character again, when we are told that illustrious men, like Œdipus and Thyestes, or even better characters[5] in preference to worse are the proper objects of tragedy.

Accordingly we find this rule universally adhered to in all serious fables whatever. Macbeth and Richard the Third, though they are objects of our detestation, never excite our contempt;[6] they have a dignity, a superiority of character which commands our respect, while their crimes are objects of our abhorrence. In this respect Milton is beyond all praise in his character of Satan.[7] Though I by no means put him in general on a footing with Shakespeare as a painter of manners, yet in this single instance he certainly goes beyond him, since he had a difficulty to encounter, which must have been pronounced insurmountable if he had not surmounted it. He was to represent a being not the creature of his own imagination, but marked by the most sacred authority as the abstract of wickedness and impiety, in such colors as to be a proper, and yet principal epic character; and this he has done in so masterly a manner, that the character of Satan alone is to me a sufficent illustration of the meaning of Aristotle in this place, and the proper distinction between poetic and moral goodness; not because the character is well marked, for that might have been as well done had he been made contemptible, and the manners of Belial and Mammon are as capable of this excellence as those of Satan; but because he never loses our respect, nor ever appears to us "less than archangel ruined."

Perhaps this subject[8] cannot be better illustrated than by a comparison between the scene in the *Fatal Curiosity* of Lillo, when the wife is exciting her husband to the murder of the

---

[4] πράξεως σπουδαίας.   [5] ἤ βελτιονος μᾶλλου ἤ χείρονος.

[6] In Chap. *v.* Aristotle in his account of comedy explains what he means by "worse persons," (φαυλοτέρων) not such, he says, as are perfectly depraved, but only those who possess that species of turpitude that will excite ridicule. Is it not natural, when he is speaking of that tragic goodness which he has already opposed to this comic turpitude, for him to mean not absolute goodness, but that species of it only which is proper to excite respect.

[7] See Beattie's "Illustrations on Sublimity," page 613; and "Essay on Poetry and Music," page 78.

[8] See Note III, Chap. XIII.

supposed stranger; and the scene between Macbeth and his wife. According to Mr. Harris, the manners in both are equally good poetically though not morally: "Because it is natural such a wife should persuade, and such a husband be persuaded; and here we have all we require, because (here he blends, or rather confounds two of Aristotle's requisites) all we require is a suitable consistence. To this we may add, that the intent in *Macbeth* is infinitely more atrocious. Wilmot, urged by extreme necessity, aggravated by the remembrance of former affluence. For,

> The needy man who has known better days,
> One whom distress has spited at the world,
> Is he, whom tempting fiends would pitch upon
> To do such deeds, as make the prosperous man
> Lift up his hands and wonder who could do them.
>
> *Douglas*

Wilmot, I say, resolves to reinstate his fortunes, by taking the life of a man he conceives a perfect stranger, with whom he is no otherwise connected, than by the common bands of nature and hospitality. But Macbeth, loaded with large possessions and newly acquired honors, is goaded by an inordinate ambition to sacrifice his kinsman, his benefactor, and his king. One who under his roof was

> —In double trust,
> First as he was his kinsman and his subject,
> Both strong against the deed; then as his host,
> Who should against the murderer shut the door,
> Not bear the knife himself.

Surely in the distinction of these two scenes the poetical *goodness of character* is sufficiently marked and makes the chief difference between them: but it obviously does not arise from moral goodness, or striking delineation of character; or if it does excel in the latter, it must be from superior merit as to one of the three last requisites, propriety, likeness, or uniformity.

In the old and middle comedy, the manners, like those in modern farce when it keeps its true character, and in the burlesque epopee, such as *Hudibras*, are represented as devoid of this poetic goodness. But in what we call genteel comedy, and the comic epopee, the manners of the principal characters at least, though drawn in general conformity to those of the age, partake of this goodness in some degree. Though Tom Jones is not drawn different from other men as Achilles is, though he is not drawn as a perfect character, and therefore as a monster, like Grandison and Clarissa, every reader will see he has no foibles that disgrace him, one only excepted, his venal amour with Lady Bellaston. And there Fielding has committed an error, and every reader feels it, against this rule which Aristotle has given, or rather transcribed from the volume of nature. I have mentioned this as relative only to the principal characters. The subordinate ones may be purely burlesque even in comedy and the comic epopee.

A character can never be respectable without possessing a sense of honor and of courage. The defect of these qualities is evident in Gil Blas, who, throughout the agreeable novel of Le Sage, for so it is in spite of this defect, can never interest us; for who can be much concerned for the welfare of a despicable character, who is both a cheat and a coward; and such a character Gil Blas certainly is.[9]

The Orphan is a striking instance of a want of this goodness of manners. Castalio and Polydore are certainly two unprincipled scoundrels, and Chamont is, as Castalio calls him, 'a noisy boisterous ruffian. The Chaplain I do not mention as he is intended for a character in love comedy. But if the reader wishes to see an instance of flagrant violation, not only of goodness but every requisite of manners, he may find it in a speech of Monimia, who when Polydore, in language too gross for quotation and which would degrade him at once from the character of gentleman, had it been addressed to a common prostitute, accuses her and her sex of every vice, the last and most conspicuous of which is unbridled lust, acquiesces in the justice of the charge, and coolly replies,

> Indeed, my lord,
> I own my sex's follies, I have 'em all;
> And to avoid its fault must fly from you.

The French poets so far from neglecting this rule of Aristotle, have pushed it to a most ridiculous excess, in which they have been but too much followed by many of our tragic

---

[9] See Beattie on "Fable and Romance," p. 570 and 572, where, speaking of Fielding's Joseph Andrews, he wonders "what could induce the author to add to the other faults of his hero's father, Wilson, the infamy of lying and cowardice."

writers. Instead of giving that natural dignity of character, which prevents even vice from becoming despicable, they have substituted an inflated and artificial character, the supposed consequence of high rank. The kings and heroes of Racine and Corneille, put us in mind of Alexander and Caesar dressed in the hoops of the Italian opera.

This false taste is well ridiculed by Lessing,[10] in a criticism on the Earl of Essex, by Banks. After quoting several passages in which Elizabeth speaks like a woman rather than a queen,[11] he proceeds:

Yes, indeed! these things are intolerable, the refined critics, and perhaps some of my readers will say, for unluckily there are Germans yet more frenchified than the French themselves. It is for their diversion that I have selected these low passages, according to their notion. I know their mode of criticising. These little negligences which are so terribly offensive to their delicate ears, and which are so difficult for the poet to find, and who has carefully scattered them here and there, to render the dialogue more natural and give the discourse an appearance of being the real inspiration of the moment; these they tack cleverly together, and then almost kill themselves with laughing at them; and shrugging their shoulders from mere pity, they gravely pronounce that the poor man knows nothing of the great world; that he has not conversed with many queens; that Racine knew much better, but then Racine had lived at court.

All this is very well, but it does not alter my opinion. If queens either do not, or dare not speak in this manner, so much the worse for them. It is not to-day I have learned, that a court is not exactly the place where a poet should study nature. But if pomp and etiquette transform men into machines, it is the duty of the poet to change these machines again into men. Let real queens speak as affectedly and politely as they please, those of the poet should speak naturally. Let him listen attentively to the Hecuba of Euripides, and console himself for having never conversed with other queens.[12]

[10] *Dramaturgie* Part I, page 96. [Article 59, of November 24, 1767 (Ed.)]
[11] Telephus aut Peleus cum pauper et exul uterque
　Projecit ampullas et sesquipedalia verba
　Si curat cor spectantis tetigisse querela.
Horace　Ep. to Pis., 96.
　Peleus and Telephus poor banish'd! each
　Drop their big six-foot words and sounding speech;
　Or else what bosom in their grief takes part.
Colman
[12] See also Beattie on "Imagination," Chap. IV, page 183; and Brumoy's "Reflections on Iphigenia."

From the principle above-mentioned arose all the absurd censures of the French critics on the simplicity of Homer, and all the misrepresentations of the French translators. It is to be lamented that Pope, who in his notes has often treated Mad. Dacier with great asperity, chose to follow her example as to this in his version. The manners of the *Iliad* are altered too much, but those of the *Odyssey* are entirely and radically changed.

NOTE II

A woman, or even a slave may be drawn with this excellence of character, though it is probable that a woman should be worse than a man, and that a slave should be absolutely bad.

This decision of Aristotle does not appear very favourable to the ladies.[1] Metastasio is angry with him for having thus without any necessity, insulted half the human race. But if the principles on which Metastasio explains this passage, as mentioned in the preceding note are right, there will be no insult at all. For if goodness of manners means manners strongly marked, it will be obvious to common observation that the remark is just, without recurring to Athens, where women were almost as much secluded from the general commerce of the world, in the time of Aristotle, as they are now, but even at the present time in western Europe, where they mix so much and take so active a part in society; I am speaking in general, there may be particular exceptions; but these it is not the province of poetry, at least of tragedy to imitate. A professed delineator of manners almost in our own time, has pronounced the same judgement on the sex. Pope says, and he quotes a lady as the author of the remark,

> Nothing so true as what you once let fall;
> Most women have no character at all.

My hypothesis it is true, will not afford this excuse for the Stagirite's want of gallantry. But whoever reflects on the situa-

---

[1] Bossu (whom Mr. Harris called Aristotle's best interpreter) observes, "As for the sex, Aristotle says in his Poetic, that there are fewer good women than others, and that they do more harm than good." In what part of the *Poetic* did he find this passage?

tion of the Grecian women, must know they could not possess that goodness of character which I imagine Aristotle to mean, in an equal degree with men. For they were very little better than in a state of domestic servitude, and therefore could seldom have opportunities of exerting dignity of character. This is by no means the case with the modern female character. Their manners, indeed, are not so strongly marked as those of men, nor afford so much variety, but they are equally capable of this poetical goodness, as far as they are marked, with those of men. I do not mean such characters as Lady Macbeth and Medea, who do not properly possess female manners, but such as Juliet, as Constance, as Desdemona, and as Belvidera. As for a slave, our tragic drama knows no such character as existed under that name in the *free* republic of Athens. Zanga and Oroonoko are captive heroes.

I would not be understood however, either as wishing to palliate or apologize, for the opinion of Aristotle in this or any other place where I think him absolutely in the wrong. Of the unfavourable idea he entertained of the fair sex there can be no doubt. This is proved beyond contradiction, from a passage in his natural history of animals,[2] which Mr. Twining has quoted, and I shall venture to translate, as a compleat specimen of the purest absurdity.

Woman is more apt to pity and fall into tears than man. She is more given to envy, more ready to find fault, fonder of scandal, and more apt to give blows. She is also more addicted to anxiety and despondency, more impudent, more false, more easily deceived and less apt to forget, also more wakeful,[3] and yet more slothful, and on the whole more obstinate than men.

Perhaps I may be thought to take up the cause of the most amiable part of our species too warmly, when I declare this passage alone is a sufficient answer to all those, who think Aristotle never in the wrong. The philosopher is not here

---

[2] Aristotle, *Historia Animalium*, ix. i. [608ᵇ 8 ff.]

[3] Ἀγρυπνότερον καὶ ὀκνηρότερον. [*Hist. An. IX.* i. 608ᵃ 33 ff.] Of this apparent paradox, Mr. Twining gives the following humorous solution. "More able to keep late hours, and at the same time more lazy than men," might not this be rendered "fonder of sitting up late, and lying in bed late"; perhaps this may be the case in general at present, as the ladies are fonder of dancing, and as yet at least, though I doubt if that will continue, not quite so fond of sporting as the men.

speaking of the civil but the natural character of woman, considered as an animal, as the female of the human race. He is enquiring into the nature of females in general throughout the whole of animated nature. These are his words:

Females (he says, with an exception as to tigers and bears) are less ferocious but more malicious, deceitful, and insidious than males, and more attentive in nourishing their young.—The traces of these manners are to be found, as I may say, in all animals, but they are most conspicuous in those whose manners are most marked, and especially in mankind whose nature is most perfect, so that these habits will be most conspicuous in them.

And then follows the definition above quoted. Here therefore the ladies are marked as the representatives of the whole creation, with the flattering exception indeed of tigresses and she-bears; but certainly most of the distinctions between the sexes mentioned by Aristotle are distinctions of artificial habit, the consequences of custom and education, and not natural habit or instinct. In some of them, as timidity and softness, the ancient and modern females agree; in others, as impudence and dissimulation, they differ, on account of their different mode of life. But wherever male jealousy and tyranny, in modern times, reduces females to the situation of slaves, the qualities of slaves will still be found in them. Surely there is not more difference between the characters of men and women, as stated by Aristotle, than there is between a soldier and an attorney.[4] And I should hardly impute this to natural instinct. I have heard it observed, that on examining the ruins either of Pompeia or Herculaneum, the bodies of the men were found in the attitude of resistance, the women in that of resignation, which I conceive to be as much the consequence of habit as the discovery said to have been made of a young man in women's cloaths, by attempting to draw a chair in a method which his dress would not permit.[5]

[4] I do not mean to say, that there are not particular instances of good or bad disposition resisting the force of habit; there are certainly rapacious and cunning soldiers, masculine women, and honest and even liberal-minded attorneys, for I cannot agree with Mr. Shenstone, or at least am more lucky in my acquaintance with them, as I know several in whom the gentleman, the christian, and the man is *not* (as he asserts) swallowed up in the lawyer.

[5] Is not the imputation of these distinctions to natural causes something on the same principle with the remark of the old groom, who had found, from long experience, that cropped horses were naturally good?

In a note on the former edition of my translation, I have said a more perfect character might be found among women than men. To trace the causes of this, may perhaps throw some light on the subject of the preceding note.

The qualities that raise men in the esteem of the world, that render them in the general opinion of mankind great and respectable on which poetical goodness of character depends, are often not connected, but frequently even in opposition to what may strictly be called moral virtue. That a degree of this poetical goodness is not incompatible even with atrocious crimes, has already been observed; and we may add, that in modern times it frequently depends on acknowledged vices, as a certain degree of gallantry and duelling. In regard to the first, how nearly has Fielding made Joseph Andrews an object of ridicule; and what pains is he obliged to employ to excuse him, by his violent attachment to another woman. The same may be observed as to duelling, in the character of Sir Charles Grandison, who, after all the trouble Richardson has taken to draw him perfect, is neither the object of our love or our respect. Indeed the poet's pencil is not always true to his intention.[6] I have no doubt that Rowe, in the *Fair Penitent*, meant to make Altamont the object of our esteem, and Lothario of our detestation. But he has so contrived in the execution, that we despise Altamont, and the gallant gay Lothario is the favorite of the spectators, though he is an unprincipled, and in one instance a despicable villain, for no crime can be more truly despicable than boasting of a woman's favors. The same may be said of two other characters in different works, Lovelace and Sir Charles Grandison. But a woman may be drawn perfectly good, and at the same time perfectly interesting, for there is no virtue in the catalogue of moral or christian duties that is not becoming, and does not both give and receive additional lustre, when possessed by that amiable sex. The utmost exertions of patience, and meekness, which at least sink the dignity of the tragic hero, raise the tragic heroine in our esteem. The characters of Imogen, of Desdemona, and of Cordelia, are as nearly patterns of perfection as human nature will admit, erring only as to that passion which we have already mentioned as furnishing that $\mu\epsilon\gamma\acute{a}\lambda\eta$ $\acute{a}\mu\alpha\rho\tau\acute{\iota}a$, that great frailty which causes the distress of virtuous characters without awakening our disgust, or sinking them in our esteem.

[6] Massinger has succeeded in this in his *Fatal Dowry*, from which Rowe entirely borrowed his plot, though without any acknowledgement. See a comparison between these plays in the *Observer*, No. 89, 90, 91.

Before I quit this part of the subject I must make one observation, though it partly anticipates the subject of the next note. It relates to the tendency my fair countrywomen have to violate in real life an example of Aristotle given to enforce the necessity of poetical propriety of manners. He tells us "there is a character of courage and fierceness adapted to men, which would be very improper in a woman." My own feelings on this head are so much in unison with those of the Stagirite, that I am as much disgusted at seeing a delicate and accomplished woman drawing a bow, or managing a spirited hunter, as I should be at a man's working a pair of ruffles, or embroidering a waistcoat. These exercises are not only unfit for female delicacy but even destructive of female beauty, as they tend to make the arm muscular, and consequently to rob it of its first grace, rotundity, and softness of outline. There is even something repugnant to our sensations in seeing a woman skilful in things that do not become her sex. In such cases there is a beauty even in awkwardness. There is a masterly stroke in Rousseau's *Emilius* exemplifying this.

Sophia could not sit still. She rose with vivacity. She ran over the whole shop, examined the tools, felt the smoothness of the planks, picked up the shavings, looked at our hands, and said she liked this kind of work because it was so clean. She playfully attempted even to imitate Emilius. With her white and delicate hand she run a plane over a board, the plane slid on without having any effect. I thought I beheld the god of love in the air laughing and beating his wings. I thought I heard him shout with delight, and say, "Hercules is revenged."

Homer who lived in more natural times than Aristotle, or the Greek tragic writers, was much more favorable to the characters of women. In what amiable colors has he drawn Helen, the cause of so much war and bloodshed. How different is the behaviour of Hector to her, and that of the pious Aeneas of Virgil! Her lamentation over the body of Hector, in the last book of the *Iliad*, is beyond expression beautiful.[7]

[7] Madam Dacier's criticism on this speech is the very βαθος of the absurd. Homer does not say this only to shew the goodness and humanity of Hector, but also to support the probability of the poem. For if Hector, who was master in Troy, both on account of his own valor and the old age of Priam, had not been in the interests of Helen, there would have been no likelihood of her not being delivered up to the Greeks in the course of so fatal a war.
Madam Dacier in this remark omits the testimony Helen bears to the

The case with regard to slavery was different, and Homer expresses himself on that head with nearly as much strength as Aristotle.[8]

> Jove fix'd it certain that whatever day
> Makes man a slave, takes half his worth away.
>
> Pope's *Odyssey*, l. xvii. v. 393

NOTE III

The next requisite is their being characteristic.

By characteristic is meant consonant with the profession, rank, sex, and age of the person. This is clearly defined as to the last condition by Horace in his *Epistle to the Pisos*.[1] The celebrated speech of Jaques in *As You Like It,* describing the seven ages of man's life, seems an imitation of this passage in Horace. But with all the veneration I have for Shakespeare, I cannot agree with Mr. Colman in thinking his alteration in making *two* of his examples characteristic of station, instead of age, an improvement; since comparatively considered, so few men are ever either soldiers or justices. I say two examples, though Mr. Colman makes them three, enumerating the lover in them. But here I think Shakespeare has adhered more to general nature than Horace. Love is certainly more naturally characteristic of youth than hunting.

An objection has been made to Iago as a deviation from this rule, as the character of an artful revengeful villain is very opposite to that of a soldier: and had Iago been the only soldier in the play the objection would have been just, as in that case he must have been considered as representing the general manners of the profession. But as in *Othello* all the principal persons of the drama are soldiers, the manners are characteristic of the individual not of the profession. From national prejudice we are

---

paternal tenderness shewn her by Priam.

Ἑκυρὸς δὲ, πατὴρ ὡς, ἤπιος αἰεί.

There is the same omission in Pope's translation.

[8] ''Ἥμισυ γάρ τ' ἀρετῆς ἀποαίνυται εὐρύοπα Ζεὺς
Ἀνέρος, εὖτ' ἄν μιν κατὰ δούλιον ἦμαρ ἕλησιν.

Odyssey l. XVII. v. 322

[1] See v. 156 to v. 178 in the original, and v. 230 to v. 265 in Mr. Colman's translation.

apt to be rather unfavorable in our representation of French characters; and had Parolles been the only Frenchman in *All's Well that Ends Well*, we should not scruple to consider him as an example of such prejudice; but as the scene lies in France chiefly, no such idea is ever entertained.[2]

As to the propriety of character, the ghosts, witches, and fairies of Shakespeare, are deservedly allowed superior excellence, as they certainly act in conformity with the manners, we impute to such imaginary beings did they really exist. Yet Shakespeare had here some archetype to follow; for popular opinion had already marked the outline of their habits, which was as advantageous to him in giving them characteristic manners as it was disadvantageous to Milton[3] in giving Satan poetical excellence of manners. But how Shakespeare[4] has contrived in such characters as Caliban, the pure creation of his own imagination, to give to what never did, and never was supposed to exist, such manners as we are irresistibly impelled by our feelings to pronounce truly characteristic, is a power of art that criticism is as inadequate to investigate, as genius to imitate.

NOTE IV

The third essential is likeness. There is a distinction between this and what we have already mentioned about their being good and characteristic.

These words obviously imply that though there is a distinction between them they are liable to be confounded, which is exactly the case with being like and characteristic. But there seems to be almost a direct opposition between likeness and goodness. "For," as is very justly remarked by Mr. Twining, "there was more danger of a reader's thinking the ὅμοιον too different from the χρηστὸν, and as a general precept incompatible with it." I can find no other way of solving this difficulty than by the common effort of unsuccessful and bold commentators, alteration of the text, and leaving out the word χρηστὸν as supposing it added by a transcriber in conformity to ὥσπερ εἴρηται, as both goodness and propriety have just been mentioned.

[2] See Bishop Warburton's *Defence of Shakespear* in this instance against the hypercriticism of Rhymer.
[3] See Note i. on this chapter.
[4] See Morgann, *An Essay on the Dramatic Character of Falstaff*, p. 75, note.

The difference between propriety and likeness consists merely in this, that the one relates to what is becoming and natural in a person of such an age, sex, or profession; the other, to what is appropriated to any particular character, from history or tradition. Mr. Twining illustrates this by the example of Medea, "where the violence and fierceness which form her traditional character, and therefore the likeness of the poet's picture may be said to be proper, or suitable with respect to the individual, though improper and unsuitable to the general character of the sex."

Mr. Mason, as he has drawn his Elfrida, whose historical character is one of the worst in the annals of human kind, has preferred general propriety of character to individual resemblance.

This subject is discussed at large by M. Lessing, in a criticism on a comedy called *Solyman the Second*,[1] taken from one of Mormontel's tales, from which I shall make a considerable extract, as it in many places applies strongly to the Elfrida of Mr. Mason, and without design, and consequently without partiality, urges what may be said on both sides as to such a delineation of an historical character.

M. Lessing first quotes the following extract from the *Journal Encyclopedique* for January, 1762, page 79:

Solyman, say they, was one of the greatest princes of his age. His victories, his talents, his virtues, rendered him an object of veneration even to the enemies he triumphed over. But this hero so sensible to glory was not insensible to love; though delicate in his pleasures, he felt amid the corruption of a seraglio, that pleasure unaccompanied by sentiment is contemptible. He imagined he had found this in Roxelana, a young Italian captive, not perhaps incapable of tenderness but nevertheless artful and ambitious, and skilled in the means of making her pleasures the source of her elevation. By feigning sensibility herself, she induced Solyman who really felt it, to violate a law of the empire which forbad the sultan to marry. She ascended the throne with him, an ambition in itself pardonable, if she had not employed her ascendancy over her lover to force him to sully his glory by the sacrifice of an innocent son. This woman M. Marmontel has chosen for the heroine of one of his tales. But how he has changed

---

[1] *Dramaturgie*, Part II, page 70, *et. seq.* [Article 33, August 21, 1767. (Ed.)]
We have a very pleasing after-piece on the same subject, in which the character of Roxelana has received additional interest from the powers of Mrs. Abingdon and Mrs. Jordan.

her! Instead of Italian he has made her French. Instead of an artful woman affecting sensiblity he has made her the coquet of a Parisian circle; and instead of a soul overwhelmed by ambition, and capable of the boldest and most atrocious actions to satisfy it, he has given her an undesigning head and an excellent heart. Are such changes allowable? Can a poet or a novellist extend the license, whatever it may be, that is given him, to known characters? Though permitted to change facts, has he a right to paint Lucretia as a coquet, and Socrates as a fine gentleman?"

To this M. Lessing replies:

I do not chuse to charge myself with the justification of M. Marmontel on this point. I have already observed,[2] that characters should be more sacred to the poet than facts. First, because when the characters are well observed, the facts as being the consequence of such characters can never vary much,[3] as on the contrary the same facts may be derived from characters entirely different. Secondly, because the instruction does not lie in the facts themselves, but in the knowledge that such characters in such circumstances do and can only produce such facts.[4] Nevertheless Marmontel has done just the reverse. The fact is, that there was formerly in the seraglio an European female slave, who had art enough to get herself declared legally married to the emperor. The character of this slave, and that of the emperor, determine the manner in which this fact really happened; and because there might have been many different characters by whose means it might really have happened, it certainly depends only on the poet, as poet, which, either of the characters established by history, or of others, he chuses to employ, according

[2] *Dramaturgie*, Part I, page 57, [*Art*. 23, July 17, 1767] where he defends the anachronisms as to the age of Elizabeth in Corneille's *Comte de Essex*, against the *Criticisms* of Voltaire. Corneille represents her as young when Essex is executed, which really happened near the close of her reign. Lessing says, "If her character gives the poetic idea of that which history attributes to that queen the poet has fulfilled his duty, and we have no business to bring the work to the strict tribunal of chronology or history." In confirmation of this doctrine we have had three tragedies on this subject on our theatre, to which the history of Elizabeth must be much better known than it can be to a French audience, which have all the same defect without its producing any ill consequence as to their reception on the stage.

[3] This I think will hardly be granted, and indeed seems confuted by the other member of the sentence. As the leading facts of the story of Elfrida not only might have been, but actually were nearly the same as represented by Mr. Mason, so had Elfrida been drawn as she really was, undoubtedly the consequential facts might have been entirely different.

[4] The reader will observe that part of the reasoning here arises from M. Lessing's mistake as to the meaning of the *Contes Moraux*, or moral tales.

as the moral he has in view, requires one or the other. All that is expected of him, in case he chuses other characters than those which are furnished by history, or even such as absolutely contradict it, is to abstain also from historical names, and rather ascribe known facts to unknown persons than give to known persons manners which do not belong to them. The first encreases our knowledge, or at least seems to encrease it, and pleases even on that account; the second contradicts the knowledge we already have, and displeases for that reason. We consider facts as accidental, and what may happen in commmon to many different persons, but characters on the contrary as something essential and particular. We permit the poet therefore to arrange the first according to his fancy, provided he does not make them contradictory to his characters. But as the second he may put them indeed in the best light, but he must not alter them. The least variation seems to destroy the individuality, and give us fictitious and deceitful persons, who usurp the names of other people, and try to pass on us for characters they in reality are not.

Notwithstanding this, it appears to me a much more pardonable fault not to preserve in the persons those characters which history has given them, than to err either as to probability or the moral intended to be conveyed in such characters as are chosen at will; for the first defect may very well be united with genius, but not the second. It is allowed to be ignorant of a thousand things that every school boy knows. It is not the acquisitions of memory, but the power of drawing from our own proper funds that constitutes riches. As to what a poet has heard, or seen, or read, he either forgets it, or does not choose to know it, just as suits his purpose. He errs then sometimes through too much security, sometimes through contempt, sometimes through premeditated design, and sometimes not; and he does it so grossly, and so often, that we poor souls can never wonder enough at it. Lifting up our hands we cry, How could so great a man have been ignorant of this? How could it have escaped his recollection? Did not he take it into consideration? O let us be silent on the subject. While we are trying to debase him, we only make ourselves ridiculous in his eyes; all that we know more than him amounts solely to what we learned at school, without which we should have been completely stupid and ignorant indeed.

NOTE V

The Fourth is consistency.

By consistency is meant keeping the character uniform with itself in every respect. Without this it is impossible for the manners to excel in the other qualities; for a character can never be said to have poetical goodness, or general propriety of manners, or individual likeness, if these qualities are not uniformly kept up.

Horace seems to conceive this admonition chiefly necessary to those poets who draw original characters from their own imagination.[1]

> Should you adventuring novelty, engage
> Some bold original to walk the stage,
> Preserve it well, continued as begun
> True to itself in every scene, and one.
> Colman's Horace *Epistle to the Pisos* 186.

Indeed though this rule is equally essential to all characters, original ones will be most liable to offend against it. As there the poet will have nothing to guide him but his own genius, and besides he will be more tempted to take liberties with what he esteems particularly his property, as being the creature of his own invention. He also will esteem himself to be, and indeed actually will be, less liable to detection.

The example that Aristotle gives of failure in this point is the character of Iphigenia in the *Iphigenia in Aulis* of Euripides.

Modern instances of the breach of this rule will be amply furnished by our best poets, serious and comic, epic and dramatic.

The character of Hamlet[2] cannot certainly be allowed to be uniform throughout. Besides the neglect or forgetfulness of the poet in making Hamlet, who is only supposed to affect madness, appear often really mad, (an error carefully and effectually

---

[1] Si quid inexpertum scenae committis, & audes
Personam formare novam; servetur ad imum
Qualis ab incepto processerit et sibi constet.
Ep. to Pis. 125.

[2] I have been informed that by order of Mrs. Garrick the tragedy of *Hamlet* was thrown into Garrick's grave. I think though he was undoubtedly great in that character he was equally so in many of Shakespeare's characters, and superior in *Lear*. The comic characters I presume were thought too light for so solemn an occasion. If by burying that tragedy with Garrick it was meant to infer that it was lost to the stage with him, a complete edition of Shakespeare might, with the utmost propriety, have been interred with that inimitable actor: for what Cardinal Bembo has said of Nature on the tomb of Raffael, may be said of Shakespeare on the tomb of Garrick.

guarded against in Edgar,[3]) there are many improprieties which I shall not enlarge upon as they are sufficiently obvious.

Romeo also surely acts contrary to the general tendency of his character when after the fall of Paris,[4] on being requested by his dying rival to lay his body by Juliet, he answers coolly, and rather lightly, "In faith I will." And on recognizing his face he considers him as an object of pity, and seems really concerned for him though his rival, and the occasion of Juliet's death.

Valentine's offer of resigning Sylvia to Protheus is a striking instance of the same impropriety in our great dramatic poet; if that play,[5] which I greatly doubt, is really a production of Shakespeare. Farquhar has added to this impropriety when he makes Aimwell say to Archer in the *Beaux Stratagem*, "Take the ten thousand or the Lady"; and in Archer's brutal answer to Dorinda, when she expresses her surprize at the offer.

In the song supposed to be written by Lovemore for the widow Belmour in the *Way to Keep Him*, and which is supposed to give his own sentiments, there is a strong instance not only of inconsistency but absolutely of opposition in this line.

Turn the chief of your care from your face to your mind.

Now the only cause of Lovemore's indifference to his wife is her having done this very thing; and the whole tenor of the

[3] When one of the persons assumes a character different from his own it is the business of the actor to mark the distinction, and make the real character appear through the feigned one. Johnson has observed, "that Garrick did not play Archer in the *Beaux Stratagem* well. The gentleman should break out through the footman, which was not the case as he did it." Boswell's *Life of Johnson*, Vol. ii, p. 62.

[4] The author of the *Remarks* makes a curious observation on these lines spoken by the prince.

And I for winking at your discords too
Have lost a brace of kinsmen.

His kinsmen he says are Mercutio and Benvolio, and therefore proposes to restore a line which mentions the death of the latter. This ought to be a good lesson to commentators, as it shews how they are able sometimes to see what is invisible, and to shut their eyes against what stares them in the face. Mercutio and Paris are obviously the prince's relations. Romeo on first seeing the face of Paris, calls him Mercutio's kinsman. And in the dramatis personae, which is arranged rather according to political than poetical rank, the first character mentioned is Escalus, prince of Verona: the second Paris, kinsman to the prince.

[5] If the hand of Shakespeare is to be traced in any part of the *Two Gentlemen of Verona*, I think it is in the characters of Launce and Speed, which must resemble Lancelot in the *Merchant of Venice*.

drama is to enforce the contrary conduct, and shew a woman that she ought, after marriage, to sacrifice to the graces as well as to the virtues.

There is a similar neglect in that excellent comedy the *School for Scandal*, when Charles Surface says to Sir Oliver on his being discovered, "Believe me when I tell you, (and upon my soul I would not say it if it was not so,) if I do not feel mortified at the exposure of my follies; it is because I feel at this moment the warmest satisfaction at seeing you my liberal benefactor." This is quite inconsistent with the character of Charles, and would have exactly suited Joseph in the same situation, as it conveys a premeditated sentiment, and is besides obviously an untruth.

I will now produce three instances from works of narrative imitation, and those justly in the highest class of estimation. To begin with *Don Quixote*. In the part first published by Cervantes, and his subsequent addition in consequence of a spurious attempt by another hand, he has two distinct characters.

In the first part it is true he is not drawn as an absolute maniac, when he is not discoursing of knight errantry, but all his conversation is tinged with singularity; and the pertinent things he says are incoherently arranged, and themselves out of place; as for instance, his long speech to the goatherds about the golden age: but in the second part he is made a man of sound judgment and elegant literature when the immediate subject of his madness is not touched upon.[6]

My next instance is from a work which is of undoubted excellence indeed, leaving every work of the same nature far behind. I mean the character of Allworthy in *Tom Jones*. He has always appeared to me a striking instance of a character at opposition with himself, though more perhaps in general with that which the author tells you in his own person he is, than with his own conduct in those parts where the author suffers him to act from himself. The author is at great pains to inform us frequently that he is, though no scholar, a man of sense and discernment, with a benevolence almost angelic; and to press this more forcibly on our minds, he has given him a name strongly expressive of his moral goodness, though all his other characters have common names. But how is he really drawn?

---

[6] See Andrew's *Anecdotes*, p. 31. Article Books.

He is the dupe of every insinuating rascal he meets; and a dupe not of the most amiable kind, since he is always led to acts of justice and feverity. The consequence of his pliability is oftener the punishment of the innocent than the acquittal of the guilty; and in such punishment he is severe and implacable. As in the case of Jones himself, his supposed father and mother, and black George. He suffers his adopted son and his foundling to be ill treated by an imperious pedagogue, whose whole character and conversation is a satire on christianity, and to have their principles corrupted by a hypocritical infidel.

The third instance is not so striking, but is I think to be found in a character, whose singularity as well as general uniformity with itself is universally and deservedly admired, and was a particular favorite with its author on this very account. I mean Sir Roger de Coverly[7] in the *Spectator*. But is his conduct throughout the work consonant with the original delineation of his character? Or can his singularities, however amiable and however entertaining, be at all said to "proceed from his good sense, and be contradictions to the manners of the world, only as he thinks the world is in the wrong?"[8]

There are many comedies whose catastrophe depends entirely on this want of uniformity of manners. I mean those in which the event of the fable turns on an entire and radical change of character in one of the principal persons. Where, as Mr. Harris observes, with as much humour as justice:

The old gentleman of the drama, after having frettted and stormed through the first four acts, towards the conclusion of the fifth is unaccountably appeased. At the same time the dissipated coquette, and the dissolute fine gentleman whose vices cannot be occasional but must clearly be habitual, are in the space of half a scene miraculously reformed, and grow at once as completely good as if they had never been otherwise.

Some instances may however be produced in which a sudden and yet lasting reformation may not be improbable, as in Lady

---

[7] The character of Sir Roger did not, it seems, suit the delicacy of Shenstone. In his *Essays on Men, Manners, and Things*, where he chuses to draw what he calls a character, and a most insipid one it is, and make him talk common-place nonsense among the tombs at Westminster, he concludes by saying he "sometimes boasted that he was a distant relation of Sir Roger de Coverly." If he was, "I am afraid his lady mother played false," for there is not the most distant family likeness.

[8] *Spectator*, No. II.

Townly. We may conceive a young woman of good natural disposition, but led into habits of dissipation by company and fashion, to be really convinced of her error by one striking incident: but we can never believe that any thing can cure the brutal suspicion of Strictland.[9]

[9] No two passions can be more different than jealousy and suspicion. The one is the offspring of brutality, and may be unconnected with love; the other is the certain proof of a most violent and unreasonable passion. Hoadley in the *Suspicious Husband* has once, and I believe once only, confounded these characters when he makes Strictland say he cannot bear that even a woman should partake in his wife's love. This is jealousy though pushed to excess. Mrs. Brooks in *Emily Montague* makes Colonel Rivers express the violence of his passion in these words: "I would engross, I would employ, I would absorb every faculty of that lovely mind." Othello reasons, if I may use the expression, in the same manner, when he says,

> —I'd rather be a toad,
> And feed upon the vapor of a dungeon,
> Than keep a corner in the thing I love
> For other's uses.—

III

THOMAS TWINING

On Poetry Considered as an Imitative Art

The word *Imitation*, like many others, is used, sometimes in a strict and proper sense, and sometimes in a sense more or less extended and improper. Its application to poetry is chiefly of the latter kind. Its precise meaning, therefore, when applied to poetry *in general*, is by no means obvious. No one who has seen a picture is at any loss to understand how painting is imitation. But no man, I believe, ever heard or read, for the first time, that poetry is imitation, without being conscious in some degree, of that "confusion of thought" which an ingenious writer complains of having felt whenever he has attempted to explain the imitative nature of Music.[1] It is easy to see whence this confusion arises, if we consider the process of the mind when words thus extended from their *proper* significations are presented to it. We are told that "Poetry is an imitative art." In order to conceive how it is so, we naturally compare it with painting, sculpture, and such arts as are strictly and clearly imitative. But, in this comparison, the *difference* is so much more obvious and striking than the *resemblance*—we see so much more readily in what respects poetry is *not* properly imitation, than in what respects it *is;*—that the mind, at last, is left in that sort of perplexity which must always arise from words thus loosely and analogically applied, when the analogy is not sufficiently clear and obvious; that is, when, of that mixture of circumstances, *like* and *unlike*, which constitutes analogy, the latter are the most apparent.

In order to understand the following Treatise on Poetry, in which *imitation* is considered as the very essence of the art,[2] it

Reprinted from *Aristotle's Treatise on Poetry* by Thomas Twining, edited by Daniel Twining (2d ed., 2 vols.; London: Luke Hansard & Sons, 1812), I, 3–65.

[1] Dr. Beattie, *Essay on Poetry*, etc. ch. vi. § 1.

[2] See the *Second part* of this Dissertation.

seems necessary to satisfy ourselves, if possible, with respect to two points: i. in what senses the word *Imitation* is, or *may* be, applied to Poetry; ii. in what senses it was so applied by Aristotle.

The only circumstance, I think, common to *everything* we denominate *imitation*, whether properly or improperly, is *resemblance*, of some sort or other.

In every imitation, strictly and properly so called, two conditions seem essential: the resemblance must be immediate, i.e. between *the imitation, or imitative work, itself,* and the object imitated; and, it must also be *obvious.* Thus, in sculpture, figure is represented by similar figure; in painting, colour and figure, by similar colour and figure; in personal imitation, or mimicry, voice and gesture, by similar voice and gesture. In all these instances, the resemblance is *obvious;* we recognize the object imitated: and it is, also, *immediate;* it lies in the imitative *work,* or *energy, itself;* or, in other words, in the very materials, or *sensible media,*[3] by which the imitation is conveyed. All *these* copies, therefore, are called, strictly and intelligibly, imitations.

1. The materials of poetic imitation are *words.* These may be considered in two views: as sounds *merely,* and as sounds *significant,* or arbitrary and conventional *signs* of ideas. It is evidently, in the *first* view only, that words can bear any real resemblance to the *things expressed;* and, accordingly, that kind of imitation which consists in the resemblance of words considered as mere *sound,* to the *sounds* and *motions* of the objects imitated,[4] has usually been assigned as the only instance in which the term *imitative* is, in its strict and proper sense, applicable to Poetry.[5] But setting aside all that is the effect of fancy and of accommodated pronunciation in the reader, to which, I fear, many passages, repeatedly quoted and admired as the happiest coincidences of sound and sense, may be reduced;[6]

---

[3] See Mr. Harris's *Treatise on Music,* etc. ch. i.

[4] Mr. Harris's *Treatise,* etc. ch. iii.

[5] Mr. Harris.—Lord Kaims, *Elements of Criticism* vol. ii. p. 1.

[6] The reader may see this sufficiently proved by Dr. Johnson in his *Lives of the Poets,* vol. iv, p. 183, 8vo, and in the *Rambler,* No. 92. "In such resemblances," as he well observes, "the mind often governs the ear, and the sounds are estimated by their meaning." See also Lord Kaims, *El. of Crit.,* vol. ii.. p. 84, 85.

setting this aside, even in such words, and such arrangements of words, as are actually in some degree, analogous in sound or motion to the thing signified or described, the resemblance is so faint and distant, and of so general and vague a nature, that it would never, *of itself*, lead us to recognize the object imitated. We discover not the *likeness* till we know the *meaning*. The natural relation of the word to the thing signified, is pointed out only by its arbitrary or conventional relation.[7]—I do not here

---

[7] See Harris on *Music*, etc., ch. iii. § 1, 2. This verse of Virgil,
        Stridenti miserum stipulâ disperdere carmen—
is commonly cited as an example of this sort of imitation. I question, however, whether this line would have been remarked by any one as particularly harsh, if a harsh sound had not been described in it. At least, many verses full as harshly constructed might, I believe, be produced, in which no such imitation can be supposed. But, even admitting that such imitation was here intended, it seems to me almost ridiculous to talk of the *"natural relation* between the sound of this verse, and *that of a vile hautboy."* [Harris, in the chapter above referred to.] All that can be said is, that the sounds are, both of them, harsh sounds; but, certainly no one species of harsh sound can well be more unlike another, than the sound of a rough verse is to the tone of a bad hautboy, or, indeed, of any other musical instrument.—That, in the clearest and most acknowledged instances of such imitative vocal sound, the resemblance is, or can possibly be, so exact as to lead a person unacquainted with the language, *by the sound alone*, to the *signification*, no man in his senses would assert. Yet Dr. Beattie, in a note, p. 304, of his *Essay on Poetry*, etc., by a mistake for which I am at a loss to account, has ascribed so extravagant a notion to Rousseau. "There is in Tasso's Gierusalemme Liberata, a famous stanza, of which Rousseau says, that a good ear and *sincere heart* are alone able to judge of *it*"; meaning, as appears from what follows, of its *sense;* for he adds, "The imitative harmony and the poetry are indeed admirable; *but I doubt whether a person who understands neither Italian nor Latin, could even guess at the meaning from the sound."* There can be no room for *doubt* in this matter; he certainly could not: nor does Rousseau appear to have even hinted the possibility of such a thing. The passage is in his admirable Letter *Sur la Musique Françoise;* where, in order to obviate the prejudices of those who regard the Italian language as wholly soft and effeminate, he produces two stanzas of Tasso, the one as an example of a sweet and tender, the other of a forcible and nervous, combination of sounds: and he adds, that to judge of *this*, i. e., of the *sound* only, not the *sense*, of the stanzas, and also of the impossibility of rendering adequately the sweetness of the one, or the force of the other, in the French language, "it is not necessary to understand Italian—it is sufficient *that we have an ear, and are impartial."* "Que ceux qui pensent que l'Italien n'est que le langage de la douceur et de la tendresse, prennent la peine de *comparer entre elles* ces deux strophes du Tasse: et s'ils desesperent de rendre en François la *douce harmonie* de l'une, qu'ils essayent d'exprimer la *rauque dureté* de l'autre: il n'est pas besoin *pour juger de ceci* d'entendre la langue, il ne faut qu' avoir *des oreilles* & *de la bonne soi."*

mean to deny that such resemblances, however slight and delicate where they really *are*, and however liable to be discovered by fancy where they are *not*, are yet a source of real beauties, of beauties *actually felt* by the reader, when they arise, or appear to arise, spontaneously from the poet's feeling, and their effect is not counteracted by the obviousness of cool intention, and deliberate artifice.[8] Nor do I mean to object to this application of the word *imitative*. My purpose is merely to shew, that when we call this kind of resemblance, imitation, we do not use the word in its *strict* sense—that, in which it is applied to a picture, or a statue. Of the two conditions above mentioned, it wants that which must be regarded as most essential. The resemblance is, indeed, real, *as far as it goes*, and immediate; but, necessarily, from its *generality*, so imperfect, that even when

---

[8] I am persuaded that many very beautiful and striking passages of this kind in the best poets were solely φυσεως αυτοματιζουσης εργα, *not* τεχνης μιμησασθαι τα γιγνομενα πειρωμενης, as it is well expressed by *Dion. Hal.* Περι συνθεσεως, § 20.—But the *Critic* is always too ready to transfer his own reflection to the *Poet;* and to consider as the *effects* of art, all those spontaneous strokes of genius which become the *causes* of art by his calm observation and discussion. Scarce any poet has, I think, so many beauties of this kind, fairly produced by strength of imagination, and delicacy of ear, as Virgil. Yet there are some verses frequently cited as fine examples in this way, which appear to me too visibly artificial to be pleasing: such as—
    Quadrupedante putrem sonitu quatit ungula campuna.
I am tempted to add to this note a passage from the first dissertation prefixed to the *Aeneid* by that excellent editor, C. G. Heyne, a man who has honourably distinguished himself from the herd of commentators, by such a degree of taste and philosophy as we do not often find united with laborious and accurate erudition. Speaking of the charms of Virgil's versification, he says, "Illud unum monebimus, in errorem inducere juvenilem animum videri eos qui nimii in eo sunt, ut ad rerum sonos et naturas accommodatos et formatos velint esse versus. Equidem non diffiteor sensum animi me refragantem habere, quotiescunque persuadere mihi volo, magnum aliquem poetam aestu tantarum rerum abreptum et magnorum phantasmatum vi inflammatum, in *sono cursus equestris* vel tubae vel aliarum rerum reddendo laborare; attenuat ea res et deprimit ingenium poetae et artis dignitatem. *Sunt tamen*, ais, *tales versus* in optimo quoque poetâ. Recte; sunt utique multi; etsi plures alios ad hoc lusus genus accommodare solet eorum ingenium qui talibus rebus indulgent. Sed mihi ad poetices indolem propius esse videtur statuere, *ipsam orationis naturam* ita esse comparatam, ut multarum rerum sonos exprimat; inflammatum autem phantasmatum specie objectâ animum, cum rerum species sibi obversantes ut *oratione vivide exprimat laborat, necessario in ista vocabula incidere, vel orationis proprietate ducente*. Ita graves et celeres, lenes ac duros sonos, *vel non id agens et curans*, ad rerum naturam accommodabit et orator quisque bonus, et multo magis poeta. [Heyne's *Virgil*, vol. ii., p. 39.]

pointed out by the *sense*, it is by no means always *obvious*, and without that, cannot possibly lead to any thing like a clear and certain recognition of the particular object imitated.[9] I must observe farther, that this kind of imitation, even supposing it much more perfect, is, by no means, that which would be likely first to occur to any one, in an enquiry concerning the nature of the imitation attributed to Poetry, were it not, that the circumstance of its real and *immediate* resemblance, has occasioned its being considered, I think not justly, as the strictest sense of the term so applied.

For the most *usual*, and the most *important* senses, and even, as will perhaps appear, for the *strictest* sense, in which Poetry has been, or may be, understood to imitate, we must have recourse to language considered in its most important point of view, as composed, not of sounds merely, but of sounds *significant*.

2. The most general and extensive of these senses, is that in which it is applied to *description*, comprehending, not only that poetic landscape-painting which is *peculiarly* called descriptive Poetry, but all such circumstantial and distinct representation as conveys to the mind a strong and clear idea of its object, whether *sensible* or *mental*.[10] Poetry, in this view, is naturally

---

[9] The causes of this imperfection are accurately pointed out by Mr. Harris; 1. The *"natural* sounds and motions which Poetry thus imitates, are themselves but *loose* and *indefinite accidents* of those *subjects* to which they belong, and consequently do but *loosely* and *indefinitely* characterise them. 2. *Poetic* sounds and motions do but *faintly* resemble those of *nature*, which are *themselves* confessed to be so *imperfect* and *vague*." [*Treatise on Music*, etc., *ch*. iii. § 2. See also *ch*. ii., § 3.] The following is a famous imitative line of Boileau:

S'en va frapper le mur, & revient en roulant.

If this line were read to any one ignorant of the language, he would be so far from guessing *what* was imitated, that it would not, I believe, occur to him that *anything* was imitated at all; unless, indeed, the idea were forced upon his mind by the pronuntiation of the reader. Now, suppose him to understand French: as the circumstance of *rolling* is mentioned in the line, he might possibly notice the effect of the letter R, and think the poet intended to express the noise of *something* that rolled. And this is all the *real* resemblance that can be discovered in this verse: a resemblance, and that too, but distant and imperfect, in the sound of a letter to the sound of *rolling* in general. For anything beyond this, we must trust to our imagination, assisted by the commentator, who assures us, that the poet "a cherché à imiter par le son des mots, *le bruit que fait une assiette en roulant*" Sat. iii. v. 216.

[10] Nothing is more common than this application of the word to description; though the writers who so apply it have not always explained the ground of the

considered as more or less *imitative*, in proportion as it is capable of raising an ideal *image* or *picture*, more or less resembling the reality of things. The more distinct and vivid the ideas are of which this picture is composed, and the more closely they correspond to the actual *impressions* received from nature, the stronger will be the resemblance, and the more perfect the imitation.

Hence it is evident that, of all description, that of *visible* objects will be the *most* imitative, the ideas of such objects being of all others, the most distinct and vivid. That *such* description, therefore, should have been called imitation, can be no wonder; and, indeed, of all the extended or analogical applications of the word, this is, perhaps, the most obivous and natural.[11] There needs no other proof of this than the very language in which we are naturally led to express our admiration of this kind of poetry, and which we perpetually borrow from the arts of strict imitation. We say the poet has *painted* his object; we talk of his *imagery*, of the lively *colours* of his description, and the masterly touches of his *pencil*.[12]

---

application, or pointed out those precise properties of description which entitle it to be considered as imitation. Mr. Addison makes use of *description* as a general term, comprehending all poetic imitation, or imitation by language, as opposed to that of painting, etc. See *Spectator* No. 416. I. C. Scaliger, though he extended *imitation* to speech in general, [see Part II. Note 1.] did not overlook the circumstances which render description peculiarly imitative. He says, with his usual spirit, speaking of poetic or verbal imitation: "At *imitatio* non uno modo; quando ne *res* quidem. Alia namque est *simplex designatio*, ut *Aeneas pugnat*: alia *modos* addit et *circumstantias;* verbi gratiâ—*armatus, in equo, iratus*. Jam hîc est pugnantis *etiam facies*, non solum *actio*. Ita *adjunctae circumstantiae, loci, affectus, occasionis* etc. *pleniorem* adhucatque *torosiorem* efficiunt *imitationem.*" [*Poetices lib. septem* cap. 2] We must not, however, confound *imitative description* with such description as is merely an *enumeration of parts*, See *note* 12 Second part of this Dissertation.

[11] Τα δε οψει γνωριμα, δια ποιητικης ἑρμηνειας ἑμφαινεται μιμητικωτερον. ὁιον, κυματων οψεις, και τοποθεσιαι, και μαχαι, και περισασεις παθων. ὡσε συνδιατιθεσθαι τας ψυχας τοις ἑιδεσι των ἁπαγγελλομενων, ὡς ὡρωμενοις. Ptolomaeus, *Harmonica.* 3. 3.

[12] It cannot be necessary to produce examples of this. They are to be found in almost every page of every writer on the subject of poetry. The reader may see Dr. Hurd's *Discourse on Poetical Imitation*, p. 10, etc.; Dr. Beattie's *Essay on Poetry and Music*, p. 97, (*Ed.* 8vo.) and the note; Dr. Warton on Pope, vol. i. p. 44, 45; vol. ii. 223, 227; Lord Kaims, *Elem. of Criticism*, vol. ii, p. 326. Nor is this manner of speaking peculiar to modern writers. φερε ὁυν says Aelian, introducing his description of the Vale of Tempe; και τα καλουμενα Τεμπη, τα θετταλικα, διαγραψομεν τω λογω, και διαπλασομεν. And he adds, as in

The objects of our other senses fall less within the power of description, in proportion as the ideas of those objects are more simple, more fleeting, and less distinct, than those of sight. The description of such objects is, therefore, called with less propriety *imitation*.[13]

Next to visible objects, *sounds* seem the most capable of descriptive imitation. Such description is, indeed, generally aided by real, though imperfect, resemblance of verbal sound; more, or less, according to the nature of the language, and the delicacy of the poet's ear. The following lines of Virgil are, I think, an instance of this.

> Lamentis gemituque et foemineo ululatu
> Tecta fremunt, resonat magnis plangoribus aether.
> *Aen.* iv. 668

But we are not, now, considering this immediate imitation of sound by sound, but such only as is merely *descriptive*, and operates, like the description of visible objects, only by the *meaning* of the words. Now if we are allowed to call description of visible objects, imitation, when it is such that *we seem to see* the object,[14] I know of no reason why we may not also consider sounds as imitated,[15] when they are so described that we *seem to hear* them. It would not be difficult to produce from the best poets, and even from prose-writers of a strong and poetical imagination, many instances of sound so imitated.

---

justification of these expressions, ὡμολογηται γαρ και ὁ λογος, ἐαν ἐχη δυναμιν φραστικην, μηδεν ασθενεστερον ὁσα βουλεται δεικνυναι των ἀνδρων των κατα χειρουργιαν δεινων. *Historiae Variae*, lib. iii. cap. I. Hence, also, the saying of Simonides, so often repeated, that "a picture is a silent poem, and a poem a speaking picture." Lucian, in that agreeable delineation of a beautiful and accomplished woman, his Εικονες, ranks the descriptive poet with the painter and the sculptor: ταυτα μεν οὖν πλαστων και γραφεων και ποιητων παιδες ἐργασονται. Homer, he denominates, τον ἀριστον των γραφεων, "the best of *painters*"; and calls upon him, even in preference to Polygnotus, Apelles, and the most eminent artists, to paint the charms of his Panthea. See also the treatise Περι της Ὁμηρου ποιησεως, towards the end. (Ει δε και Ζωγραφιας διδασκαλον Ὁμηρου φαιη τις, κ. τ. αλλ.)

[13] One obvious reason of this is, the want of that natural association just remarked, with *painting*, (the most striking of the *strictly imitative* arts,) which is peculiar to the description of *visible* objects.

[14] Ορωμενοις μαλλον ἠ ἀκουομενοις ἐοικε τα [Ὁμηρου] ποιηματα.
Treatise περι της Ὁμηρου ποιησεως, *loc. cit.*

[15] Lucian, in his *Imagines*, just now cited, has very happily described a fine female voice, and he calls the description, somewhat boldly, καλλιφονιας και ᾠδης εικον.

Those readers who are both poetical and musical will, I believe, excuse my dwelling a moment upon a subject which has not, as far as I know, been much considered.

Of our own poets I do not recollect any who have presented *musical* ideas with such feeling, force, and reality of description, as Milton, and Mr. Mason. When Milton speaks of

— Notes with many a winding bout
Of linked sweetness long drawn out.
L'Allegro

And of "a soft and solemn-breathing sound," that

Rose like a steam of rich distill'd perfumes,
And stole upon the air.
Comus

Who, that has a truly musical ear, will refuse to consider such description as, in some sort, imitative?[16]

In the same spirit both of Poetry and of Music are these beautiful lines in *Caractacus*, addressed by the Chorus to the Bards:

—Wond'rous men!
Ye, whose skill'd fingers know how best to lead,
Through all the maze of sound, the wayward step
Of Harmony, recalling oft, and oft
Permitting her unbridled course to rush
Through dissonance to concord, sweetest then
Ev'n when expected harshest.

It seems scarce possible to convey with greater clearness to the ear of imagination the effect of an artful and well-conducted harmony; of that free and varied range of modulation, in which the ear is ever wandering, yet never lost, and of that masterly and bold intertexture of discord, which leads the sense to pleasure, through paths that lie close upon the very verge of pain.

The general and confused effect of complex and aggregated sound may be said to be *described*, when the most striking and characteristic of the single sounds of which it is compounded are selected and enumerated; just as *single* sounds are described (and they can be described no otherwise) by the selection of their principal *qualities*, or *modifications*. I cannot produce a

[16] See also *Il Penseroso*, 161–166.

finer example of this than the following admirable passage of Dante, in which, with a force of representation peculiar to himself in such subjects, he describes the mingled terrors of those distant sounds that struck his ear as he entered the gates of his imaginary *Inferno;* "si mise dentro alle segrete cose."

> Quivi sospiri, pianti, ed alti guai
> Risonavan per l'aer senza stelle;
> . . . .
> Diverse lingue, orribili favelle,
> Parole di dolore, accenti d'ira,
> Voci alte fioche, e suon di man con elle.
>
> *Inferno, Canto* iii

The reader may be glad to relieve his imagination from the terrible ΕΝΑΡΓΕΙΑ of this description, by turning his ear to a far different combination of sounds; to the charming description of "the melodies of morn," in the "Minstrel,"[17] or of the *melodies of evening* in the "Deserted Village":

> Sweet was the sound, when oft at evening's close,
> Up yonder hill the village murmur rose.
> There as I past with careless steps and slow,
> The mingling notes came soften'd from below;
> The swain responsive as the milk-maid sung,
> The sober herd that low'd to meet their young;
> The noisy geese that gabbled o'er the pool,
> The playful children just let loose from school;
> The watch-dog's voice that bay'd the whisp'ring wind,
> And the loud laugh that spoke the vacant mind
> These all in soft confusion sought the shade,
> And fill'd each pause the nightingale had made.[18]

[17] Book I. *Stanzas* 40, 41.

[18] The following Stanza of Spenser has been much admired:

> The joyous birdes, shrouded in chearful shade,
> Their notes unto the voice attempred sweet,
> Th' angelical soft trembling voices made
> To th' instruments divine, respondence meet;
> The silver-sounding instruments did meet
> With the base murmur of the water's fall;
> The water's fall with difference discreet
> Now soft, now loud, unto the wind did call,
> The gentle warbling wind low answered to all.
>
> *Fairy Queen, Book* ii., *Canto* 12, *Stanza* 71

Dr. Warton says of these lines, that they "are of themselves a complete

But *single sounds* may also be so described or characterized as to produce a secondary perception, of sufficient clearness to deserve the name of imitation. It is thus that we hear the "far-off Curfeu" of Milton:

> Over some wide-water'd shore
> Swinging slow with sullen roar.[19]

And Mr. Mason's "Bell of Death," that

> —pauses now; and now with *rising knell*
> *Flings to the hollow gale* its sullen sound.
> *Elegy*, iii.

I do not know a happier descriptive line in Homer than the following, in his simile of the nightingale:

> Ἡ τε θαμα τρωπωσα χεει πολυηχεα φωνην.[20]

That which is peculiar in the singing of this bird, the variety, richness, flexibility, and liquid volubility of its notes, cannot well be

---

concert of the most delicious music." It is unwillingly that I differ from a person of so much taste. I cannot consider as *Music*, much less as "delicious music," a mixture of incompatible sounds, if I may so call them—of sounds *musical* with sounds *unmusical*. The singing of birds cannot possibly be "attempred" to the notes of a human voice. The mixture is, and must be, disagreeable. To a person listening to a concert of voices and instruments, the interruption of *singing-birds*, *wind*, and *waterfalls*, would be little better than the torment of Hogarth's enraged musician. Farther—the description itself is, like too many of Spenser's, coldly elaborate, and indiscriminately minute. Of the expressions, some are feeble and without effect—as, *"joyous* birds," some evidently improper—as, *"trembling* voices," and *"cheareful* shade"; for there cannot be a greater fault in a voice than to be tremulous; and *cheareful* is surely an unhappy epithet applied to shade; some cold and laboured, and such as betray too plainly the *necessities of rhyme*; such is,
    The water's fall with *difference discreet*.

[19] The reader who conceives the word *"swinging*," to be merely descriptive of *motion*, will be far, I think, from feeling the whole force of this passage. They who are accustomed to attend to sounds, will, I believe, agree with me, that the sound, in this case, is affected by the motion, and that the swing of a bell is actually *heard in its tone*, which is different from what it would be if the *same* bell were struck with the *same force*, but *at rest*. The experiment may be easily made with a small hand-bell.

[20] *Odyssey*, T. 521. I am surprised at Ernestus's interpretation of τρωπωσα; i.e., "de lusciniâ inter canendum SE *versante*"; [*Index* to his Homer] by which the greatest beauty of the description would be lost; and lost without necessity: for the natural construction is that which *Hesychius* gives: τρωπωσα—τρεπουσα ΤΗΝ ΦΩΝΗΝ.

more strongly characterized, more *audibly* presented to the mind, than by the πολυηχεα, the χεει, and, above all, the θαμα τρωπωσα, of this short description.[21] But, to return—

I mentioned also, description of *mental* objects; of the emotions, passions, and other internal movements and operations of the mind. Such objects may be described, either *immediately*, as they affect the mind, or through their *external* and *sensible* *effects*. Let us take the passion of Dido for an instance:

> At regina gravi jamdudum saucia curâ
> Vulnus alit venis, et caeco carpitur igni, &c.
> *Aeneid.* iv. 1

This is *immediate* description. But when Dido

> Incipit effari, mediâque in voce resistit;
> Nunc eadem, labente die, convivia quaerit,
> Iliacosque iterum, demens, audire labores
> Exposcit, pendetque iterum narrantis ab ore.
> Post, ubi digressi, lumenque obscura vicissim
> Luna premit, suadentque cadentia sidera somnos,
> Sola domo maeret vacuâ, stratisque relictis
> Incubat.—

—here, the passion is described, and most exquisitely, by its *sensible effects*. This, indeed, *may* be considered as falling under the former kind of descriptive imitation—that of *sensible* objects. There is this difference, however, between the description of a sensible object, and the description of a mental—of any passion for example—*through* that of a sensible object, that, in the former, the description is considered as terminating in the clear and distinct representation of the sensible object, the landscape, the attitude, the sound, etc.,: whereas in the other, the sensible exhibition is only, or chiefly, the *means* of effecting that which is the principal end of such description—the emotion, of whatever kind, that arises from a strong conception of

---

[21] Not a single beauty of this line is preserved in Mr. Pope's translation. The χεει, "*pours* her voice," is *entirely* dropt; and the strong and rich expression, in θαμα τρωπωσα, and πολυηχεα, is diluted into "*varied* strains." [Book xix, 607.] For the *particular* ideas of a *variety of quick turns* and *inflexions* [θαμα τρωπωσα] and a *variety of tones*, [πολυηχεα] the translator has substituted the *general*, and therefore weak idea, of *variety* in the abstract—of a song or "strains" simply *varied*. The reader may see this subject—the importance of *particular* and *determinate* ideas to the force and beauty of description—admirably illustrated in the *Discourse on Poetical Imitation*. [Hurd's Horace, vol. iii, p. 15–19.]

the passion itself. The image carries us on forcibly to the feeling of its internal cause. When this *first* effect is once produced, we may, indeed, return from it to the calmer pleasure, of contemplating the imagery itself with a painter's eye.

It is undoubtedly, *this* description of passions and emotions, by their *sensible* effects, that principally deserves the name of *imitative;* and it is a great and fertile source of some of the highest and most touching beauties of poetry.[22] With respect to *immediate* descriptions of this kind, they are from their very nature, far more weak and indistinct, and do not, perhaps, often possess that degree of forcible representation that amounts to what we call *imitative* description.—But here some distinctions seem necessary. In a strict and philosophical view, a *single* passion or emotion does not admit of description at all. Considered in itself, it is a simple internal feeling, and, as such, can no more be *described*, than a simple idea can be *defined*. It can be described no otherwise than in its *effects*, of *some* kind or other. But the effects of a passion are of two kinds, *internal* and *external*. Now, popularly speaking, by *the passion* of love, for example, we mean the whole operation of that passion upon the *mind*—we include all its internal workings; and when it is described in these internal and invisible effects only, we consider it as *immediately* described by these internal effects being included in our general idea of the passion. *Mental objects*, then, admit of immediate description, only when they are, more or less, complex; and such description may be considered as more or less *imitative*, in proportion as its impression on the mind approaches more or less closely to the real impression of the passion or emotion itself.—Thus, in the passage above referred to as an instance of such immediate description, the mental object described is a complex object—the passion of love, including some of its internal effects; that is, some *other* passions or feelings which it excites, or with which it is accompanied:

> At regina gravi jamdudum saucia curâ
> Vulnus alit venis, et caeco carpitur igni.
> Multa viri virtus animo, multusque recursat
> Gentis honos: haerent infixi pectore vultus,
> Verbaque: nec placidam membris dat cura quietem.
> *Aen.* iv. *initio.*

[22] See the *Discourse on Poetical Imitation*, of Dr. Hurd, p. 39, etc.

53

Reduce this passage to the mere mention of the passion *itself*—the simple feeling or emotion of *love* in the precise and strict acceptation of the word, abstractedly from its concomitant effects, it will not even be *description*, much less *imitative* description. It will be mere attribution, or predication. It will say only—"Dido was in love."

Thus, again, a complication of *different passions* admits of forcible and *imitative* description:

> —aestuat ingens
> Imo in corde pudor, mixtoqu insania luctu,
> Et furiis agitatus amor, et conscia virtus.
> *Aen.* xii. 666.

Here, the mental object described is not any single passion, but the complex passion, if I may call it so, that results from the mixture and fermentation of all the passions *attributed* to Turnus.

To give one example more: The mind of a reader can hardly, I think, be flung into an imaginary situation more closely resembling the real situation of a mind distressed by the *complicated* movements of irresolute, fluctuating, and anxious deliberation, than it is by these lines of Virgil:

> —magno curarum fluctuat aestu;
> Atque animum nunc huc celerem, nunc dividit illuc,
> In partesque rapit varias, perque omnia versat.
> *Aen.* viii. 19.

It may be necessary, also, for clearness, to observe, that description, as applied to mental objects, is sometimes used in a more loose and improper sense, and the Poet is said to *describe*, in general, all the passions or manners which he, in any way, exhibits; whether, in the proper sense of the word, *described*, or merely *expressed;* as, for example, in the lines quoted from the opening of the fourth book of the *Aeneid*, the passion of Dido is *described* by the *Poet*. In these—

> Quis novus hic nostris successit sedibus hospes?
> Quem sese ore ferens!—quam forti pectore et armis!—

—it is *expressed* by herself. But is not this, it may be asked, still *imitation?* It is; but not *descriptive* imitation. As *expressive of passion*, it is no farther imitative, than as the passion expressed is imaginary, and makes a part of the Poet's *fiction:* otherwise, we must apply the word *imitative*, as nobody ever thought of applying it, to *all* cases in which we are made, by sympathy, to feel strongly the passion of another expressed by words. The passage is, indeed, also *imitative* in another view—as *dramatic*. But for an explanation of both these heads of imitation, I must refer to what follows.—I shall only add, for fear of mistake, that there is also, in the second of those lines, *descriptive imitation;* but descriptive of *Aeneas* only; not of Dido's *passion*, though it strongly *indicates* that passion.—All I mean to assert is, that those lines are not *descriptive imitation of a mental object*.

So much, then, for the subject of *descriptive imitation*, which has, perhaps, detained us too long upon a single point of our general inquiry.

3. The word *imitation* is also, in a more particular, but well-known, sense, applied to Poetry when considered as *fiction*—to stories, actions, incidents, and characters, as far as they are *feigned* or *invented* by the Poet *in imitation*, as we find it commonly, and obviously enough, expressed, of nature, of real life, of truth, in *general*, as opposed to that individual reality of things which is the province of the historian.[23] Of this imitation the epic and dramatic poems are the principal examples.

That this sense of the term, as applied to fiction, is entirely distinct from that in which it is applied to description, will evidently appear from the following considerations.—In descriptive imitation, the resemblance is between the ideas raised, and the actual *impressions*, whether external or internal, received from the things themselves. In fictive imitation, the resemblance is, strictly speaking, between the ideas raised, and other ideas; the ideas raised—the ideas of the *Poem*—being no other than copies, resemblances, or, more philosophically, new, though similar, combinations of that general stock of ideas, collected from experience, observation, and reading, and reposited in the Poet's mind. In description, *imitation* is opposed to actual *impression*, external or internal: in fiction, it is opposed to *fact*.—In their *effects*, some degree of illusion is implied; but the illusion is not of the same kind in both. Descriptive imtiation may be said to produce *illusive perception*,—fictive, *illusive belief*.

Farther—descriptive imitation may subsist without fictive,

and fictive, without descriptive. The first of these assertions is too obvious to stand in need of proof. The other may require some explanation. It seems evident that fiction may even subsist in mere *narration*, without any degree of *description*, properly so called; much more, without *such* description as I have called *imitative;* that is, without any greater degree of resemblance to the things expressed, than that which is implied in *all* ideas, and produced by *all* language, considered merely as *intelligible*. Let a story be invented, and related in the plainest manner possible; in short and general expressions, amounting, in the incidents, to mere assertion, and in the account of passions and characters, as far as possible, to mere attribution: this, as fiction, is still *imitation*—an invented resemblance of real life, or, if you please, of history[24]—though without a single *imitative description*, a single *picture*, a single instance of strong and visible colouring, throughout the whole.[25] I mean, by this, only to shew the distinct and independent senses in which *imitation* is applied to description and to fiction, by shewing how each species of imitation *may* subsist without the other: but, that fictive imitation, though it does not, in any degree, depend on descriptive for its existence, does, in a very great degree, depend on it for its beauty, is too obvious to be called in question.[26]

The two senses last mentioned of the word *imitative*, as

[24] "Historiae imitatio ad placitum." Bacon, *De augm. Scient.*, lib. ii., c. 13.

[25] The *Aeneid* in this view, is equally *imitation* in every part where it is not, or is not *supposed* to be, historically true; even in the simplest and barest narration. In point of fiction, "tres littore cervos prospicit errantes," is as much imitation, though not as *poetical*, as the fine description of the storm in the same book, or of Dido's conflicting passions, in the fourth.

[26] Yet even here a distinction obviously suggests itself. A work of fiction may be considered in two views; in the whole, or in its parts: in the general story, the Μῦθος, fable, series of *events*, etc., or, in the detail and circumstances of the story, the account of such places, persons, and things, as the fable necessarily involves. Now, in the first view, nothing farther seems requisite to make the fictive imitation *good*, than that the events be, in *themselves*, important, interesting, and affecting, and so *connected* as to appear credible, probable, and natural to the reader, and, by that means, to produce the illusion, and give the pleasure, that is expected: and this purpose may be answered by mere *narration*. But in the detail this is not the case. When the Poet proceeds to fill up and distend the outline of his general plan by the exhibition of places, characters, or passions, these also, as well as the *events*, must appear probable and natural: but, being more *complex* objects, they can no otherwise be made to appear so than by some degree of *description*, and that description will not be *good* de-

applied to description, and to fiction, are manifestly extended, or improper senses, as well as that first mentioned, in which it is applied to language considered as mere sound. In *all* these imitations, *one* of the essential conditions of whatever is *strictly* so denominated is wanting;—in sonorous imitation, the resemblance is *immediate,* but not *obvious;* in the others, it is *obvious,* but not *immediate;* that is, it lies, not in the *words* themselves, but in the *ideas* which they raise as *signs:*[27] yet as the circumstance of *obvious* resemblance, which may be regarded as the most striking and distinctive property of Imitation, is here found, this extension of the word seems to have more propriety than that in which it is applied to those faint and evanescent resemblances which have, not without reason, been called the echo of sound to sense.[28]

4. There seems to be but *one* view in which Poetry can be considered as *Imitation,* in the strict and proper sense of the word. If we look for both *immediate* and *obvious* resemblance, we shall find it only in *dramatic*—or to use a more general term—*personative* Poetry; that is, all Poetry in which, whether essentially or occasionally, the Poet personates; for here, *speech* is imitated by *speech.*[29] The difference between this, and mere narration or description, is obvious. When, in common discourse, we *relate,* or *describe,* in our own persons, we *imitate* in no other sense than as we raise *ideas* which resemble the things related or described. But when we speak *as another person,* we become mimics, and not only the ideas we convey, but the words, the discourse itself, in which we convey them, are imitations; they resemble, or are supposed to resemble, those of the person we represent. Now this is the case not only with the

---

scription, that is, will not give the pleasure expected from a work of imagination, unless it be *imitative*—such as makes us see the *place,* feel the *passion,* enter thoroughly into the *character* described. Here, the *fictive* imitation itself, cannot produce its proper *effect,* and therefore cannot be considered as *good,* without the assistance of *descriptive.*

[27] See above, p. 43.

[28] Pope's *Essay on Crit.* 365.—Indeed, what Ovid says of the nymph *Echo* [*Met.* iii. 358.] may be applied to this echo of imitative words and construction: Nec *prior ipsa loqui* didicit. The *sense* of the words must *speak first.*

[29] The drama, indeed, is said also to imitate *action* by *action;* but this is only in actual representation, where the players are the immediate imitators. In the poem itself nothing but *words* can be immediately copied. Gravina says well, "Non è *imitazione poetica* quella, che non è fatta *dalle parole.*"—[*Della Trag. sect.* 13.]

Tragic and Comic Poet, but also with the Epic Poet, and even the Historian, when either of these quits his own character, and *writes* a speech in the character of another person. He is then an imitator, in as strict a sense as the personal mimic. In *dramatic*, and all *personative* Poetry, then, both the conditions of what is *properly* denominated Imitation, are fulfilled.

And now, the question—"in what senses the word *Imitation* is, or may be applied to Poetry,"—seems to have received its answer. It appears, I think, that the term ought not to be extended beyond the *four* different applications which have been mentioned; and that Poetry can be justly considered as *imitative*, only by *sound*, by *description*, by *fiction*, or by *personation*. Whenever the Poet speaks in his own person, and, at the same time, does not either feign, or make "the sound an echo to the sense," or stay to impress his ideas upon the fancy with some degree of that force and distinctness which we call description, he cannot, in any sense that I am aware of, be said to *imitate;* unless we extend imitation to *all* speech—to every mode of expressing our thoughts by words—merely because all words are signs of ideas, and those ideas images of *things*.[30]

It is scarce necessary to observe, that these different species of imitation often run into, and are mixed with each other. They are, indeed, more properly speaking, only so many distinct, abstracted *views*, in which Poetry may be considered as imitating. It is seldom that any of them are to be found separately; and in some of them, others are necessarily implied. Thus, dramatic imitation implies fiction, and sonorous imitation, description; though conversely, it is plainly otherwise. Descriptive imitation is, manifestly, that which is most independent on all the others. The passages in which they are all united are frequent; and those in which all are excluded, are, in the best Poetry, very rare: for the Poet of genius rarely forgets his proper *language;* and that can scarcely be retained, at least while he *relates*, without more or less of colouring, of imagery, of that *descriptive* force which makes us see and hear. A total suspension of all his functions as an imitator is hardly to be found, but in the simple proposal of his subject,[31] in his invoca-

---

[30] See *Hermes* iii. 3. 329, etc. And Part II. of this *Diss.* note 48.

[31] Arma virumque cano, Trojae qui primus ab oris
Italiam, fato profugus, Lavinaque venit
Litora.   *Aeneid*, i.

tion,[32] the expression of his own sentiments,[33] or, in those calm beginnings of narration where, now and then, the Poet stoops to *fact*, and becomes, for a moment, little more than a metrical historian.[34]

The full illustration of all this by examples, would draw out to greater length a discussion, which the reader, I fear, has already thought too long. If he will open the *Aeneid*, or any other epic poem, and apply these remarks, he may, perhaps, find it amusing to trace the different kinds of imitation as they successively occur, in their various combinations and degrees; and to observe the Poet varying, from page to page, and sometimes even from line to line, the *quantity*, if I may so speak, of his imitation; sometimes shifting, and sometimes, though rarely and for a moment, throwing off altogether, his imitative form.

It has been often said that *all Poetry is Imitation.*[35] But from the preceding inquiry it appears, that, if we take *Poetry* in its common acceptation, for all *metrical composition*, the assertion is not ture; not, at least, in any sense of the term *Imitation* but such as will make it equally true of all *Speech.*[36] If, on the other hand, we depart from that common acceptation of the word *Poetry*, the assertion that "all Poetry is Imitation," seems only an improper and confused way of saying, that no composition that is not imitative *ought* to be *called* Poetry. To examine the truth of this, would be to engage in a fresh discussion totally distinct from the object of this dissertation. We have not, now, been considering *what* Poetry *is*, or how it should be *defined;* but only, in what sense it is an *Imitative Art:* or, rather, we have

---

[32] Musa, mihi causas memora, etc.   *Ibid.*

[33] Tantaene animis caelestibus irae?

. . . .

Tantae molis erat Romanam condere gentem.
                                        Ibid.

[34] Urbs antiqua fuit, (Tyrii tenuêre coloni,)
    Carthago, Italiam contra, Tiberinaque longe
    Ostia, etc.   *Ibid.*

[35] This expression is nowhere, that I know of, used by Aristotle. In the beginning of his treatise he asserts only that the *Epic, Tragic, Comic,* and *Dithyrambic Poems* are imitations. Le Bossu, not content with saying that "*every sort of Poem in general is an Imitation,*" goes so far as even to alter the text of Aristotle in his marginal quotation. He makes him say, ποιησεις πασαι τυγχανουσιν ουσαι μιμησεις το συνολον.

[36] See p. 58, note 30.

been examining the nature and extent of VERBAL IMITATION in general.[37]

II

The preceding *general* inquiry, "in what senses the word *Imitation* is, or may be, applied to Poetry," brings us with some advantage to the other question proposed, of more immediate concern to the reader of this treatise of Aristotle—"in what senses it was so applied by *him*."

1. It is clearly so applied by him in the sense which, from him, has, I think, most generally been adopted by modern writers—that of *fiction*, as above explained,[38] whether conveyed in the dramatic or personative form, or, by mere narration in the person of the Poet himself.[39] This appears from the whole sixth section of Part II. [of the original, ch. ix] but especially from the last paragraph, where he expressly says, that what constitutes the Poet an *imitator*, is the *invention of a Fable*: ποιητην μαλλον ΤΩΝ ΜΥΘΩΝ εἶναι δει ΠΟΙΗΤΗΝ———ὅσῳ ποιητης ΚΑΤΑ ΜΙΜΗΣΙΝ ἐστι, μιμειται δε ΤΑΣ ΠΡΑΞΕΙΣ.[40] He repeatedly calls the fable, or Μυθος, "*an imitation of an action*"; but this it can be in no other sense than as it is feigned, either entirely, or in part. A history, as far, at least, as it is strictly history, is not an *imitation* of an action.

2. It seems equally clear, that he considered *dramatic* Poetry as *peculiarly* imitative, above every other species. Hence his *first* rule concerning the epic or narrative imitation, that its fable "should be *dramatically* constructed, like that of *tragedy*";[41] τους μυθους, καθαπερ ἐν ταις τραγῳδιαις, ΔΡΑΜΑΤΙΚΟΥΣ; his praise of Homer for "the *dramatic* spirit of his imitations"; ὅτι και ΜΙΜΗΣΕΙΣ ΔΡΑΜΑΤΙΚΑΣ ἐποιησε;[42] and above all, the remarkable expression he uses, where, having laid it down as a precept that the epic Poet "should speak as little as possible in his *own person*," (ΑΥΤΟΝ δει τον ποιητην ἐλαχιστα λεγειν) he gives this rea-

---

[37] Imitation, in every sense of the word that has been mentioned, is manifestly independent on *metre*, though being more eminently adapted to the nature and end of metrical composition, it has thence been peculiarly denominated *Poetic* imitation, and attributed to the *Poetic Art.*

[38] P. 55.

[39] μιμεισθαι ἐστιν—ὡς τον αυτον και μη μεταβαλλοντα. cap. 3. "The Poet may *imitate*, etc.—*or, in his own person throughout, without change.*" Part I. Sect. 4.

[40] See Mr. Harris, *Philological Inquiries* p. 139.

[41] Part III, Sect. 1. Of the orig. ch. xxiii.

[42] Part I, Sect. 6. Orig. cap. iv.

son: ΟΥ γαρ ἐστι κατα ταυτα ΜΙΜΗΤΗΣ—"for he is not *then* the
IMITATOR."[43] But, he had before expressly allowed the Poet to be an
imitator even while he retains his own person.[44] I see no other way
of removing this apparent inconsistence, than by supposing him to
speak comparatively, and to mean no more, than that the Poet is
not then *truly* and *strictly* an imitator;[45] or, in other words, that
imitation is applicable in its *strict* and *proper* sense, only to *personative*
poetry, as above explained; to that Poetry in which speech is represented by speech, and the resemblance, as in painting and sculpture,
is immediate. I am not conscious that I am here forcing upon
Aristotle a meaning that may not be his. I seem to be only drawing
a clear inference from a clear fact. It cannot be denied, that, in the
passages alleged, he plainly speaks of personative Poetry as that
which *peculiarly* deserves the name of imitation. The inference
seems obvious—that he speaks of it as *peculiarly* imitative, in the
only sense in which it is so, as being the only species of Poetry that
is *strictly* imitative.

I do not find in Aristotle any express application of the term,
except these two. Of the other two senses in which Poetry may
be, and by modern writers has been, considered as
imitation—*resemblance* of *sound,* and *description*—he says
nothing.

With respect, indeed, to the former of these, *sonorous* imitation, it cannot appear in any degree surprising that he should
pass it over in total silence. I have already observed, that even in
a *general* inquiry concerning the nature of the imitation attributed to Poetry, it is by no means that sense of the word which
would be likely first to occur; and it would, perhaps, never have
occurred at all, if, in such inquiries, we were not naturally led
to compare Poetry with Painting, and other arts *strictly* imita-

---

[43] Part III, Sect. 3. Orig. cap. xxiv.   [44] See above, note 39.

[45] So Victorius: "amittit *pené* eo tempore nomen Poetae." Castelvetro's solution of this difficulty is the same; and I find his ideas of this matter so coin-
cident with my own, that I am induced to transcribe his words: In his comment
upon the passage, he says, speaking of the dramatic part of epic poetry. "Si
domanda qui *solo rassomigliativo,* (i. e., *imitative*) non perché ancora quando il
Poeta narra senza introducimento di persone à favellare, non rassomigli, ma
perché *le parole diritte poste in luogo di parole diritte, figurano, rappresentano, e
rassomigliano* MEGLIO *le parole,* che le parole poste in luogo di COSE non figurano,
non rappresentano, non rassomigliano le *cose;* in guisa che, *in certo modo si puo
dire* che il rappresentare *parole con parole* sia rassomigliare; e il rappresentare
cose con parole non sia rassomigliare, *paragonando l'un rassomigliare con l'altro,*
& *non semplicemente.*" P. 554.

tive,[46] and as naturally led by that comparison to admit *sonorous* imitation as one species, from its agreement with those strictly imitative arts in the circumstance of *immediate* resemblance. But no such general inquiry was the object of Aristotle's work, which is not a treatise *on Poetic Imitation*, but *on Poetry*. His subject, therefore, led him to consider, not *all* that *might* without impropriety be denominated imitation in Poetry, but *that* imitation only which he regarded as essential to the art; as the source of its greatest beauties, and the foundation of its most important rules. With respect, then, to that casual and subordinate kind of imitation which is produced merely by the *sound* of words, it was not likely even that the idea of it should occur to him. Indeed, it is to be considered as a property of language in general, rather than of Poetry; and of *speech*—of actual pronunciation—rather than of language.[47] Besides that the beauties arising from this source are of too delicate and fugitive a nature to be held by rule. They *must* be left to the ear of the reader for their effect, and *ought* to be left to that of the Poet for their production.

But neither does Aristotle appear to have included *description* in his notion of Poetic imitation; which, as far as he has explained it, seems to have been simply that of the imitation of human actions, manners, passions, events, etc., in *feigned story;* and that, *principally*, when conveyed in a dramatic form. Of description, indeed, important as it is to the beauty of Poetry in general, and to that of fiction itself, more particularly in the *epic* form, he has not said one word throughout his treatise: so far was he from extending Poetic imitation, as some have done, to that general sense which comprehends all speech.[48]

But here, to avoid confusion, the sense in which I have used the term *description* must be kept in view. When it is said that

---

[46] See above, p. 43.   [47] See above p. 43.

[48] Thus I. C. Scaliger, *Poetices Libri Septem* vii. *cap* 2. "Denique *imitationem* esse in *omni sermone, quia verba sunt imagines rerum.*" He is followed by Isaac Casaubon; *De Satira Graecorum Poesi et de Romanorum Satira,* cap. v. p. 340. Both these acute critics dispute warmly against Aristotle's principle, that the essence of Poetry is imitation. And they are, undoubtedly, so far in the right, that *if*, as they contend, the only proper sense of *Poetry* is that in which it is opposed to *prose* ("omnem *metro astrictam* orationem et posse et "debere *Poema* dici." *Cas. ubi sup.*) then, there can be no other imitation common to *all Poetry* than that which is common to *all speech*. See above, pp. 57, 58.

Aristotle did not include description in his notion of "imitation," it is not meant that he did not consider the descriptive parts of narrative Poetry as *in any respect* imitative. The subject of a description may be either real, or feigned. Almost all the descriptions of the higher Poetry, the Poetry of invention, are of the latter kind. These Aristotle, unquestionably, considered as imitation; but it was *as fiction, not as description;* as falsehood resembling truth, or nature, in general, not as verbal expression resembling, by its force and clearness, the visible representations of painting, or the perception of the thing itself. Had he considered description in *this* sense as imitation, he must necessarily have admitted imitation without fiction.[49] But this seems clearly contrary to the whole tenor of

[49] It is obvious, that, if the *imitation* attributed to description consists in the clear and distinct image of the object described, every description conveying such an image to the mind must be equally considered as imitative, whether that object be real, or imaginary; that is, whether the imitation be of individual, or general nature; just as in painting, a portrait, or a landscape from nature, is as much imitation, as an historical figure, or an ideal scene of Claude Lorrain, though certainly of an inferior kind. Indeed, that which presents a real, sensible, and precise object of comparison, may even be said to be more obviously and properly *imitation*, than that which refers us, for its original, to a vague and general idea. It may be objected, that this will extend *imitation* to *all* exact description; and it may be asked, whether every such description of a building, or of a machine, for instance, is to be called an imitation? I answer, that descriptions may be *too* exact to be imitative; too detailed and minute to present *the whole* strongly, as a picture. Technical descriptions are such. They may be said to describe *every part* without describing the *whole*. To give a complete idea of all the *parts*, for the mere purpose of information, and to give a strong and vivid *general* idea in order to please the imagination, are very different things. It is by *selection*, not by *enumeration*, that the latter purpose is to be effected. (See Dr. Beattie's *Essay on Poetry and Music*, Part I, ch. v, sect. 4.) I believe it will be found, on examination, that every description, whatever be its purpose, or its subject, which does actually convey such a lively and distinct idea of the *whole* of any object, affords *some* degree of pleasure to the imagination, and is, so far, imitative; but whether it affords *such* a degree of that pleasure, or whether it be such in *other* respects, as to amount, on the whole, to what may properly be called *Poetical* imitation, is another question. I must again remind the reader, that the object of this Dissertation is to inquire *in what senses* the word *imitation* is applied to *language* in general—not to examine all the requisites of *such* imitation as deserves the name of *Poetry*. Though it has been said that all Poetry is imitation, it has never, I think, been said that all imitation is Poetry. See above, pp. 56, 57, and note 24.

What I said above, of the difference between the description of *all* the *parts* or *circumstances*, and the description of the *whole* by the selection of *those parts* or *circumstances* which are most striking, and characteristic of the thing de-his treatise. The beauty, indeed, of such description was well known to the antients, and frequent examples of it are to be found in their best writers—their orators and historians, as well as Poets; and, particularly, in Homer.[50] But there is one particular kind of description that may be said to be, in a great measure at least, peculiar to modern times; I mean that which answers to *landscape* in painting, and of which the subject is, prospects, views, rural scenery, etc., considered merely as *pictures*—as beautiful objects to the *eye*.[51] As the truth of this observation

---

scribed, may be illustrated by a single description of a *machine*, in Virgil— I mean the description of a *plough*, in his *Georgics*.

> Continuo in sylvis magnâ vi *flexa domatur*
> In burim, & CURVI *formam accipit ulmus aratri.*
> Huic ab stirpe pedes temo protentus in octo,
> Binae aures, duplici aptantur dentalia dorso.
> Caeditur & tilia ante jugo levis, altaque fagus,
> Stivaque, quae currus à tergo torqueat imos, etc.

I believe every reader will agree with me that the second line of this description conveys, alone, a clearer *picture* of a plough to the imagination, than all that follows; which indeed differs little, if we except the *metre*, from a mere technical description in a dictionary of arts.

[50] Indeed, the very existence of an appropriated term, ἐνάργεια, to denote the *clearness* and *visibility* of description, would alone furnish a sufficient proof of this, though every work in which it was exemplified had been lost.

[51] Descriptions of rural objects in the antient writers, are almost always, what may be called *sensual* descriptions. They describe them not as *beautiful*, but as *pleasant;* as pleasures, not of the *imagination*, but of the *external senses*. Of this kind is the description of a Sicilian scene in the 7th Pastoral of Theocritus, from ver. 131 to 146. Refreshing shades, cool fountains, the singing of birds, sweet smells, boughs laden with fruit, the hum of bees, etc.—all this is charming, but it is not a *landscape*. (See Dr. Warton's *Essay on Pope*, vol. i. p. 4.) Nor does Virgil paint a landscape, though his reader may paint one for himself, when he exclaims,

> —O qui me *gelidis* in vallibus Haemi
> Sistat, & ingenti ramorum *protegat umbrâ.*

Of the same kind is the famous description, in the *Phaedrus* of Plato, of that spot on the banks of the Ilissus to which Socrates and Phaedrus retire to read and converse together in the heat of a summer's day. The broad shade of a plane-tree, refreshing breezes, a spring, μαλα ψυχρου ὑδατος, to *cool their feet*, and, *what is best of all*, says Socrates—(παντων κομψοτατον) a bed of grass in which they could recline at their ease—these are the materials of the description: not a single allusion to the pleasure of the *eye*. We learn from a passage that follows this description, that the country had no charms for Socrates. His apology is curious. He could *"learn nothing from fields and trees."* Συγγινωσκε δε μοι, ὦ ἀριστε, he says to Phaedrus, who had rallied him on that subject, φιλομαθης γαρ ειμι. τα μεν ουν χωρια και τα δενδρα ουδεν με θελει διδασκειν, ὁι δ' ἐν τῳ ἀστει ἀνθρωποι. *Phaedrus*, p. 230. *Ed. Serrani*.

may not be readily admitted, and as the subject is curious, and has not, that I know of, been discussed, the reader will, perhaps, pardon me, if I suffer it to detain us from our direct path, in a digression of some length.

I do not mean to deny that there are some beautiful, though slight, touches of local description to be found in the antient Poets. But it must be confessed, I think, that they scattered these beauties with a sparing hand, in comparison with that rich profusion of picturesque ideas which every reader of Poetry recollects in Shakespeare, Milton, Spenser, Thomson, and almost all the modern Poets of any name. Nor can I say that I am able to point out anything of this sort in the most descriptive of the *Greek* Poets—in Theocritus, or even in Homer—that fairly amounts to such picturesque *landscape-description* (if I may call it so), as I mean, and as we find so frequently in the Poets just mentioned. In Mr. Pope's *Poetical Index* to his Homer, we are referred, indeed, to descriptions of *"prospects,"* and *"landscapes of a fine country"*; but, if we turn to the original, we shall seldom, or never, find these landscapes. They are of Mr. Pope's painting; sometimes suggested by a single epithet, as his

—grassy Pteleon *deck'd with chearful greens,*
The bow'rs of Ceres and the sylvan scenes.
Iliad. ii. 850.

One word only of this description is Homer's property, *"grassy,"* λεχεποιην.[52] Many other instances may be found, particularly in his catalogue of the ships, which indeed he professes to have endeavoured to "make appear as much a *landscape or piece of painting* as possible." [Obs. on the catalogue.] Sometimes he does more than *"open the prospect a little,"* as he expresses it; he creates it. In his *perfidious* version ("Perfida—sed quamvis perfida, cara tamen!") *"lofty* Sesamus *invades the sky"*; and the river Parthenius

[52] Il. B. 697. The adjective, *grassy*, however, is by no means adequate to—λεχεποιην—i. e., την πολλην ποαν ἐχουσαν και βαθειαν, εὐαυξη, ἐν ᾗ ἐστι και λεξασθαι, τουτεστι, κοιμηθηναι. Hesych. Hence, probably, Mr. Pope's *bowers*, etc. A *single* word perfectly equivalent to a *single* word of the original cannot always be found. In this case, a translator, unwilling to fall short of the Poet's meaning, naturally endeavours to express in *more* words what *he* has said in one; but in doing this, he will often be unavoidably reduced to the dilemma, of either misrepresenting the original, if he admits *different* or *additional* ideas, or, of weakening it by diffusion, if he does not.

> —*roll'd thro' banks of flowers*
> *Reflects her bord'ring palaces and bowers.*
> Ib. 1040.

In Homer, the mountain and the river are simply *named;* not a single epithet attends them.[53] In the Index to the Odyssey, we find, among other descriptions, one of *"the landscape about Ithaca."* This has a promising appearance. Mr. Pope indeed has done his utmost to *make* a landscape of this description; yet, even his translation, though certainly beautiful, and even *picturesque*, will hardly, I believe, be thought to come up to what a modern reader would expect from *"the landscape about Ithaca."* Still less is this title applicable to the original.[54] All that can be said of it without exaggeration is, that it is a very pleasing scene, though described, as many things in Homer are described, with that simplicity which leaves a great deal, and *may* suggest a great deal, to the fancy of the reader. Though it does not answer to the idea given of it in Pope's index, or in the *note* upon the place,[55] yet it must be allowed to furnish, at least, some good *materials* for a landscape, such as, a grove,[56] water falling from a rock, and a rustic altar. If the description itself is too simple, short, and *general*, to be, properly speaking, *picturesque description*, yet it is such as wants nothing, to become so, but a little more colouring of expression, a little more distinctness and *speciality* of touch. This, and more than this, Mr. Pope has given it; and that *his* description is, at least, highly *picturesque*, will scarce be disputed. Homer gives us simply—"an altar to the nymphs."[57] Pope covers it with *moss*, and *embowers it deep in shades;* and in his concluding line, he goes beyond the description of the *place*, to the description of the "religio loci"—of the *effect* of the place upon the minds of those who approached it.

> Beneath, *sequester'd* to the nymphs is seen
> A *mossy* altar, *deep-embower'd in green;*
> Where constant vows by travellers are paid,
> *And holy horrors solemnize the shade.*
> V. 242.

[53] *Il.* B. 853, 854.   [54] *Od.*, P. 204–11.

[55] "It is observable that Homer gives us *an exact draught of the country;* he sets before us, *as in a picture, the city,*" etc. *Od.*, Book xvii, note on v. 224.

[56] Homer's grove is *circular*, ἄλσος παντόσε κυκλοτερές, ver. 209. A circumstance rather unpicturesque. Mr. Pope knew what to suppress, as well as what to add. He softens this into a *"surrounding* grove."

[57] βωμός—νυμφάων. *V.* 210.

The additions of Mr. Pope's pencil are distinguished, in the above quotations, by *Italics*.[58] But, to *prove* the inferiority of the antients in this species of description, by an accurate and comparative examination of all those passages which are commonly produced as examples of it, would be a task of considerable length, though, I think, of no great difficulty. The few instances here given from Homer are intended rather as illustrations of the difference I meant to point out, than as proofs of the *general* fact, which I leave to the recollection and the judgment of the reader. To me, I confess, nothing appears more evident.

And may we not account for this defect in antient Poetry, from a similar defect in the sister art of *painting?* For it appears, I think, from all that has been transmitted to us of the history of that art among the antients, that *landscape-painting* either did not exist, or, at least, was very little cultivated or regarded among the Greeks.[59] In Pliny's account of Grecian artists we

[58] Many such additions and improvements the reader will also find in his translation of Homer's description of the shield, in the 18th book. To give one remarkable specimen: The *eleventh compartment* of the shield, he tells us in his *Observations on the Shield* at the end of that book, is, "an *entire, landscape* without human figures, an image of nature solitary and undisturbed," etc. Let us first view this landscape in the original. *Il.* Σ. 587.

Ἐν δε νομον ποιησε περικλυτος Ἀμφιγυηεις
Ἐν καλῃ βησσῃ, μεγαν οιων ἀργενναων
Σταθμους τε κλισιας τε κατηρεφεας ἰδε σηκους.

What I said of the simplicity and *generality* of the description last mentioned, in the Odyssey, is exactly applicable to this. Even in his *prose* translation of these lines, (Obs. p. 123.) Mr. Pope could not perfectly command his fancy. "The divine artist then engraved a large flock of white sheep, *feeding along* a beautiful valley. *Innumerable* folds, *cottages* and enclosed shelters, were *scattered through the prospect.*" The expressions I have distinguished are Mr. Pope's; their effect on the *visibility* and distinctness of the picture, I need not point out. The last addition, *scattered through* the *prospect*," is particularly picturesque. Now, let us turn to his *poetic* version, and there, indeed, we shall find that finished landscape of which Homer furnished only the simple sketch:

Next this, *the eye* the art of Vulcan *leads*
Deep through fair *forests*, and *a length of meads;*
And stalls, and folds, and *scatter'd cots between,*
And *fleecy* flocks that *whiten all the scene.*

[59] The Abbé Winckelmann, eminent for the accuracy of his researches into every thing relative to the subject of ancient arts, gives it as his opinion, that the paintings discovered in the ruins of Herculanum, (*four* only excepted,) are not older than the times of the Emperors; and he assigns this reason, among others, that most of them are only *landscapes:* "Paysages, ports, maisons de campagne, chasses, pêches, vues, et que le premier qui travailla dans ce genre fut un certain Ludio qui vivoit du tems d'Auguste." He adds, "Les *anciens*

find no landscape-painter mentioned; nor anything like a land-scape described in his catalogue of their principal works. The first, and the only landscapes he mentions, are those said to be painted *in fresco* by one *Ludius* in the time of Augustus; "qui *primus instituit* amoenissimam parietum picturam; villas, et por-ticus, ac topiaria opera—*lucos, nemora, colles,—amnes, littora*—varias ibi obambulantium species, aut navigantium, *terráque villas adeuntium asellis aut vehiculis,*" etc. He likewise painted seaports; "idemque—maritimas urbes pingere *instituit,* blandissimo aspectu."[60] He seems to have been the Claude Lor-rain of antient painting. But, that *landscape* was not, even in Pliny's time, a common and established branch of painting, may perhaps be presumed from the single circumstance of its not having acquired a name. In the passage just quoted, Pliny calls it only, periphrastically, "an *agreeable kind* of painting, or sub-ject," "amoenissimam picturam."[61] He is not sparing of techni-cal terms upon other occasions; as, *rhyparographus, anthropo-graphus, catagrapha, monocromata,* etc. With respect to the *Greeks,* at least, this may be allowed to afford somewhat more than a presumption of the fact.

The Greek Poets, then, did not *describe* the scenery of nature in a picturesque manner, because they were not accus-tomed to *see* it with a painter's eye. Undoubtedly they were not blind to all the beauties of such scenes; but those beauties were not heightened to them, as they are to us, by comparison with painting—with those models of *improved* and *selected* nature, which it is the business of the landscape-painter to exhibit. They had no Thomsons, because they had no Claudes. Indeed, the influence of painting, in this respect, not only on Poetry, but on the *general taste* for the visible beauties of rural nature, seems obvious and indisputable.[62] Shew the most beautiful pros-

---

Grecs ne s'amusoient pas à peindre des objets *inanimés, uniquement propres á rejouir agreablement la vue sans occuper l'esprit* (*Histoire de l Art chez les Anciens, tome* ii., *p.* 104.) The remark seems just. *Men* and *manners,* were the only ob-jects which the Greeks seem to have thought worth regarding, either in paint-ing, or poetry.

[60] Plin. Hist. Nat. xxxv. 10.

[61] It is remarkable also, that the younger Pliny, where he describes the view from one of his villas, and compares it to a painted landscape, expresses him-self, probably for want of an appropriated term, (such as *paysage,* etc.) by a periphrasis;— *formam aliquam ad eximiam pulchritudinem pictam;*"—i.e. "a beautiful ideal *landscape.*" Plin. *Ep. lib.* v. *ep.* 6.

[62] I do not know that there is, either in the Greek or Roman language, any single term appropriated to express exactly what *we* mean by *a prospect.* Pliny,

pect to a peasant, who never saw a landscape, or read a description: I do not say that he will absolutely feel *no* pleasure from it; but I will venture to say, that the pleasure he will feel is very different in *kind*, and very inferior in *degree*, compared with that which is felt by a person of a cultivated imagination, accustomed to the representation of such objects, either in painting, or in picturesque Poetry. Such beauty does imitation reflect back upon the object imitated.[63] What may serve to confirm the truth of these remarks, is, that from the time of Augustus, when, according to Pliny, landscape painting was first cultivated, descriptions of prospects, picturesque imagery, and allusions to that kind of painting, seem to have become more common. I do not pretend, however, to have accurately examined this matter. I shall only remind the reader of the acknowledged superority of Virgil in touches of this kind; of Pliny's description of the view from his villa, mentioned above; and of Aelian's description of the Vale of Tempe, and his allusion to painting in the introduction to it.[64]

To return to *description in general;* this, as I observed above, Aristotle was so far from including in his notion of *imitation,* that he is even totally silent concerning it; unless he may be thought slightly to allude to it in one passage, where he recommends it to the Poet to reserve his highest colouring of language for the *inactive,* that is, the merely narrative, or *descriptive,* parts of his poem.[65] Several obvious circumstances help to account for this silence. Intent on the higher precepts, and on what he regarded as the more essential beauties of the art —the internal construction and contrivance of the fable, the artful dependence and close connection of the incidents, the union of the wonderful and the probable, the natural delineation of character and passion, and whatever tended most

---

in the epistle referred to in note 61, and in the 17th of 2d book, has frequent occasion for such a term, but is obliged to have recourse to circumlocution— *regionis forma—regionis situm—facies—facies locorum.* "Tot *facies locorum* totidem fenestris et distinguit et miscet." [ii. 17.] *Ang.*—"so many *prospects.*"

[63] "Elegant imitation has strange powers of interesting us in certain views of nature. These we consider but transiently, till the Poet, or *Painter,* awake our attention, and send us back to life with a new curiosity, which we owe entirely to the copies which they lay before us." Preface to Wood's Essay on Homer, p. 13.

[64] See above, Part I, note 12, p. 47.

[65] Ἐν τοις ἀργοις μερεσι, και μητε ἠθικοις, μητε διανοητικοις. Cap. xxiv. Translation, Part III. Sect. 6.

effectually to arrest the attention, and secure the emotion, of the spectator or the reader—intent on these, he seems to have thought the beauties of language and expression a matter of inferior consideration scarce worthy of his attention. The chapters on *diction* seem to afford some proof of this. The manner in which he has treated that subject, will be found, if I mistake not, to bear strong marks of this comparative negligence, and to be, in several respects, not such as the reader, from the former parts of the work, would naturally expect. To this it should be added, that Aristotle's principal object was, evidently, Tragedy. Now in Tragedy, where the Poet himself appears not—where all is action, emotion, imitation—where the succession of incidents is close and rapid, and rarely admits those ἀργα μερη, those *"idle or inactive parts,"* of which the philosopher speaks— there is, of course, but little occasion, and little room, for description. It is in the open and extended plan, the varied and disgressive narration, of the Epic form, that the descriptive powers of the Poet have full range to display themselves within their proper province.

I have attempted, in the preceding discussion, to make my way through a subject, which I have never seen treated in a manner perfectly clear and satisfactory by others, and which I am therefore far from confident that I have treated clearly myself. I can only hope that I have, at least, left it less embarrassed than I found it.[66] I shall venture, with the same view, to terminate this inquiry by a few remarks on the *origin* of this doctrine of poetic *imitation*.

Its history may be sketched in few words. We find it first in Plato; alluded to in many parts of his works, but no where so clearly and particularly developed, as in the *third* and *tenth* books of his *Republic*. Aristotle followed; applying, and pursuing to its consequences, with the enlarged view of a philosopher and a critic, the principle which his master had considered with the severity of a moral censor, and had described, as we de-

[66] Some writers, by *imitation* understand *fiction* only: others explain it only by the general term *description;* and others, again, give it a greater extent, and seem to consider language as *imitating* whatever it can *express*. [See above, note 48, and Harris *on Music*, etc. ch. i.] Some speak of it as the imitation of *nature*, in general; others seem to confine it to the imitation of *la belle nature*.— By some writers, the proposition, that "all poetry is imitation," is considered as too plain a point to need any explanation; while others are unable to see why *any* Poetry, except the *dramatic only*, should be so denominated. [See Wood's Essay on Homer, p. 240, *octavo*, and the note.]

scribe an imposter or a robber, only, that being known, it might be avoided.[67]

From these sources, but principally from the treatise of Aristotle, this doctrine was derived, through the later antient, to the latest modern writers. In general, however, it must be confessed, that the way in which the subject has been explained is not such as is calculated to give perfect satisfaction to those fastidious understandings that are not to be contented with anything less than distinct ideas; that, like the sundial in the fable, allow of no medium between knowing clearly, and knowing nothing.

> Si je ne vois bien clair, je dis—Je n'en sçais rien.[68]

It is one question, in what senses, and from what original ideas, Poetry was *first* called imitation by Plato and Aristotle; and another, what senses may have suggested themselves to modern writers, who finding Poetry denominated an imitative art, instead of carefully investigating the original meaning of the expression, have had recourse, for its explication, to their own ideas, and have, accordingly, extended it to every sense which the widest and most distant analogy would bear.

With respect to the *origin* of the appellation—the very idea that Poetry is *imitation*, may, I think, evidently be traced to the *theatre* as to its natural source; and it may, perhaps, very reasonably be questioned, whether, if the drama had never been invented, Poetry would ever have been placed in the class of *Imitative* Arts.

That Aristotle drew his ideas of Poetic imitation chiefly from the drama, is evident from what has been already said. His preference, indeed, of dramatic Poetry, is not only openly declared in his concluding chapter, but strongly marked throughout, and by the very plan and texture of his work. The Epic—that "'greatest work," as Dryden extravagantly calls it, "which *the soul of man* is capable to perform,"[69] is slightly touched and soon dismissed. Our eye is still kept on Tragedy. The form and features of the Epic Muse are rather described by

---

[67] The chief objections of Plato to *imitative* Poetry, particularly Tragedy, may be seen in the 10th book of his Republic, from πραττοντας, φαμεν, ἀνθρωπους—p. 603, C. to ξυμφημι, p. 608, B. *Ed. Serrani.*

[68] *La Montre et le Quadran*, in the ingenious and philosophical fables of La Motte. Livre iii. fab. 2.

[69] *Pref.* to his Aeneid.

comparison with those of her sister, than delineated as they are in themselves; and though that preference which is the result of the comparison seems justly given on the whole, yet it must, perhaps, be confessed, that the comparison is not *completely* stated, and that the advantages and privileges of the Epic are touched with some reserve.[70] It is, indeed, no wonder, that he, who held imitation to be the essence of Poetry, should prefer that species which, being more strictly imitative, was, in his view, more strictly *Poetry*, than any other.

With respect to Plato the case is still plainer. In the *third* book of his *Republic*, where he treats the subject most fully, and is most clear and explicit, he is so far from considering *"all Poetry"* as imitation, that he expressly distinguishes *imitative Poetry* from *"Poetry without imitation."*[71] Nor does he leave us in any uncertainty about his meaning. His *imitative* Poetry is no other than that which I have called *personative*, and which the reader will find clearly and precisely described in the passage referred to.[72] Imitation, then, he confines to the drama, and the dramatic part of the epic poem; and that, which with Aristotle is the *principal*, with Plato is the *only*, sense of *imitation* applied to Poetry. In short, that Plato drew his idea of the ΜΙΜΗΣΙΣ of Poetry from the theatre itself, and from the personal imitations of *represented* tragedy, is evident from the manner in which he explains the term, and from the general cast and language of all his illustrations and allusions. "When the Poet," he says, "quitting his narration, makes any speech in the character of *another person*, does he not then assimilate, as much as possible, his language to that of the person introduced as speaking?—Certainly.—But to assimilate one's self to another person, *either in* voice *or* gesture—is not this to imitate that person?"[73] And in many other passages we find the same allusion

---

[70] For example: in Part III. sect. 2. [*Orig. ch.* xxiv.] he had allowed the greater *extent* of the Epic Poem to give it an advantage over Tragedy in point of *variety* and *magnificence*. But, in the comparison between them in his last chapter, this important advantage is entirely passed over, and only the *disadvantages* of the epic extent of plan are mentioned; its *variety*, the want of which he had before allowed to be a great defect, and even a frequent cause of ill success, in tragedy, is here stated only as a fault—as want of *unity*. [See Part V. sect. 3. *Orig.* cap. xxvi.]

[71] Rep. 3. *ed. Ser.* p. 393. ἄνευ μιμήσεως ποιησις. and *lib.* x. p. 605. ὁ μιμητικος ποιητης.

[72] Rep. 3, from D. p. 392, to D. p. 394. *ed. Ser.*

[73] Ἀλλ' ὅταν γε τινα λεγῃ ῥῆσιν ὡς τις ἄλλος ὤν, ἀρ' οὐ τοτε ὁμοιουν αὐτον φησομεν ὁ τι μαλιστα την ἀυτου λεξιν ἑκαστῳ, ὃν ἀν προειπῃ ὡς ἑρουντα: φησομεν. τι

to the imitations, by *voice* and *action*, of the actor and the rhapsodist; and even to ludicrous mimicry of the lowest kind.[74]

All this will scarce appear strange or surprising, if we recollect the close connection which then subsisted between *poetical* and *personal* imitation. It was by no means with the antients as

γαρ; Οὐκουν το γε ὁμοιουν ἑαυτον ἀλλῳ, ἠ κατα φωνην, ἠ κατα σχημα, μιμεισθαι ἐστιν ἐκεινον ᾡ ἀν τις ὁμοιοι. *Rep.* 3, p. 393. *ed. Serran.*

[74] *Ibid.* p. 395—κατα σωμα και φωνας.—p. 397, λεξις δια μιμησεως φωναις και σχημασι. The reader may also see p. 396 and 397; in both which places he alludes even to the lowest and most ridiculous kind of mimicry. The passages are so curious and amusing, that the reader will pardon me if I suffer them, *in a note*, to lead me into a short digression. He speaks in them of *imitating*, or, as we call it, *taking off*, "the neighing of horses, and the bellowing of bulls—the sound of thunder, the roaring of the sea and the winds—the tones of the trumpet, the flute, and all sorts of instruments—the barking of dogs, the bleating of sheep, and the singing of birds—the *rattle of a shower of hail*, and the *rumbling of wheels*." The sublime Plato was not always sublime. The expressions here are too strong to be understood merely of the imitations of poetical *description;* they are applicable only to *vocal* mimicry. Were there any doubt of this, it might be sufficiently removed by other passages of antient authors in which similar feats are recorded. Plutarch, [*De aud. Poet.* ed. H. Steph. p. 31.] commenting upon Aristotle's distinction, Part I. § 5, between the pleasure we receive from the imitation, and that which we receive from the real object, observes, that "though the grunting of a hog, the rattle of wheels, the whistling of the wind, and the roaring of the sea, for instance, are sounds, in themselves offensive and disagreeable, yet when we hear them well and naturally imitated, *they give us pleasure.*" And he records the names of two eminent performers in this way, *Parmeno*, and *Theodorus;* the first of whom possessed the grunt of the hog, and the other the rattle of the wheel, in high perfection. This *Theodorus* was, probably, a different person from the tragic actor of the same name, whose vocal talents of a higher kind are mentioned by Aristotle in his Rhetoric (*lib.* iii. *cap.* 1.) and who was eminent for the power of accommodating the tone of his voice to the various characters he represented. "The voice," says the philosopher, "of Theodorus appears always to be that of the very person supposed to speak: not so the voices of other actors." In order fully to understand which praise, it is necessary to recollect, that this vocal flexibility in an actor had far greater room to display itself among the antients, than it has with us, on account of the exclusion of women from their stage. Hence one of the objections of Plato to the admission of dramatic Poetry into his Republic: Οὐ δη ἐπιτρεψομεν ὡν φαμεν κηδεσθαι, και δειν αὐτους ἀνδρας ἀγαθους γενεσθαι, γυναικα μιμεισθαι, ἀνδρας ὀντας, κ.τ. αλ. [*Rep.* 3. p. 395, D.] —a passage which may also serve to confirm what has been asserted, that Plato, in speaking of Poetry as imitation, constantly kept his eye on the personal imitation of the actor or the rhapsodist. To return to the art of vocal mimicry: the passages above produced shew it to have been of very respectable antiquity. But there are two other passages that make it still more venerable; one in the hymn to Apollo attributed to Homer, *v.* 162, 3, 4, where the musical *imitations* of the Delian virgins are described; (see Dr. Burney's *Hist. of Music*, vol. i. p. 372.) and another very curious

it is with us. Before the multiplication of copies was facilitated by the invention of printing, *reading* was uncommon. It was not even till long after, that it became, in any degree, the general practice, as it is now. Yet Poetry, we know, among the Greeks, was the common food even of the vulgar. But they *heard* it only. The philosopher, the critic, and the few who collected books when they could be obtained only by the labour or expence of transcription, might, indeed, take a tragedy or an epic poem into their closets; but, to the generality, all was action, representation, and recital. The tragic, and even the epic poet, were, in a manner, lost in the actor and the rhapsodist.[75] A tragedy not intended for the stage, would have

passage in the Odyssey, Δ. 279, by which it appears, that the art was practised even in the Trojan times, and that the beauteous Helen herself, among her other charms, possessed the talent of vocal mimicry in a degree that would, in modern times, have qualified her to make no inconsiderable figure at Bartholomew-fair. She is described as walking round the wooden horse, after its admission within the walls of Troy, calling, by name, upon each of the Grecian chiefs, and *"imitating the voices of their wives."* Παντων Αργειων φωνην ισκους' αλοχοισι. And so well did she *take them off*, that their husbands were on the point of betraying themselves by answering, or coming out. Anticlus, in particular, would have spoken, if Ulysses had not, by main force, *stopped his mouth with his hand*, till Minerva came to their relief, and took Helen away.

- - - ἀλλ' Ὀδυσευς ἐπι μαστακα χερσι πιεζε
Νωλεμεως κρατερῃσι, σαωσε δε παντας Αχαιους.—

Od. Δ. 287, 8.

A line *added* in Pope's translation of this passage, affords a curious example of misapplied ornament:

Firm to his lips his forceful hands apply'd,
Till *on his tongue the flutt'ring murmurs dy'd.*

B. iv. v. 391.

—one instance out of many that might be quoted, of the ridiculous effect produced, (especially in the Odyssey,) by continual efforts to elevate what neither *should* nor *can* be elevated. In the version of the 16th book, (a version *approved* at least by Mr. Pope) we have this line:

They reach'd the *dome*; the *dome with marble shin'd.*

v. 41.

—who would suspect this to be a description of the rude building which Eumaeus, *"αυτος δειμαθ' υεσσιν?"* [Lib. xiv. 8.] All that is to be found of this *marble dome* in Homer is a *"stone threshold."* ὑπερβη λαινον οὐδον! v. 41.

[75] The rhapsodist was defined to be, *the actor of an epic Poem.* Ραψῳδοι— ὑποκριται ἐπων. Hesychius. Ραψῳδοι—ὁι τα Ὁμηρου ἐπη ἐν τοις θεατροις απαγγελλοντες.—Suidas. "Homer's Poems," says the ingenious and entertaining author of the *Enquiry into the Life and Writings of Homer*, were made to be *recited*, or sung to a *company*; and not read in private, or perused in a book, which few were then capable of doing: and I will venture to affirm, that whoever reads not *Homer* in *this view*, loses a great part of the delight he might receive from the Poet."—Blackwell's Enquiry, etc. p. 122.

appeared to the antients as great an absurdity as an ode not written for music. With *them*, there could be no difficulty in conceiving Poetry to be an *Imitative Art*, when it was scarce known to them but through the visible medium of arts, strictly and literally, mimetic.

IV

THOMAS TAYLOR

From the Introduction to his Translation of the *Rhetoric, Poetic,* and *Nicomachean Ethics* of Aristotle

The three treatises of which the present volume consists have been deservedly considered by the ancients as ranking in the first class of the most exquisite productions of human wit; and even in the present frivolous age they maintain so high a degree of reputation as to be studied at the University of Oxford. Indeed, so much penetration and profundity of thought are displayed in the composition of each, that the reader by whom they are thoroughly understood will immediately subscribe to the encomium given to the Stagirite by the great Syrianus, *that he was the most skilful and the most prolific in his conceptions of all men* (δεινοτατος και γονιμωτατος); and also to the assertion of another of the ancients, which may be considered as the *ne plus ultra* of eulogy, *that he dipped his pen in intellect*.

I. With respect to *Rhetoric*, which forms the first of these treatises, it is very nearly allied to dialectic[1] properly so called, and which is the subject of the *Topics* of Aristotle; and, therefore, in order to explain the nature of rhetoric, it will be requisite to compare it with dialectic, and see in what they both agree, and in what they differ.

Dialectic then is denominated from disputing and is the art of disputing; but rhetoric derives its name from speaking and is the art of speaking. The art of disputing, however, consists in the ability of arguing on and defending each side of a proposed question. But the art of speaking consists in the ability of persuading the hearer to assent to either side of a question.

From this definition, it may be inferred that the subject of

Reprinted from *The Rhetoric Poetic and Nicomachean Ethics of Aristotle*, translated by Thomas Taylor (2 vols.; London: James Black & Son, 1818), I, i–ix, 295–96.

[1] Aristotle calls *dialectic* that art which is explained by him in his Topics and Sophistical Elenchi.

dialectic is every thing, so far as it is disputable with probability on each side; and that the subject of rhetoric is every thing so far as it can be influenced by persuasion.

In the second place, it may be inferred that dialectic and rhetoric agree in this, that each discusses every thing; that each discusses both sides of a question; and that each proceeds not from what is true, but from what is probable. For of the two parts of a problem contradictorily opposed to each other, the one is necessarily false; but dialectic and rhetoric discuss and defend each part of a problem. Hence they not only prove and defend what is true, but also what is false. As what is false, however, cannot be proved and defended from true, but only from probable assertions, rhetoric and dialectic do not proceed from true but from probable arguments. They also agree in this, that each does not proceed from things that are proper or peculiar, but from such as are common. For if it were requisite that they should discuss any proposed problem from peculiarities, they would be confounded with all sciences. To which it may be added, that they ought to use principles adapted to discuss the proposed problems in each part, and that common principles alone possess this adaption. Another reason is, that they ought to discuss things from principles known to all men, and known even to those who are ignorant of particular sciences.

Again, dialectic and rhetoric agree in this, that it is the business of each to deliver certain common places, or principles, from which we may be able to dispute on any proposed problem, or speak in a manner adapted to persuade on each side of a question. They likewise agree in this, that they are not sciences, but certain powers and faculties. For sciences neither prove, nor persuade to the assent of, each part of contradiction, but that part only which is true, and is, therefore, demonstrable; but the power of effecting this is possessed both by dialectic and rhetoric. Hence, they are not sciences, but powers and faculties; for those things are properly said to be powers, which are equally affected to opposites.

Dialectic and rhetoric, however, differ in this, that it is the business of the former to dispute with probability before those who are partially wise; but of the latter, to speak in a manner adapted to persuade the multitude. And because it is usual to dispute with those who are partially wise, about universal problems, abstracting from particular circumstances of persons, places and times, etc.; but to dispute with the multitude about moral or political subjects, and about problems restricted to particular persons, places and times; hence dialectic for the most part discusses *universal*, and rhetoric *restricted* problems. They also differ in this, that dialectic employs a strict and contracted form of arguing; but rhetoric a more ample and dilated form. And they differ in the third place in this, that dialectic employs arguments alone in proof of what it wishes to establish; but rhetoric for the purpose of persuading not only employs arguments, but likewise manners and passions, as Aristotle copiously evinces in the course of this treatise.

II. With respect to the *Poetic*, the next of the treatises, it is requisite to observe that *poetry is the art of imitating in measured diction so as to produce delight*. The proximate *genus*, therefore, of poetry is, that it is an imitative art; and the difference, through which it differs from other imitative arts, is the mode of imitating. For as the other imitative arts imitate in different modes, poetry imitates by metre, or measured diction alone.

From this definition, explaining the nature of poetry, it may be briefly inferred what the subject of it is and what its employment and end. The *subject* of poetry are *things, so far as they can be imitated in measured diction and produce delight*. The *employment* of poetry is, *the imitation itself*. And *the end* is, *the delight produced by the metrical imitation of things*. Hence it follows that poetry ought expecially to imitate those things, the imitation of which is most delightful. But the imitation of admirable and probable deeds is most delightful, and which, therefore, poetry ought principally to imitate. In order, however, to imitate these, it is requisite, in the first place, that it should devise admirable and probable deeds; and in the next place, that it should express them in admirable diction, such as is the metrical. Hence the labour of poetry ought especially to be conversant in these two things; first in the invention of the fable, viz. of admirable and probable deeds; and secondly, in expressing such deeds in a measured diction which is eminently adapted to them, or in other words, which is eminently imitative of the several particulars.

It is much to be regretted that this treatise, which was perhaps originally only the first of three books written by

Aristotle on poetry, is all that is left of a work, the whole of which was doubtless as admirable as the part that remains. And the loss of the second and third books is particularly to be regretted, because there can be no doubt of Aristotle having treated in one of these books of the purification of the mind from depraved affections, and of the correction of the manners, as the principal and proper end, according to the ancients, of right poetical imitation. I say this loss is particularly to be regretted, not only on account of the importance of the matter, and the very able manner in which it was discussed, but because an elucidation of the mode in which the mind is to be purified from depraved affections, would have fully solved a difficulty which occurs in the present treatise, and which has been insuperable to modern commentators. The difficulty I allude to is the assertion of Aristotle *that the terror and pity excited by tragedy purify the spectator from such-like passions.* For, according to the modern commentators on this treatise, the meaning of Aristotle is that the terror and pity excited by tragedy purify the spectator from terror and pity. The reader, however, will find in a note on this passage in the following translation that this cannot be the meaning of Aristotle, as it contradicts what he asserts in his *Ethics;* and I also trust that he will subscribe to the opinion of the translator, that Aristotle meant to say, *that the terror and pity excited by tragedy purify the spectator from those perturbations which form the catastrophe of the tragedy.* Thus in the *Ajax* of Sophocles, the terror and pity excited by the catastrophe, purify the spectator from anger and impiety towards divinity; and in a similar manner purification is effected in other tragedies.

Note on Catharsis

When Aristotle says that tragedy through pity and fear effects a purification from such-like passions, his meaning is, that it purifies from those perturbations, which happen in the fable, and which for the most part are the cause of the peripetia, and of the unhappy event of the fable. Thus for instance, Sophocles, through pity and terror excited by the character of Ajax, intends a purification from anger and impiety towards the gods, because through this anger and impiety those misfortunes happened to Ajax; and thus in other instances. For it must by no means be said that the meaning of Aristotle is that tragedy through terror and pity purifies the spectators from terror and pity; since he says in the 2d book of his Ethics, "that he who is accustomed to timid things becomes timid, and to anger becomes angry, because habit is produced from energies." Hence, we are so far from being able, through the medium of terror and pity in tragedy, to remove terror and pity from the spectators, that by accustoming them to objects of commiseration and terror, we shall in a greater degree subject them to these passions. Indeed, if tragedy intended through pity to purify from pity, and through fear to purify from fear, it would follow that the same passion of the soul would be contrary to itself; for contraries are cured by contraries. Hence, fear would be contrary to itself, and pity would be contrary to pity. Hence, also, energies would be contrary to their proper habits, or rather the same energies and habits would be contrary to each other, which is repugnant to reason and experience. For we see that energies and habits are increased and established from similar energies.

By no means, therefore, does Aristotle oppose Plato, in ascribing this purifying effect to tragedy. For when Plato expels tragic poets from his Republic, it is because they are not servicable to youth who are to be educated philosophically. For a purification from all the passions is effected by philosophic discipline; but tragedy only purifies from some of the passions, by the assistance of others, viz. by terror and pity; since it is so far from purifying the spectators from terror and pity, that it increases them. To which we may add, that philosophic discipline is not attended with the mythological imitation of ancient tragedy, which though it harmonizes with divine natures, and leads those who possess a naturally good disposition to the contemplation of them, yet it is not useful to legislators for the purposes of virtue and education, nor for the proper tuition of youth. For the good which such fables contain is not disciplinative, but mystic; nor does it regard a juvenile, but an aged habit of soul. For Socrates in the *Republic* justly observes, "The young person is not able to judge what is allegory, and what is not; but whatever opinions he receives at such an age, are with difficulty washed away, and are generally immoveable."

Introduction to his translations of Aristotle

None of the English translators and commentators On the *Poetic* of Aristotle, that I have seen, appear to have had the least glimpse of this meaning of the passage, though I trust it is sufficiently obvious that it is the genuine meaning of Aristotle.

V

JOHN HENRY CARDINAL NEWMAN

Poetry, with Reference to
Aristotle's *Poetics*

We propose to offer some speculations of our own on Greek Tragedy, and on Poetry in general, as suggested by the doctrine of Aristotle on the subject.

Aristotle considers the excellence of a tragedy to depend upon its plot—and, since a tragedy, as such, is obviously the exhibition of an action, no one can deny his statement to be abstractedly true. Accordingly, he directs his principal attention to the economy of the fable; determines its range of subjects, delineates its proportions, traces its progress from a complication of incidents to their just and satisfactory settlement, investigates the means of making a train of events striking or affecting, and shows how the exhibition of character may be made subservient to the purpose of the action. His treatise is throughout interesting and valuable. It is one thing, however, to form the *beau ideal* of a tragedy on scientific principles; another to point out the actual beauty of a particular school of dramatic composition. The Greek tragedians are not generally felicitous in the construction of their plots. Aristotle, then, rather tells us what Tragedy should be, than what Greek Tragedy really was. And this doubtless was the intention of the philosopher. Since, however, the Greek drama has obtained so extended and lasting a celebrity, and yet its excellence does not fall under the strict rules of the critical art, we have to inquire in what it consists.

That the charm of Greek Tragedy does not ordinarily arise from scientific correctness of plot, is certain as a matter of fact. Seldom does any great interest arise from the action; which,

Reprinted from *Essays Critical and Historical* (London: Longmans, Green & Co., 1890), I,1–26.

instead of being progressive and sustained, is commonly either a mere necessary condition of the drama, or a convenience for the introduction of matter more important than itself. It is often stationary—often irregular—sometimes either wants or outlives the catastrophe. In the plays of Aeschylus it is always simple and inartificial; in four out of the seven there is hardly any plot at all; and, though it is of more prominent importance in those of Sophocles, yet even here the *Oedipus at Colonus* is a mere series of incidents, and the *Ajax* a union of two separate subjects; while in the *Philoctetes*, which is apparently busy, the circumstances of the action are but slightly connected with the *dénouement*. The carelessness of Euripides in the construction of his plots is well known. The action then will be more justly viewed as the vehicle for introducing the personages of the drama, than as the principal object of the poet's art; it is not in the plot, but in the characters, sentiments, and diction, that the actual merit and poetry of the composition are found. To show this to the satisfaction of the reader, would require a minuter investigation of details than our present purpose admits; yet a few instances in point may suggest others to the memory.

For instance, in neither the *Oedipus Coloneus* nor the *Philoctetes*, the two most beautiful plays of Sophocles, is the plot striking; but how exquisite is the delineation of the characters of Antigone and Oedipus, in the former tragedy, particularly in their interview with Polynices, and the various descriptions of the scene itself which the Chorus furnishes! In the *Philoctetes*, again, it is the contrast between the worldly wisdom of Ulysses, the inexperienced frankness of Neoptolemus, and the simplicity of the afflicted Philoctetes, which constitutes the principal charm of the drama. Or we may instance the spirit and nature displayed in the grouping of the characters in the *Prometheus*, which is almost without action; the stubborn enemy of the new dynasty of gods; Oceanus trimming, as an accomplished politician, with the change of affairs; the single-hearted and generous Nereids; and Hermes, the favourite and instrument of the usurping potentate. So again, the beauties of the Thebae are almost independent of the plot; it is the Chorus which imparts grace and interest to the actionless scene; and the speech of Antigone at the end, one of the most simply striking in any play, has, scientifically speaking, no place in the tragedy, which should already have been brought to its conclusion. Then again, amid the multitude of the beauties of the irregular Euripides, it would be obvious to notice the character of Alcestis, and of Clytemnestra in the *Electra;* the soliloquies of Medea; the picturesque situation of Ion, the minister of the Pythian temple; the opening scene of the *Orestes;* and the dialogues between Phaedra and her attendant in the *Hippolytus,* and the old man and Antigone in the *Phoenissae*—passages nevertheless which are either unconnected with the development of the plot, or of an importance superior to it.

Thus the Greek drama, as a fact, was modelled on no scientific principle. It was a pure recreation of the imagination, revelling without object or meaning beyond its own exhibition. Gods, heroes, kings, and dames, enter and retire: they may have a good reason for appearing, they may have a very poor one; whatever it is, still we have no right to ask for it; the question is impertinent. Let us listen to their harmonious and majestic language, to the voices of sorrow, joy, compassion, or religious emotion, to the animated odes of the chorus. Why interrupt so transcendent a display of poetical genius by inquiries degrading it to the level of every-day events, and implying incompleteness in the action till a catastrophe arrives? The very spirit of beauty breathes through every part of the composition. We may liken the Greek drama to the music of the Italian school in which the wonder is, how so much richness of invention in detail can be accommodated to a style so simple and uniform. Each is the development of grace, fancy, pathos, and taste, in the respective media of representation and sound.

However true then it may be, that one or two of the most celebrated dramas answer to the requisitions of Aristotle's doctrine, still, for the most part, Greek Tragedy has its own distinct and peculiar praise, which must not be lessened by a criticism conducted on principles, whether correct or not, still leading to excellence of another character. This being as we hope shown, we shall be still bolder, and proceed to question even the sufficiency of the rules of Aristotle for the production of dramas of the highest order. These rules, it would appear, require a fable not merely natural and unaffected, as a vehicle of more poetical matter, but one laboured and complicated, as the sole legitimate channel of tragic effect; and thus tend to withdraw the mind of the poet from the spontaneous exhibition of pathos or imagination to a minute diligence in the formation of a plot.

To explain our views on the subject, we will institute a short comparison between three tragedies, the *Agamemnon*, the *Oedipus*, and the *Bacchae*, one of each of the tragic poets, as to which, by reference to Aristotle's principles, we think it will be found that the most perfect in plot is not the most poetical.

1. Of these, the action of the *Oedipus Tyrannus* is frequently instanced by the critic as a specimen of judgment and skill in the selection and combination of the incidents; and in this point of view it is truly a masterly composition. The clearness, precision, certainty, and vigour with which the line of the action moves on to its termination is admirable. The character of Oedipus, too, is finely drawn, and identified with the development of the action.

2. The *Agamemnon* of Aeschylus presents us with the slow and difficult birth of a portentous secret—an event of old written in the resolves of destiny, a crime long meditated in the bosom of the human agents. The Chorus here has an importance altogether wanting in the Chorus of the *Oedipus*. They throw a pall of ancestral honour over the bier of the hereditary monarch, which would have been unbecoming in the case of the upstart king of Thebes. Till the arrival of Agamemnon, they occupy our attention, as the prophetic organ, not commissioned indeed, but employed by heaven, to proclaim the impending horrors. Succeeding to the brief intimation of the watcher who opens the play, they seem oppressed with forebodings of woe and crime which they can neither justify nor analyze. The expression of their anxiety forms the stream in which the plot flows—everything, even news of joy, takes a colouring from the depth of their gloom. On the arrival of the king, they retire before Cassandra, a more regularly commissioned prophetess; who, speaking first in figure, then in plain terms, only ceases that we may hear the voice of the betrayed monarch himself, informing us of the striking of the fatal blow. Here, then, the very simplicity of the fable constitutes its especial beauty. The death of Agamemnon is intimated at first—it is accomplished at last; throughout we find but the growing in volume and intensity of one and the same note—it is

a working up of one musical ground, by figure and imitation, into the richness of combined harmony. But we look in vain for the progressive and thickening incidents of the *Oedipus*.

3. The action of the *Bacchae* is also simple. It is the history of the reception of the worship of Bacchus in Thebes; who, first depriving Pentheus of his reason, and thereby drawing him on to his ruin, reveals his own divinity. The interest of the scene arises from the gradual process by which the derangement of the Theban king is effected, which is powerfully and originally described. It would be comic, were it unconnected with religion. As it is, it exhibits the grave irony of a god triumphing over the impotent presumption of man, the sport and terrible mischievousness of an insulted deity. It is an exemplification of the adage, "Quem deus vult perdere, prius dementat." So delicately balanced is the action along the verge of the sublime and grotesque, that it is both solemn and humorous, without violence to the propriety of the composition: the mad fire of the Chorus, the imbecile mirth of old Cadmus and Tiresias, and the infatuation of Pentheus, who is ultimately induced to dress himself in female garb to gain admittance among the Bacchae, are made to harmonize with the terrible catastrophe which concludes the life of the intruder. Perhaps the victim's first discovery of the disguised deity is the finest conception in this splendid drama. His madness enables him to discern the emblematic horns on the head of Bacchus, which were hid from him when in his sound mind; yet this discovery, instead of leading him to an acknowledgment of the divinity, provides him only with matter for a stupid and perplexed astonishment:

> A Bull, thou seem'st to lead us; on thy head
> Horns have grown forth: wast heretofore a beast?
> For such thy semblance now.

This play is on the whole the most favourable specimen of the genius of Euripides—not breathing the sweet composure, the melodious fulness, the majesty and grace of Sophocles; nor rudely and overpoweringly tragic as Aeschylus; but brilliant, versatile, imaginative, as well as deeply pathetic. Here then are two dramas of extreme poetical power, but deficient in skilfulness of plot. Are they on that account to be rated below the *Oedipus*, which, in spite of its many beauties, has not even a share of the richness and sublimity of either?

Aristotle, then, it must be allowed, treats dramatic composition more as an exhibition of ingenious workmanship, than as a free and unfettered effusion of genius. The inferior poem may, on his principle, be the better tragedy. He may indeed have intended solely to delineate the outward framework most suitable to the reception of the spirit of poetry, not to discuss the nature of poetry itself. If so, it cannot be denied that, the poetry being given equal in the two cases, the more perfect plot will merit the greater share of praise. And it may seem to agree with this view of his meaning, that he pronounces Euripides, in spite of the irregularity of his plots, to be, after all, the most tragic of the Greek dramatists, that is, inasmuch as he excels in his appeal to those passions which the outward form of the drama merely subserves. Still there is surely too much stress laid by the philosopher upon the artificial part; which, after all, leads to negative, more than to positive excellence; and should rather be the natural and, so to say, unintentional result of the poet's feeling and imagination, than be separated from them as the direct object of his care. Perhaps it is hardly fair to judge of Aristotle's sentiments by the fragment of his work which has come down to us. Yet as his natural taste led him to delight in the explication of systems, and in those absolute decisions which came of his vigorous talent for thinking through large subjects, we may be allowed to suspect him of entertaining too cold and formal conceptions of the nature of poetical composition, as if its beauties were less subtile and delicate than they really are. A word has power to convey a world of information to the imagination, and to act as a spell upon the feelings; there is no need of sustained fiction, often no room for it. The sudden inspiration, surely, of the blind Oedipus, in the second play bearing his name, by which he is enabled, "without a guide," to lead the way to his place of death, in our judgment, produces more poetical effect than all the skilful intricacy of the plot of the *Tyrannus*. The latter excites an interest which scarcely lasts beyond the first reading—the former *"decies repetita placebit."*

Some confirmation of the judgment we have ventured to pass on the greatest of analytical philosophers, is the account he gives of the source of poetical pleasure; which he almost identifies with a gratification of the reasoning faculty, placing it in the satisfaction derived from recognizing in fiction a resemblance to the realities of life—"The spectators are led to recognize and to syllogize what each thing is."

But as we have treated, rather unceremoniously, a deservedly high authority, we will try to compensate for our rudeness by illustrating his general doctrine of the nature of Poetry, which we hold to be most true and philosophical.

Poetry, according to Aristotle, is a representation of the ideal. Biography and history represent individual characters and actual facts; poetry, on the contrary, generalizing from the phenomenon of nature and life, supplies us with pictures drawn, not after an existing pattern, but after a creation of the mind. Fidelity is the primary merit of biography and history; the essence of poetry is fiction. "Poesis nihil aliud est," says Bacon, "quam historiae imitatio ad placitum." It delineates that perfection which the imagination suggests, and to which as a limit the present system of Divine Providence actually tends. Moreover, by confining the attention to one series of events and scene of action, it bounds and finishes off the confused luxuriance of real nature; while, by a skilful adjustment of circumstances, it brings into sight the connexion of cause and effect, completes the dependence of the parts one on another, and harmonizes the proportions of the whole. It is then but the type and model of history or biography, if we may be allowed the comparison, bearing some resemblance to the abstract mathematical formulae of physics, before they are modified by the contingencies of atmosphere and friction. Hence, while it recreates the imagination by the superhuman loveliness of its views, it provides a solace for the mind broken by the disappointments and sufferings of actual life; and becomes, moreover, the utterance of the inward emotions of a right moral feeling, seeking a purity and a truth which this world will not give.

It follows that the poetical mind is one full of the eternal forms of beauty and perfection; these are its material of thought, its instrument and medium of observation, these colour each object to which it directs its view. It is called imaginative or creative, from the originality and independence of its modes of thinking, compared with the commonplace and matter-of-fact conceptions of ordinary minds, which are fettered down to the particular and individual. At the same time it feels a natural sympathy with everything great and splendid in the physical and moral world; and selecting such from the mass of common phenomena, incorporates them, as it were, into the substance of its own creations. From living thus in a world of its own, it speaks the language of dignity, emotion, and refinement. Figure is its necessary medium of communication with man; for in the feebleness of ordinary words to express its ideas, and in the absence of terms of abstract perfection, the adoption of metaphorical language is the only poor means allowed it for imparting to others its intense feelings. A metrical garb has, in all languages, been appropriated to poetry—it is but the outward development of the music and harmony within. The verse, far from being a restraint on the true poet, is the suitable index of his sense, and is adopted by his free and deliberate choice. We shall presently show the applicability of our doctrine to the various departments of poetical composition; first, however, it will be right to volunteer an explanation which may save it from much misconception and objection. Let not our notion be thought arbitrarily to limit the number of poets, generally considered such. It will be found to lower particular works, or parts of works, rather than the authors themselves; sometimes to disparage only the vehicle in which the poetry is conveyed. There is an ambiguity in the word "poetry," which is taken to signify both the gift itself, and the written composition which is the result of it. Thus there is an apparent, but no real contradiction, in saying a poem may be but partially poetical; in some passages more so than in others; and sometimes not poetical at all. We only maintain, not that the writers forfeit the name of poet who fail at times to answer to our requisitions, but that they are poets only so far forth, and inasmuch as they do answer to them. We may grant, for instance, that the vulgarities of old Phoenix in the ninth *Iliad*, or of the nurse of Orestes in the *Choephoroe*, are in themselves unworthy of their respective authors, and refer them to the wantonness of exuberant genius; and yet maintain that the scenes in question contain much incidental poetry. Now and then the lustre of the true metal catches the eye, redeeming whatever is unseemly and worthless in the rude ore; still the ore is not the metal. Nay, sometimes, and not unfrequently in Shakspeare, the introduction of unpoetical matter may be necessary for the sake of relief, or as a vivid expression of recondite conceptions, and, as it were, to make friends with the reader's imagination. This necessity, however, cannot make the additions in themselves beautiful and pleasing. Sometimes, on the other hand, while we do not deny the incidental beauty of a poem, we are ashamed and indignant on witnessing the unworthy substance in which that beauty is imbedded. This remark applies strongly to the immoral compositions to which Lord Byron devoted his last years.

Now to proceed with our proposed investigation.

1. We will notice *descriptive poetry* first. Empedocles wrote his physics in verse, and Oppian his history of animals. Neither were poets—the one was an historian of nature, the other a sort of biographer of brutes. Yet a poet may make natural history or philosophy the material of his composition. But under his hands they are no longer a bare collection of facts or principles, but are painted with a meaning, beauty, and harmonious order not their own. Thomson has sometimes been commended for the novelty and minuteness of his remarks upon nature. This is not the praise of a poet; whose office rather is to represent known phenomena in a new connection or medium. In *L'Allegro* and *Il Penseroso* the poetical magician invests the commonest scenes of a country life with the hues, first of a cheerful, then of a pensive imagination. It is the charm of the descriptive poetry of a religious mind, that nature is viewed in a moral connexion. Ordinary writers, for instance, compare aged men to trees in autumn—a gifted poet will in the fading trees discern the fading men.[1] Pastoral poetry is a description of rustics, agriculture, and cattle, softened off and corrected from the rude health of nature. Virgil, and much more Pope and others, have run into the fault of colouring too highly; instead of drawing generalized and ideal forms of shepherds, they have given us pictures of gentlemen and beaux.

Their composition may be poetry, but it is not pastoral poetry.

2. The difference between poetical and historical *narrative* may be illustrated by the Tales Founded on Facts, generally of

---

[1] Thus:

> "How quiet shows the woodland scene!
> Each flower and tree, its duty done,
> Reposing in decay serene,
> Like weary men when age is won," etc.

a religious character, so common in the present day, which we must not be thought to approve, because we use them for our purpose. The author finds in the circumstances of the case many particulars too trivial for public notice, or irrelevant to the main story, or partaking perhaps too much of the peculiarity of individual minds: these he omits. He finds connected events separated from each other by time or place, or a course of action distributed among a multitude of agents; he limits the scene or duration of the tale, and dispenses with his host of characters by condensing the mass of incident and action in the history of a few. He compresses long controversies into a concise argument, and exhibits characters by dialogue, and (if such be his object) brings prominently forward the course of Divine Providence by a fit disposition of his materials. Thus he selects, combines, refines, colours,—in fact, poetizes. His facts are no longer actual, but ideal; a tale founded on facts is a tale generalized from facts. The authors of *Peveril of the Peak*, and of *Brambletye House*, have given us their respective descriptions of the profligate times of Charles II. Both accounts are interesting, but for different reasons. That of the latter writer has the fidelity of history; Walter Scott's picture is the hideous reality, unintentionally softened and decorated by the poetry of his own mind. Miss Edgeworth sometimes apologizes for certain incidents in her tales, by stating they took place "by one of those strange chances which occur in life, but seem incredible when found in writing." Such an excuse evinces a misconception of the principle of fiction, which, being the perfection of the actual, prohibits the introduction of any such anomalies of experience. It is by a similar impropriety that painters sometimes introduce unusual sunsets, or other singular phenomena of lights and forms. Yet some of Miss Edgeworth's works contain much poetry of narrative. Manoeuvring is perfect in its way, the plot and characters are natural, without being too real to be pleasing.

3. *Character* is made poetical by a like process. The writer draws indeed from experience; but unnatural peculiarities are laid aside, and harsh contrasts reconciled. If it be said, the fidelity of the imitation is often its greatest merit, we have only to reply, that in such cases the pleasure is not poetical, but consists in the mere recognition. All novels and tales which introduce real characters, are in the same degree unpoetical.

Portrait-painting, to be poetical, should furnish an abstract representation of an individual; the abstraction being more rigid, inasmuch as the painting is confined to one point of time. The artist should draw independently of the accidents of attitude, dress, occasional feeling, and transient action. He should depict the general spirit of his subject—as if he were copying from memory, not from a few particular sittings. An ordinary painter will delineate with rigid fidelity, and will make a caricature; but the learned artist contrives so to temper his composition, as to sink all offensive peculiarities and hardnesses of individuality, without diminishing the striking effect of the likeness, or acquainting the casual spectator with the secret of his art. Miss Edgeworth's representations of the Irish character are actual, and not poetical—nor were they intended to be so. They are interesting, because they are faithful. If there is poetry about them, it exists in the personages themselves, not in her representation of them. She is only the accurate reporter in word of what was poetical in fact. Hence, moreover, when a deed or incident is striking in itself, a judicious writer is led to describe it in the most simple and colourless terms, his own being unnecessary; for instance, if the greatness of the action itself excites the imagination, or the depth of the suffering interests the feelings. In the usual phrase, the circumstances are left "to speak for themselves."

Let it not be said that our doctrine is adverse to that individuality in the delineation of character, which is a principal charm of fiction. It is not necessary for the ideality of a composition to avoid those minuter shades of difference between man and man, which give to poetry its plausibility and life; but merely such violation of general nature, such improbabilities, wanderings, or coarsenesses, as interfere with the refined and delicate enjoyment of the imagination; which would have the elements of beauty extracted out of the confused multitude of ordinary actions and habits, and combined with consistency and ease. Nor does it exclude the introduction of imperfect or odious characters. The original conception of a weak or guilty mind may have its intrinsic beauty; and much more so, when it is connected with a tale which finally adjusts whatever is reprehensible in the personages themselves. Richard and Iago are subservient to the plot. Moral excellence in some characters may become even a fault. The Clytemnestra of Euripides is so interesting, that the divine vengeance, which is the main subject of the drama, seems almost unjust. Lady Macbeth, on the contrary, is the conception of one deeply learned in the poetical art. She is polluted with the most heinous crimes, and meets the fate she deserves. Yet there is nothing in the picture to offend the taste, and much to feed the imagination. Romeo and Juliet are too good for the termination to which the plot leads; so are Ophelia and the Bride of Lammermoor. In these cases there is something inconsistent with correct beauty, and therefore unpoetical. We do not say the fault could be avoided without sacrificing more than would be gained; still it is a fault. It is scarcely possible for a poet satisfactorily to connect innocence with ultimate unhappiness, when the notion of a future life is excluded. Honours paid to the memory of the dead are some alleviation of the harshness. In his use of the doctrine of a future life, Southey is admirable. Other writers are content to conduct their heroes to temporal happiness—Southey refuses present comfort to his *Ladurlad, Thalaba,* and *Roderick,* but carries them on through suffering to another world. The death of his hero is the termination of the action; yet so little in two of them, at least, does this catastrophe excite sorrowful feelings, that some readers may be startled to be reminded of the fact. If a melancholy is thrown over the conclusion of the *Roderick,* it is from the peculiarities of the hero's previous history.

4. Opinions, feelings, manners, and customs, are made poetical by the delicacy or splendour with which they are expressed. This is seen in the *ode, elegy, sonnet,* and *ballad;* in which a single idea, perhaps, or familiar occurrence, is invested by the poet with pathos or dignity. The ballad of "Old Robin Gray" will serve for an instance, out of a multitude; again, Lord Byron's "Hebrew Melody," beginning, "Were my bosom as false," etc.; or Cowper's "Lines on his Mother's Picture"; or Milman's "Funeral Hymn" in the *Martyr of Antioch;* or Milton's "Sonnet on his Blindness"; or Bernard Barton's "Dream." As picturesque specimens, we may name Campbell's *Battle of the Baltic;* or Joanna Baillie's "Chough and Crow"; and for the more exalted and splendid style, Gray's *Bard;* or Milton's "Hymn on the Nativity"; in which facts, with which every one is familiar, are made new by the colouring of a poetical imagination. It must all along be observed, that we are not adducing instances for their own sake; but in order to illustrate our

general doctrine, and to show its applicability to those compositions which are, by universal consent, acknowledged to be poetical.

The department of poetry we are now speaking of is of much wider extent than might at first sight appear. It will include such moralizing and philosophical poems as Young's *Night Thoughts,* and Byron's *Childe Harold.* There is much bad taste, at present, in the judgment passed on compositions of this kind. It is the fault of the day to mistake mere eloquence for poetry; whereas, in direct opposition to the conciseness and simplicity of the poet, the talent of the orator consists in making much of a single idea. "Sic dicet ille ut verset saepe multis modis eandem et unam rem, ut haereat in eadem commoreturque sententia." This is the great art of Cicero himself, who, whether he is engaged in statement, argument, or raillery, never ceases till he has exhausted the subject; going round about it, and placing it in every different light, yet without repetition to offend or weary the reader. This faculty seems to consist in the power of throwing off harmonious verses, which, while they have a respectable portion of meaning, yet are especially intended to charm the ear. In popular poems, common ideas are unfolded with copiousness, and set off in polished verse—and this is called poetry. Such is the character of Campbell's *Pleasures of Hope;* it is in his minor poems that the author's poetical genius rises to its natural elevation. In *Childe Harold,* too, the writer is carried through his Spenserian stanza with the unweariness and equable fulness of accomplished eloquence; opening, illustrating, and heightening one idea, before he passes on to another. His composition is an extended funeral sermon over buried joys and pleasures. His laments over Greece, Rome, and the fallen in various engagements, have quite the character of panegyrical orations; while by the very attempt to describe the celebrated buildings and sculptures of antiquity, he seems to confess that *they* are the poetical text, his the rhetorical comment. Still it is a work of splendid talent, though, as a whole, not of the highest poetical excellence. Juvenal is perhaps the only ancient author who habitually substitutes declamation for poetry.

5. The *philosophy of mind* may equally be made subservient to poetry, as the philosophy of nature. It is a common fault to mistake a mere knowledge of the heart for poetical talent. Our

greatest masters have known better; they have subjected meta-physics to their art. In *Hamlet, Macbeth, Richard*, and *Othello*, the philosophy of mind is but the material of the poet. These personages are ideal; they are effects of the contact of a given internal character with given outward circumstances, the re-sults of combined conditions determining (so to say) a moral curve of original and inimitable properties. Philosophy is exhib-ited in the same subserviency to poetry in many parts of Crabbe's *Tales of the Hall*. In the writings of this author there is much to offend a refined taste; but, at least in the work in question, there is much of a highly poetical cast. It is a repre-sentation of the action and reaction of two minds upon each other and upon the world around them. Two brothers of different characters and fortunes, and strangers to each other, meet. Their habits of mind, the formation of those habits by external circumstances, their respective media of judgment, their points of mutual attraction and repulsion, the mental position of each in relation to a variety of trifling phenomena of every-day nature and life, are beautifully developed in a series of tales moulded into a connected narrative. We are tempted to single out the fourth book, which gives an account of the childhood and education of the younger brother, and which for variety of thought as well as fidelity of description is in our judgment beyond praise. The Waverley Novels would afford us specimens of a similar excellence. One striking peculiarity of these tales is the author's practice of describing a group of characters bearing the same general features of mind, and placed in the same general circumstances; yet so contrasted with each other in minute differences of mental constitution, that each diverges from the common starting-point into a path peculiar to himself. The brotherhood of villains in *Kenilworth*, of knights in *Ivanhoe*, and of enthusiasts in *Old Mortality*, are instances of this. This bearing of character and plot on each other is not often found in Byron's poems. *The Corsair* is intended for a remarkable personage. We pass by the incon-sistencies of his character, considered by itself. The grand fault is, that whether it be natural or not, we are obliged to accept the author's word for the fidelity of his portrait. We are told, not shown, what the hero was. There is nothing in the plot which results from his peculiar formation of mind. An every-day bravo might equally well have satisfied the requirements of the action. Childe Harold, again, if he is anything, is a being professedly isolated from the world, and uninfluenced by it. One might as well draw Tityrus's stags grazing in the air, as a character of this kind; which yet, with more or less alteration, passes through successive editions in his other poems. Byron had very little versatility or elasticity of genius; he did not know how to make poetry out of existing materials. He declaims in his own way, and has the upperhand as long as he is allowed to go on; but, if interrogated on principles of nature and good sense, he is at once put out and brought to a stand.

Yet his conception of Sardanapalus and Myrrha is fine and ideal, and in the style of excellence which we have just been admiring in Shakespeare and Scott.

These illustrations of Aristotle's doctrine may suffice.

Now let us proceed to a fresh position; which, as before, shall first be broadly stated, then modified and explained. How does originality differ from the poetical talent? Without affecting the accuracy of a definition, we may call the latter the originality of right moral feeling.

Originality may perhaps be defined the power of abstracting for one's self, and is in thought what strength of mind is in action. Our opinions are commonly derived from education and society. Common minds transmit as they receive, good and bad, true and false; minds of original talent feel a continual propensity to investigate subjects, and strike out views for themselves—so that even old and established truths do not escape modification and accidental change when subjected to this process of mental digestion. Even the style of original writers is stamped with the peculiarities of their minds. When originality is found apart from good sense, which more or less is frequently the case, it shows itself in paradox and rashness of sentiment, and eccentricity of outward conduct. Poetry, on the other hand, cannot be separated from its good sense, or taste, as it is called; which is one of its elements. It is originality energizing in the world of beauty; the originality of grace, purity, refinement, and good feeling. We do not hesitate to say, that poetry is ultimately founded on correct moral perception; that where there is no sound principle in exercise there will be no poetry; and that on the whole (originality being granted) in proportion to the standard of a writer's moral character will his compositions vary in poetical excellence. This position, however, requires some explanation.

Of course, then, we do not mean to imply that a poet must necessarily display virtuous and religious feeling; we are not speaking of the actual material of poetry, but of its sources. A right moral state of heart is the formal and scientific condition of a poetical mind. Nor does it follow from our position that every poet must in fact be a man of consistent and practical principle; except so far as good feeling commonly produces or results from good practice. Burns was a man of inconsistent life; still, it is known, of much really sound principle at bottom. Thus his acknowledged poetical talent is in nowise inconsistent with the truth of our doctrine, which will refer the beauty which exists in his compositions to the remains of a virtuous and diviner nature within him. Nay, further than this, our theory holds good, even though it be shown that a depraved man may write a poem. As motives short of the purest lead to actions intrinsically good, so frames of mind short of virtuous will produce a partial and limited poetry. But even where this is instanced, the poetry of a vicious mind will be inconsistent and debased; that is, so far only poetry as the traces and shadows of holy truth still remain upon it. On the other hand, a right moral feeling places the mind in the very centre of that circle from which all the rays have their origin and range; whereas minds otherwise placed command but a portion of the whole circuit of poetry. Allowing for human infirmity and the varieties of opinion, Milton, Spenser, Cowper, Wordsworth, and Southey, may be considered, as far as their writings go, to approximate to this moral centre. The following are added as further illustrations of our meaning. Walter Scott's centre is chivalrous honour; Shakspeare exhibits the characteristics of an unlearned and undisciplined piety; Homer the religion of nature and conscience, at times debased by polytheism. All these poets are religious. The occasional irreligion of Virgil's poetry is painful to the admirers of his general taste and delicacy. Dryden's "Alexander's Feast" is a magnificent composition, and has high poetical beauties; but to a refined judgment there is something intrinsically unpoetical in the end to which it is devoted, the praises of revel and sensuality. It corresponds to a process of clever reasoning erected on an untrue foundation—the one is a fallacy, the other is out of taste. Lord Byron's *Manfred* is in parts intensely poetical; yet the delicate mind naturally shrinks from the spirit which here and there reveals itself, and the basis on which the drama is built. From a perusal of it we should infer, according to the above theory, that there was right and fine feeling in the poet's mind, but that the central and consistent character was wanting. From the history of his life we know this to be the fact. The connexion between want of the religious principle and want of poetical feeling, is seen in the instances of Hume and Gibbon, who had radically unpoetical minds. Rousseau, it may be supposed, is an exception to our doctrine. Lucretius, too, had great poetical genius; but his work evinces that his miserable philosophy was rather the result of a bewildered judgment than a corrupt heart.

According to the above theory, Revealed Religion should be especially poetical—and it is so in fact. While its disclosures have an originality in them to engage the intellect, they have a beauty to satisfy the moral nature. It presents us with those ideal forms of excellence in which a poetical mind delights, and with which all grace and harmony are associated. It brings us into a new world—a world of overpowering interest, of the sublimest views, and the tenderest and purest feelings. The peculiar grace of mind of the New Testament writers is as striking as the actual effect produced upon the hearts of those who have imbibed their spirit. At present we are not concerned with the practical, but the poetical nature of revealed truth. With Christians, a poetical view of things is a duty, we are bid to colour all things with hues of faith, to see a Divine meaning in every event, and a superhuman tendency. Even our friends around are invested with unearthly brightness—no longer imperfect men, but beings taken into Divine favour, stamped with His seal, and in training for future happiness. It may be added, that the virtues peculiarly Christian are especially poetical—meekness, gentleness, compassion, contentment, modesty, not to mention the devotional virtues; whereas the ruder and more ordinary feelings are the instruments of rhetoric more justly than of poetry—anger, indignation, emulation, martial spirit, and love of independence.

A few remarks on poetical composition, and we have done. The art of composition is merely accessory to the poetical talent. But where that talent exists, it necessarily gives its own character to the style, and renders it perfectly different from all others. As the poet's habits of mind lead to contemplation rather than to communication with others, he is more or less obscure, according to the particular style of poetry he has adopted; less so in epic, or narrative and dramatic representation—more so in odes and choruses. He will be obscure, moreover, from the depth of his feelings, which require a congenial reader to enter into them—and from their acuteness, which shrinks from any formal accuracy in the expression of them. And he will be obscure, not only from the carelessness of genius, and from the originality of his conceptions, but it may be from natural deficiency in the power of clear and eloquent expression, which, we must repeat, is a talent distinct from poetry, though often mistaken for it.

However, dexterity in composition, or *eloquence* as it may be called in a contracted sense of the word, is manifestly more or less necessary in every branch of literature, though its elements may be different in each. Poetical eloquence consists, first, in the power of illustration; which the poet uses, not as the orator, voluntarily, for the sake of clearness or ornament, but almost by constraint, as the sole outlet and expression of intense inward feeling. This spontaneous power of comparison may, in some poetical minds, be very feeble; these of course cannot show to advantage as poets. Another talent necessary to composition is the power of unfolding the meaning in an orderly manner. A poetical mind is often too impatient to explain itself justly; it is overpowered by a rush of emotions, which sometimes want of power, sometimes the indolence of inward enjoyment, prevents it from describing. Nothing is more difficult than to analyse the feelings of our own minds; and the power of doing so, whether natural or acquired, is clearly distinct from experiencing them. Yet, though distinct from the poetical talent, it is obviously necessary to its exhibition. Hence it is a common praise bestowed upon writers, that they express what we have often felt, but could never describe. The power of arrangement, which is necessary for an extended poem, is a modification of the same talent, being to poetry what method is to logic. Besides these qualifications, poetical composition requires that command of language which is the mere effect of practice. The poet is a compositor; words are his types; he must have them within reach, and in unlimited abundance. Hence the need of careful labour to the accomplished poet—not in order that his diction may attract, but that the language may be subjected to him. He studies the art of composition as we might learn dancing or elocution; not that we may move or speak according to rule, but that, by the very exercise our voice and carriage may become so unembarrassed as to allow of our doing what we will with them.

A talent for composition, then, is no essential part of poetry, though indispensable to its exhibition. Hence it would seem that attention to the language, for its own sake, evidences not the true poet, but the mere artist. Pope is said to have tuned our tongue. We certainly owe much to him—his diction is rich, musical, and expressive: still he is not on this account a poet; he elaborated his composition for its own sake. If we give him poetical praise on this account, we may as appropriately bestow it on a tasteful cabinet-maker. This does not forbid us to ascribe the grace of his verse to an inward principle of poetry, which supplied him with archetypes of the beautiful and splendid to work by. But a similar gift must direct the skill of every fancy-artist who subserves the luxuries and elegances of life. On the other hand, though Virgil is celebrated as a master of composition, yet his style is so identified with his conceptions, as their outward development, as to preclude the possibility of our viewing the one apart from the other. In Milton, again, the harmony of the verse is but the echo of the inward music which the thoughts of the poet breathe. In Moore's style, the ornament continually outstrips the sense. Cowper and Walter Scott, on the other hand, are slovenly in their versification. Sophocles writes, on the whole, without studied attention to the style; but Euripides frequently affected a simplicity and prettiness which exposed him to the ridicule of the comic poets. Lastly, the style of Homer's poems is perfect in their particular department. It is free, manly, simple, perspicuous, energetic, and varied. It is the style of one who rhapsodized without deference to hearer or judge, in an age prior to the temptations which more or less prevailed over succeeding writers—before the theatre had degraded poetry into an exhibition, and criticism narrowed it into an art.

SIR ARTHUR QUILLER-COUCH

A Note on the *Poetics*

The *Poetics* of Aristotle can scarcely be called a treatise, or even—fragment though it is—the fragment of a revised treatise. Nevertheless, and as it stands, it has for the student of literary criticism a double historical value apart from its own inherent merit. It is the first examination known to us of the poetical art, and ever since its re-discovery it has exercised an amazing pollency upon all critical minds, throughout Europe. It has been used as Bible and misinterpreted as Bible; and its misinterpretations have, translated into laws and practice, commanded a century and more of dramatic literature. It has been slavishly obeyed, violently controverted. The historical fact remains that all critical writers have to reckon their start with it. In short it is Elementary.

Being Elementary, it is (in my experience) the very best start for a learner. But being also seminal, it suggests thoughts which, between teacher and pupil, can be carried into many paths, as well as used for friendly correction of judgment. It has that final majesty which resides in ministry, the innocent cunning to be universal while practical. It is upon some few of its quite elementary points that I invite your attention to-day.

Let us start with a very few words on its shape, scope and intention. It is (as I have said) a fragment. Laying itself out to discuss the poetic art in general, it passes on to deal with Tragedy, discusses this carefully, compares it to its advantage with Epic, and then suddenly breaks off. Everyone to-day allows that a Second Part, dealing with the Epic itself, with Comedy, if not also with the Lyric or Dithyramb, was in-

Reprinted from *The Poet as Citizen and other Papers* (New York: Cambridge University Press, 1934), pp. 86–96, by permission of the publisher. Copyright 1934 by Cambridge University Press.

tended, and possibly followed. But that Second Part has been lost.

Further, the *reliquiae*, as they have come down to us, while mostly pure Aristotle in style as in matter, are in later parts—here and there—careless, shorthand, or idly repetitive passages, which suggest that we owe what we have to no revision by the Master, but to notes by a pupil who in time yielded to that end-of-term feeling we all know so well, and was occasionally the victim of an abrupt question, thrown at him to wake him up.

As for its early fame. There is no evidence at all (or none known to me) that the Alexandrine critics, or their Roman successors in Rhetoric, esteemed it of palmary, even of considerable, importance—that is, if we cut out Horace's unacknowledged borrowings for the *Ars Poetica*. It must have impressed more oriental races somehow, for it survived in Arabic and Syriac translation; but for medieval Europe, it was, until the second half of the fifteenth century, a lost book. Even when, in the thirteenth century, the drive out of Byzantium opened up its libraries to the West and *the* Philosopher started to resume that sway over the intelligence of Europe which he has, ever since, maintained and improved, his *Rhetoric* found a translator as a matter of course, but our little treatise was 'left out in the cold', even outside the doors of the great Aldine Aristotle of 1495–8.

It does not fall within the scope of my purpose to-day, Gentlemen, to rehearse the story of this Cinderella. One could easily embroider it with many historical ornaments—as, for a single instance, with the story of the first real commentator—Castelvetro—one of those diabolical crossword-puzzle men, camp-followers in the commissariat of any humanistic movement since time began—who, with his numerous brothers and their wives, held supper-parties at Modena, high-brow gatherings at which every guest had to compose a Greek or a Latin epigram, or at least an Italian sonnet or a madrigal, and all had to discourse in the language selected by the President of the Feast for that evening. Picture these feasts. I instance Castelvetro—*pedantuccio e grammataccio* as a testy contemporary called him—only because, as about the earliest to squeeze a foot into the glass slipper, he exhibited the resultant corns of Rules, imposed them as such upon the Great French tragedians of the seventeenth century, and had to be exposed in England by the common sense of Dryden, later by Samuel Johnson, until it remained only for my predecessor in this Chair to enquire, with a beautiful simplicity, 'How did this nonsense ever come to be talked by men of sense?'

But Castelvetro's and other men's vagaries are but parentheses in the statement of an undeniable fact—that from the moment this little, unshapely book was re-born into our Western world it has simply taken charge of all the art of Criticising, constraining all critics. They may contradict, confute, cut themselves with knives; they may misinterpret with Castelvetro, partly interpret with Milton or Lessing, misunderstand with Edgar Allen Poe and George Henry Lewes, curse with Dallas, patronise with Croce. But not one of them can disregard or get away from it.

And why?

Well, for three good reasons, of which the first is the most trivial. It happens to be, so far as is known, the earliest attempt to treat Poetry as a branch of man's Natural History. Even for this it has more than an antiquarian interest; being an actual datum for any study on man's development as a thinking animal. As Newman put it in a slightly different connection, 'In a language's earlier times, while it is yet unformed, to write in it at all is almost a work of genius. It is like crossing a country before roads are made communicating between place and place. The authors of that age deserve to be Classics, both because of what they do and because they can do it'. Newman was speaking in particular of pioneers in pure *literature,* early framers of a nation's verse or prose. But his words apply just as well to those who break the ground and draw the first furrow in any field of human thought.

Our business to-day, however, does not lie with this historical precedence of the *Poetics*. I but remind you of it, and pass on to some points which more nearly concern us as learners in the Art of Criticising.

For the first, there is that virtue of his method which I commended to you in my preceding lecture—the simple, direct way of taking poetry as the actual 'stuff the poets wrote' and 'getting on to *that*' as a naturalist would: a thing to be wondered at, no doubt as a spider's web might be wondered at, or the convolutions of a sea-shell, or the starry pattern of a crystal; but first of all to be observed, noted, with a curiosity in the thing for its own sake; also, no doubt, in the permanent hope of all men of science, that by accumulating observed facts and divining their right arrangement some general conclusions may be drawn—with this difference, of course, that Poetry, the object examined, being a *human* faculty or activity, these conclusions may be of use to future men, as no observations by a naturalist can as yet (so far as we know) instruct the future spider or mollusc to rise on stepping-stones of his dead self to higher things. I speak cautiously here; since there is no telling what the Mendelians may or may not do some day—and an oyster may then be eugenically crossed in love. And I speak, of course, under Aristotle's own insistent reservation that no study of man's doings—be it in politics, ethics, any form of his industry or art or worldly activity—can be conducted on any line of mathematical demonstration: the whole business must depend on induction, a process so complicated by individual freaks of reason or passion that whereas Poetry, for instance, can persuade you convincingly of what, in given circumstances, Alcibiades would have done and suffered, History at any moment may produce evidence that he did precisely the opposite, and escaped the fatal consequences.

But, this granted, who can help admiring the way Aristotle goes to work? He is always, as I put it last time, 'on the ball', and that ball, Epic or Tragedy, always close to his toe. You may dissent from this or that opinion of his on this play or that passage in it. But there it is: you know just where you are, and why. You may hold, for instance (as I humbly do), that his insistence on *Plot* in a drama tempts him to over-estimate his pet *Oedipus* ('Cover his face'), to ignore the calm cruelty of so much in its 'perfect' author. But there you have his preference and his reason for it, chapter and verse.

And that is why, though he could only deal with the poetry existing in his day, his book remains the norm of the art in which we are learners. I dare not prophesy that it always will so remain, but will rather imitate the caution which he used in speaking of the development of Tragedy.

If it be asked whether Tragedy has yet arrived at being all that it need be in form—to decide that theoretically in relation to the

Theatre is another question—all we can say is that its advance was by little and little, as the poets discovered improvements, until it reached its natural metre, and there stopped.

Not even an Aristotle could foretell a Shakespeare, or deal with that which Time took almost two thousand years in bringing to birth. Nevertheless, by working on the evidence he had, and working on the method of examining definite concrete works, he derived conclusions by which we can test Shakespeare himself again and again, always with profit and no small wonder. For an example, if you take his reasoned definition of the Tragic Hero, as

a man of high prosperity, good but not eminently good nor just, whose misfortune is brought about by no vice or depravity, but through some error (ἁμαρτία) of frailty. . .

and apply this successively to Macbeth, Coriolanus, Brutus, Hamlet, Othello, Lear, Antony (all great, all even noble, all so different in their ways), and you will hardly withhold your wonder at the man or—my immediate point—your respectful admiration of his method.

Next, I will ask you to consider how, throughout the little treatise—sometimes explicitly, but ever as a thing understood —Aristotle handles Poetry as no mere ornament but a natural function of man, to create or enjoy, and, as a beautiful function, therefore a natural grace of life. It is no 'Criticism of Life', save and in so far as all Art is that. I suppose there are few now but would condemn Matthew Arnold's as an ill-fitting definition, at once too loose and too strait—while none the more ingratiating by that smatch of the Schoolmaster which unregenerate man so properly abhors. Nor on the other hand shall I who spent some of my youth in combating 'Art for Art's Sake' waste any fraction of your youth, or of my own declining years, in discussing that other extreme of doctrine. We are talking of Aristotle, who—understanding most things—would scarcely have understood what 'Art for Art's Sake' meant. Indeed I have always regretted that Butcher's most useful edition of the *Poetics* should be labelled *Aristotle's Theory of Poetry and Fine Art*. It misleads. To Aristotle *any* art—that of Poetry included—would be a fine art just in proportion as it was fine; as carpentry, for instance, or pottery, would be a fine art if finely practised. One art could, and did, serve another—as, let us say, statuary serves architecture. But as for separating the arts by invidious category, into arts fine in themselves, and arts not fine in themselves, Aristotle had no idea of it. Indeed I am ready to assert that nowhere in his published works can you find a term translatable as 'Fine Art'; and I am reasonably certain that had he felt any need for any such term, he had the capacity to invent one.

No the arts—all of them—to him, as to any other Greek—were just parts in the education of a gentleman; that is to say, of a perfect citizen.

You may get at this—to take an example most pertinent to us—by considering his famous definition of the use of Tragedy as 'through Pity and Terror purging these emotions in us'. The word Katharsis or 'purge'—'pill' if you like—is now generally, and after much delicate paraphrasing in more squeamish times, recognised for what it is—a straight medical word used by a naturalist to convey that Tragedy operates on the mind, to cleanse it, as certain laxatives will do on the body. (And Apollo, let me again remind you, was father alike of Song and of Medicine.) That is all; and almost all the fuss about it just clears itself away when you compare this supposedly difficult passage with others in other works of the Master. Then you will perceive that the purpose of all the separate arts is to cleanse a man of his 'humours' and recall his system to the normal. Tragedy, by its dose of pity and terror, showing him over-weening pride, ambition, lust, exaggerated in a spectacle of kings and princes, will teach him to discharge these accretions of self-pity, self-esteem, vaulting ambition, tyrannical pride, unreasonable terrors from his soul, and dismiss him with

calm of mind, all passion spent.

But even such an operation—if you will look into the *Politics*—does Music. Music, by its regulated beat, effects a Katharsis of 'enthusiasm'. Music, if I may use the illustration, corrects the sort of vocality to which unbridled man gives way in his bath. Rhetoric similarly (if rightly employed) corrects to genuine persuasiveness the tendency on the one hand to gush, on the other to legal hairsplitting and making the worse argument seem the better. Comedy canalises the right man's mirth between laughter at things not properly ridiculous and the mere hysterical *fou rire*. Even dancing regulates, by rhythm, the less moderate tendencies of the human leg.

All these, in short, coalesce into one system of the arts—that of using for good man's emotions regulated and controlled by reason: all together moulding him back to that temperance, that σωφροσύνη which results in a cultivated man who is also an exemplary citizen.

Let us turn, now, to a more particular lesson of the *Poetics*. Aristotle starts off by telling us that 'Epic Poetry and Tragedy, Comedy, Lyric, even flute-playing and lyre-playing are all, speaking generally, modes of *Imitation*.' The word *Mimesis*, translated literally as 'Imitation' of course, is just as defensibly accurate as the late Mr. Paley's habitual rapturous rendering of γυναῖκες in a Greek chorus by 'the female population.'

That, of course, is the trouble with all our efforts to convey any word from one language to another with its exact meaning or its shades of meaning. As Professor Ker (*valde deflendus*) complained ten years since—

In the other Arts there is nothing like the curse of Babel; but the divine Idea of Poetry, abiding the same with itself in essence, shining with the same light, as Drummond sees it in Homer and Virgil, Ronsard and Garcillasso de la Vega, is actually seen by very few votaries in each and all of these several lamps. The light of Poetry may be all over the world and belong to the whole human race, yet how little of it is really available, compared with the other arts! It is broken up among the various languages. . . .

In a previous lecture I have asked you to accept 'Representation' as the nearest word in English for Aristotle's 'Mimesis'. It does not, it cannot, as I have tried to show, preclude originality or personality, however modest of himself an author may be. So *he* be true, a pattern will push up through his weaving. As my late friend Sir Walter Raleigh has put it, speaking of Shakespeare, 'No man can walk save in his own shadow', and an author friend, Sir Henry Newbolt, in an epistle dedicatory to one of his books—

I have heard [he says] of certain mirrors made in the far East which show not only a reflection of the scene before them but a picture of their own as well, a constant and inseparable pattern appearing from beneath their visible surface and interweaving itself with every representation of the outer world. Surely the mind of man is such a mirror, and that which he writes just such a constant and inevitable transformation of that which he has seen.

VII

JOHN GASSNER

Catharsis and the Modern Theater

It is difficult to think of a more academic concept than that of
catharsis. It is encrusted with antiquity and bears the rust of
much speculation justly suspect to the practical worker. The
concept is, nevertheless, one of those insights that philosophers
sometimes achieve in spite of themselves. Aristotle touched
bottom when he declared the effect of tragedy to be purgation
of the soul by pity and fear.

The Aristotelian formula, supremely empirical, has a dual
importance: the spectator is given a definition of his experience,
and the playwright is provided with a goal for which certain
means are requisite, the goal set for him being no other than
the effect he must achieve if he is to hold an audience with high
and serious matter of a painful nature. Unfortunately, however,
Aristotle's analysis was altogether too fragmentary, and his
Poetics has come down to us as little more than a collection of
notes. We do not even know precisely what catharsis meant for
him and how he thought "pity and fear" produced the purgation.

The subject has exercised commentators since the Renaissance when they seized upon the short passage: "Tragedy
through pity and fear effects a purgation of such emotions."
Each age has added its own interpretation, naturally reflecting
its own interests and its own kind of drama. According to the
Sixteenth Century pundits, including the famous Castelvetro,
tragedy hardened the spectator to suffering by subjecting him
to pity- and fear-inducing scenes of misery and violence. Corneille, who gave much thought to his craft, held that tragedy
forced the spectator to fear for himself when he observed a
character's passions causing disaster and that the resolve to rule
one's own passions effected the purgation. Others, including

Reprinted from *European Theories of the Drama*, edited by Barret H. Clark
(New York: Crown Publishers, 1964), pp. 549–52, by permission of the
publisher. Copyright 1964 by Crown Publishers.

John Milton, took the homeopathic view that pity and terror on the stage counteracted the disturbing elements of pity and terror in the spectator. For the liberals or humanitarians of the Enlightenment, including the author of *Nathan the Wise*, tragedy purified the observer by enabling him to exercise his sympathies. For Hegel tragedy reconciled conflicting views, thereby effecting catharsis. And so it went until Jacob Bernays, Wilhelm Stekel, and other psychologists arrived at the view that accords most easily with both the findings of psychopathology and common sense—namely, that catharsis is simply the expulsion of disturbing drives and conflicts.

Without adhering to any specific school of psychopathology, it is safe to say that if Aristotelian catharsis is a valid definition of tragic effect (and I believe it is), it means one thing above all: In the tragic experience we temporarily expel troublesome inner complications. We expel "pity" and "fear," to use Aristotle's terms, and the terms are broad enough to cover the most pathological or near-pathological elements—namely, anxieties, fears, morbid grief or self-pity, sadistic or masochistic desires, and the sense of guilt that these engender and are engendered by. In a successful tragedy we see these drives enacted on the stage directly or through their results by characters with whom we can identify ourselves. They are our proxies, so to speak.

We must observe, however, that the expulsion would certainly prove ephemeral and perhaps even incomplete or ineffective if the expelled matter were merely brought to the surface (to our "pre-conscious," if you will) instead of being fully recognized by our consciousness. Evoked "pity and fear" on the tragic stage may effect expulsion, but at least one other force is needed if real recognition is to be effectuated.

That something more is needed is evidenced by the whole history of the theater. The distinction between tragedy and melodrama is grounded in the opinion that excitement is not enough, that it does not produce the most satisfactory effects. Where the excitement emanates plausibly and serves an end beyond itself there is, we say, tragedy. Where the excitement exists solely for itself and is accomplished without the operation of reason or credibility we have melodrama. If purgation in tragedy were confined solely to the effects of pity and fear there could be little dramatic distinction between *Hamlet* and *The Bat*.

Has it not always been recognized that the superiority of the great tragedies, if we exclude purely stylistic differences, has resided in their powerful blending of passion with enlightenment? This is what we mean when we attribute their superiority to the significance of their content, the depth and scope of their conflict, or the relevance of their action to the major aspects and problems of humanity. In tragedy there is always a precipitate of final enlightenment—some inherent, cumulatively realized, understanding. We have seen an experience enacted on the stage, and have externalized its inner counterpart in ourselves by the process of vibrating to the acted passions; or possibly by some other means, since unconscious processes are open to infinite debate. Then, ensuring the externalization of the inner drives, we have given them form and meaning—that is, understood their causes and effects, which brings us to the furthest point from the unconscious, or from nebulous emotion, ever reached by the individual. Enlightenment is, therefore, the third component of the process of purgation.

It exists in perfect harmony with the components of "pity and fear," and it is even supported by them. "Pity and fear," (using these terms to cover the emotional experience) are the *fixatives* of tragic enlightenment, for without their agency the meaning of a play would be superficial and fleeting; enlightenment unrooted in the emotions or unsupported and unevoked by them would be something imposed from without, unprecipitated from the struggle of the drama, and devoid of persuasive growth or cumulative effect. Moreover, pity and terror have mnemonic values which the drama cannot dispense with, because of its rapid course of action. Who would remember the significances of *Hamlet* without its anguish?

Finally, but keeping the above qualifications strictly in mind, we can maintain that enlightenment is not only the third element in catharsis, but the decisive one. The ultimate relief comes when the dramatist brings the tragic struggle to a state of rest. This cannot occur so long as we are left in a state of tension. No matter how well the action or the main character's destiny is resolved and concluded, the anarchic forces, "the pity and fear," evoked by the tragedy cannot establish a suitable inner equilibrium. Only enlightenment, a clear comprehension of what was involved in the struggle, an understanding of cause and effect, a judgment on what we have witnessed, and an induced state of mind that places it above the riot of passion—can effect this necessary equilibrium. And it is a necessary one if there is to be purgation, and if for the moment we are to be healed of the wounds self-inflicted in the unconscious, inflicted on us from without by external circumstance before they settle our inmost self, then inflicted once more by the tragic story enacted before our eyes on the stage. Only enlightenment can therefore round out the esthetic experience in tragedy, can actually ensure complete esthetic gratification. True tragic exaltation, which we require of a tragedy, also lies in this. For the exaltation comes only if we have prevailed over the anarchy of our inner life and the ever present and ever pressing life around us; and how can we master this anarchy without understanding it, without putting order into this house of disorder?

Had Aristotle pursued his investigation of classic drama further, he would have surely arrived at this view himself. The author of the *Nichomachean Ethics* and the *Politics* could not have failed to discover the conclusive element of enlightenment in the purgation afforded by the tragedies of Aeschylus, Sophocles, and Euripides. To adopt Nietzschean (*The Birth of Tragedy*) terminology, Greek tragedy imposed the Apollonian world of light and reason upon the dynamic Dionysian world of passion. The Apollonian element in the warp and woof of the plays, including the great choral passages, ordered and so mastered the Dionysiac excitement or disequilibrium. I believe the same thing can be demonstrated in Elizabethan tragedy, in the work of Corneille and Racine, and in modern tragedy.

To conclude this argument, I should, I suppose, try to disabuse anyone who would look askance at this insistence on enlightenment because it suggests a moral in the outmoded Victorian sense. The "moral" is imposed from without by a convention; that was the prime limitation of William Winter's criticism. Enlightenment is not actually imposed, but wells up from the stream of the play itself, from the enacted events, actions, and reactions. The moral, in other words, is a predigested judgement, whereas enlightenment is empirical. The moral is a summation or tag; enlightenment is a process. The moral of a play can be put into a sententious sentence. The element of enlightenment can also be summarized, but the summary is only a portion of the whole. It is a state of grace, so to speak, a civilized attitude achieved in the course of experiencing the play: an Apollonian attitude, Santayana's "life of reason," a clarity of mind and spirit, a resilience and cheerfulness even. The moral is a law. The enlightenment is a state of mind, and includes specific conclusions only as a necessary concomitant of every state of mind that is now vacuous. It is even a kind of poetry of the mind, no matter how earnest, somber or sultry.

Acceptance of the function of enlightenment in tragic catharsis is particularly essential if we are to cope with the modern drama, if we are to understand, write, and produce it. In the case of modern drama, many problems arise and many distinctions must be made. For instance, we must realize that many serious modern plays are not tragedies at all but a new form of tragi-comedy for which no term has yet been found. In this essay let us, however, continue to hew close to the matter of enlightenment.

The fact is that many who would grant my premise, out of conviction or from sheer exhaustion, will stickle at one other point as much as they would at the possibility that "enlightenment" is just an undercover term for a moral. They will insist on confining the matter of enlightenment to "universals" and proceed to flail post-Ibsen drama because it so often treats immediate issues and problems.

I have nothing against "universals," but it seems to me that the only universals these critics favor are *dead* ones; or let us say that, for reasons that could bear some scrutiny, they prefer them to be conveniently remote from contemporary social conflicts. Otherwise a universal is not universal for them. A fallacy, I believe, since how can something be universal if it no longer functions, what life is there in it if it lacks direct applicability to what pinches us, and what is left in it but a platitude that fobs us off with a cold compress while the diseased body teems with microbes.

A hard and fast distinction between the topical and the universal is impossible in practice. We live amid the immediacies of our time and place. Are these distinguishable, can these be separated from, fundamental realities and human drives? The immediate realities contain and project the universal ones. Even our most unvarnished economic and political struggles relate to the universals of anxiety, fear of deprivation, pain and extinction; they involve love and hate, loyalty and treason, selfishness and self-sacrifice, honor and dishonor, falsehood and truth, good and evil. And all this is also only another way of saying that anything we call universal is only a generalization of immediate and specific interests or concerns. If we could put ourselves in the place of an Athenian spectator at the first performance of *The Trojan Women,* the Oresteian trilogy, or any other tragedy that stirred that spectator either as an individual or as a member of a group, we would not speak so glibly of universals. It is safe to conjecture that everything we consider universal in these plays was once very immediate—socially, politically, psychologically.

No, the failure of any contemporary topical or even downright propaganda play as tragic art has other causes than the substitution of the "topical" for the "universal." These cannot be examined in this essay; they are many, and they also require particularization in individual cases. Still hewing to my theme, I should like to add only that perhaps the overall cause will be found in the social dramatist's and the propagandist's failure to achieve a catharsis. He fails chiefly because in striving so conscientiously for enlightenment, he so often substitutes statement for dramatic process and neglects to effectuate the "pity and fear"—that is, the tensions and emotional rapport or identification implicit in the Aristotelian terms. Although it is the combination of "pity," "fear," and "enlightenment" that produces tragic catharsis, his assault strategy makes the frontal attack with "enlightenment" but forgest about the flanks. The general assault fails, and the unsupported frontal attack soon crumbles, since there is no effective enlightenment when the play fails. There is even a school of social drama that in one way or other denies the value of catharsis. According to Berthold Brecht, the champion of the epic or "learning-play" (*Lehrstück*), sympathy and emotional identification (*Einfühlung*) represent enticements or evasions of social understanding and action. He objects to "all the illusion which whips up the spectator for two hours and leaves him exhausted and full of vague recollection and vaguer hope." Brecht's view is only a forthright version of an attitude that underlies much social drama which, regardless of its merits, must remain fundamentally untragic. Perhaps proponents of anti-emotional drama should go one step further and arraign tragedy itself as wrong for their purposes.

VIII

MAXWELL ANDERSON

The Essence of Tragedy

Anybody who dares to discuss the making of tragedy lays himself open to critical assault and general barrage, for the theorists have been hunting for the essence of tragedy since Aristotle without entire success. There is no doubt that playwrights have occasionally written tragedy successfully, from Aeschylus on, and there is no doubt that Aristotle came very close to a definition of what tragedy is in his famous passage on catharsis. But why the performance of a tragedy should have a cleansing effect on the audience, why an audience is willing to listen to tragedy, why tragedy has a place in the education of men, has never, to my knowledge, been convincingly stated. I must begin by saying that I have not solved the Sphinx's riddle which fifty generations of skillful brains have left in shadow. But I have one suggestion which I think might lead to a solution if it were put to laboratory tests by those who know something about philosophical analysis and dialectic.

There seems no way to get at this suggestion except through a reference to my own adventures in playwriting, so I ask your tolerance while I use myself as an instance. A man who has written successful plays is usually supposed to know something about the theory of playwriting, and perhaps he usually does. In my own case, however, I must confess that I came into the theatre unexpectedly, without preparation, and stayed in it because I had a certain amount of rather accidental success. It was not until after I had fumbled my way through a good many successes and an appalling number of failures that I began to doubt the sufficiency of dramatic instinct and to wonder whether or not there were general laws governing dramatic structure which so poor a head for theory as my own might

Reprinted from *The Essence of Tragedy and Other Footnotes and Papers* (Washington: Anderson Press, 1939), pp. 3–14, by permission of the publisher. Copyright 1939 by Anderson House.

grasp and use. I had read the *Poetics* long before I tried play-writing, and I had looked doubtfully into a few well-known handbooks on dramatic structure, but the maxims and theories propounded always drifted by me in a luminous haze—brilliant, true, profound in context, yet quite without meaning for me when I considered the plan for a play or tried to clarify an emotion in dialogue. So far as I could make out every play was a new problem, and the old rules were inapplicable. There were so many rules, so many landmarks, so many pitfalls, so many essential reckonings, that it seemed impossible to find your way through the jungle except by plunging ahead, trusting to your sense of direction and keeping your wits about you as you went.

But as the seasons went by and my failures fell as regularly as the leaves in autumn I began to search again among the theorists of the past for a word of wisdom that might take some of the gamble out of playwriting. What I needed most of all, I felt, was a working definition of what a play is, or perhaps a formula which would include all the elements necessary to a play structure. A play is almost always, probably, an attempt to recapture a vision for the stage. But when you are working in the theatre it's most unsatisfactory to follow the gleam without a compass, quite risky to trust "the light that never was on sea or land" without making sure beforehand that you are not being led straight into a slough of despond. In other words you must make a choice among visions, and you must check your chosen vision carefully before assuming that it will make a play. But by what rules, what maps, what fields of reference can you check so intangible a substance as a revelation, a dream, an inspiration, or any similar nudge from the subconscious mind?

I shan't trouble you with the details of my search for a criterion, partly because I can't remember it in detail. But I reread Aristotle's *Poetics* in the light of some bitter experience, and one of his observations led me to a comparison of ancient and modern playwriting methods. In discussing construction he made a point of the recognition scene as essential to tragedy. The recognition scene, as Aristotle isolated it in the tragedies of the Greeks, was generally an artificial device, a central scene in which the leading character saw through a disguise, recognized as a friend or as an enemy, perhaps as a lover or a member of his own family, some person whose identity had been hidden.

Iphigeneia, for example, receives a victim for sacrifice and then recognizes her own brother in this victim. There is an instant and profound emotional reaction, instantly her direction in the play is altered. But occasionally, in the greatest of the plays, the recognition turned on a situation far more convincing, though no less contrived. Oedipus, hunting savagely for the criminal who has brought the plague upon Thebes, discovers that he is himself that criminal—and since this is a discovery that affects not only the physical well-being and happiness of the hero, but the whole structure of his life, the effect on him and on the direction of the story is incalculably greater than could result from the more superficial revelation made to Iphigeneia.

Now scenes of exactly this sort are rare in the modern drama except in detective stories adapted for the stage. But when I probed a little more deeply into the memorable pieces of Shakespeare's theatre and our own I began to see that though modern recognition scenes are subtler and harder to find, they are none the less present in the plays we choose to remember. They seldom have to do with anything so naïve as disguise or the unveiling of a personal identity. But the element of discovery is just as important as ever. For the mainspring in the mechanism of a modern play is almost invariably a discovery by the hero of some element in his environment or in his own soul of which he has not been aware—or which he has not taken sufficiently into account. Moreover, nearly every teacher of playwriting has had some inkling of this, though it was not until after I had worked out my own theory that what they said on this point took on accurate meaning for me. I still think that the rule which I formulated for my own guidance is more concise than any other, and so I give it here: A play should lead up to and away from a central crisis, and this crisis should consist in a discovery by the leading character which has an indelible effect on his thought and emotion and completely alters his course of action. The leading character, let me say again, must make the discovery; it must affect him emotionally; and it must alter his direction in the play.

Try that formula on any play you think worthy of study, and you will find that, with few exceptions, it follows this pattern or some variation of this pattern. The turning point of *The Green Pastures*, for example, is the discovery of God, who is the leading character, that even he must learn and grow, that a God who is to endure must conform to the laws of change. The turning point of *Hamlet* is Hamlet's discovery, in the play-scene, that his uncle was unquestionably the murderer of his father. In *Abe Lincoln in Illinois* Lincoln's discovery is that he has been a coward, that he has stayed out of the fight for the Union because he was afraid. In each case, you will note, the discovery has a profound emotional effect on the hero, and gives an entirely new direction to his action in the play.

I'm not writing a disquisition on playwriting and wouldn't be competent to write one, but I do want to make a point of the superlative usefulness of this one touchstone for play-structure. When a man sets out to write a play his first problem is his subject and the possibilities of that subject as a story to be projected from the stage. His choice of subject matter is his personal problem, and one that takes its answer from his personal relation to his times. But if he wants to know a possible play subject when he finds it, if he wants to know how to mould the subject into play form after he has found it, I doubt that he'll ever discover another standard as satisfactory as the modern version of Aristotle which I have suggested. If the plot he has in mind does not contain a playable episode in which the hero or heroine makes an emotional discovery, a discovery that practically dictates the end of the story, then such an episode must be inserted—and if no place can be found for it the subject is almost certainly a poor one for the theatre. If this emotional discovery is contained in the story, but is not central, then it must be made central, and the whole action must revolve around it. In a three-act play it should fall near the end of the second act, though it may be delayed till the last; in a five-act play it will usually be found near the end of the third, though here also it can be delayed. Everything else in the play should be subordinated to this one episode—should lead up to or away from it.

Now this prime rule has a corollary which is just as important as the rule itself. The hero who is to make the central discovery in a play must not be a perfect man. He must have some variation of what Aristotle calls a tragic fault—and the reason he must have it is that when he makes his discovery he must change both in himself and in his action—and he must change for the better. The fault can be a very simple one—a mere unawareness, for example—but if he has no fault he cannot change for the better, but only for the worse, and for a reason which I shall discuss later, it is necessary that he must become more admirable, and not less so, at the end of the play. In other words, a hero must pass through an experience which opens his eyes to an error of his own. He must learn through suffering. In a tragedy he suffers death itself as a consequence of his fault or his attempt to correct it, but before he dies he has become a nobler person because of his recognition of his fault and the consequent alteration of his course of action. In a serious play which does not end in death he suffers a lesser punishment, but the pattern remains the same. In both forms he has a fault to begin with, he discovers that fault during the course of the action, and he does what he can to rectify it at the end. In *The Green Pastures* God's fault was that he believed himself perfect. He discovered that he was not perfect, and he resolved to change and grow. Hamlet's fault was that he could not make up his mind to act. He offers many excuses for his indecision until he discovers that there is no real reason for hesitation and that he has delayed out of cowardice. Lincoln, in *Abe Lincoln in Illinois*, has exactly the same difficulty. In the climactic scene it is revealed to him that he has hesitated to take sides through fear of the consequences to himself, and he then chooses to go ahead without regard for what may be in store for him. From the point of view of the playwright, then, the essence of a tragedy, or even of a serious play, is the spiritual awakening, or regeneration, of his hero.

When a playwright attempts to reverse the formula, when his hero makes a discovery which has an evil effect, or one which the audience interprets as evil, on his character, the play is inevitably a failure on the stage. In *Troilus and Cressida* Troilus discovers that Cressida is a light woman. He draws from her defection the inference that all women are faithless—that faith in woman is the possession of fools. As a consequence he turns away from life and seeks death in a cause as empty as the love he has given up, the cause of the strumpet Helen. All the glory of Shakespeare's verse cannot rescue the play for an audience, and save in *Macbeth* Shakespeare nowhere wrote so richly, so wisely, or with such a flow of brilliant metaphor.

For the audience will always insist that the alteration in the hero be for the better—or for what it believes to be the better.

As audiences change the standards of good and evil change, though slowly and unpredictably, and the meanings of plays change with the centuries. One thing only is certain: that an audience watching a play will go along with it only when the leading character responds in the end to what it considers a higher moral impulse than moved him at the beginning of the story, though the audience will of course define morality as it pleases and in the terms of its own day. It may be that there is no absolute up or down in this world, but the race believes that there is, and will not hear of any denial.

And now at last I come to the point toward which I've been struggling so laboriously. Why does the audience come to the theatre to look on while an imaginary hero is put to an imaginary trial and comes out of it with credit to the race and to himself? It was this question that prompted my essay, and unless I've been led astray by my own predilections there is a very possible answer in the rules for playwriting which I have just cited. The theatre originated in two complementary religious ceremonies, one celebrating the animal in man and one celebrating the god. Old Greek Comedy was dedicated to the spirits of lust and riot and earth, spirits which are certainly necessary to the health and continuance of the race. Greek tragedy was dedicated to man's aspiration, to his kinship with the gods, to his unending, blind attempt to lift himself above his lusts and his pure animalism into a world where there are other values than pleasure and survival. However unaware of it we may be, our theatre has followed the Greek patterns with no change in essence, from Aristophanes and Euripides to our own day. Our more ribald musical comedies are simply our approximation of the Bacchic rites of Old Comedy. In the rest of our theatre we sometimes follow Sophocles, whose tragedy is always an exaltation of the human spirit, sometimes Euripides, whose tragicomedy follows the same pattern of an excellence achieved through suffering. The forms of both tragedy and comedy have changed a good deal in non-essentials, but in essentials—and especially in the core of meaning which they must have for audiences—they are in the main the same religious rites which grew up around the altars of Attica long ago.

It is for this reason that when you write for the theatre you must choose between your version of a phallic revel and your vision of what mankind may or should become. Your vision may be faulty, or shallow, or sentimental, but it must conform to some aspiration in the audience, or the audience will reject it. Old Comedy, the celebration of the animal in us, still has a place in our theatre, as it had in Athens, but here, as there, that part of the theatre which celebrated man's virtue and his regeneration in hours of crisis is accepted as having the more important function. Our comedy is largely the Greek New Comedy, which grew out of Euripides' tragi-comedy, and is separated from tragedy only in that it presents a happier scene and puts its protagonist through an ordeal which is less than lethal.

And since our plays, aside from those which are basically Old Comedy, are exaltations of the human spirit, since that is what an audience expects when it comes to the theatre, the playwright gradually discovers, as he puts plays before audiences, that he must follow the ancient Aristotelian rule: he must build his plot around a scene wherein his hero discovers some mortal frailty or stupidity in himself and faces life armed with a new wisdom. He must so arrange his story that it will prove to the audience that men pass through suffering purified, that, animal though we are, despicable though we are in many ways, there is in us all some divine, incalculable fire that urges us to be better than we are.

It could be argued that what the audience demands of a hero is only conformity to race morality, to the code which seems to the spectators most likely to make for race survival. In many cases, especially in comedy, and obviously in the comedy of Molière, this is true. But in the majority of ancient and modern plays it seems to me that what the audience wants to believe is that men have a desire to break the moulds of earth which encase them and claim a kinship with a higher morality than that which hems them in. The rebellion of Antigone, who breaks the laws of men through adherence to a higher law of affection, the rebellion of Prometheus, who breaks the law of the gods to bring fire to men, the rebellion of God in *The Green Pastures* against the rigid doctrine of the Old Testament, the rebellion of Tony in *They Knew What they Wanted* against the convention that called on him to repudiate his cuckold child, the rebellion of Liliom against the heavenly law which asked him to betray his own integrity and make a hypocrisy of his affection, even the repudiation of the old

forms and the affirmation of new by the heroes of Ibsen and
Shaw, these are all instances to me of the groping of men
toward an excellence dimly apprehended, seldom possible of
definition. They are evidence to me that the theatre at its best is
a religious affirmation, an age-old rite restating and reassuring
man's belief in his own destiny and his ultimate hope. The
theatre is much older than the doctrine of evolution, but its one
faith, asseverated again and again for every age and every year,
is a faith in evolution, in the reaching and the climb of men
toward distant goals, glimpsed but never seen, perhaps never
achieved, or achieved only to be passed impatiently on the way
to a more distant horizon.

IX

KENNETH BURKE

The Problem of the Intrinsic
(as reflected in the Neo-Aristotelian
School)

There is a *rhetorical* explanation for doctrines proclaiming the eternity of art. We can say that, esthetic standards being transitory, men try to compensate for this changefulness by denying its existence. Then we might fill out this explanation on the rhetorical level by sociological considerations, noting for instance that the doctrine would fit well with a collector's or antiquarian's attitude towards art, and thus with the business of selling art objects to customers in search of sound esthetic investments. And when art is approached from the antiquarian point of view, men may ask so little of it that it can easily meet the requirements. Thus a work that, in its original context, might have seemed "terrifying" or "divine," could at least remain eternally "interesting" or "odd," thereby possessing a kind of permanence as tested by dilettantish criteria. Much esthetic theory stressing the appreciation of "form" would doubtless fall under this head.

Or noting how much of art has been a secularized variant of religious processes, particularly since the rise of the romantic reaction against capitalism and technology, we may offer a *symbolical* interpretation. A doctrine proclaiming the eternity of art would, from the symbolic point of view, be the natural secular analogue of a belief in the eternity of God.

But we may discuss motives on three levels. Besides Rhetoric

Reprinted from *A Grammar of Motives* (Englewood Cliffs, N.J.: Prentice-Hall, Inc., 1945) pp. 465–84, by permission of the publisher. Copyright 1945 by Prentice-Hall, Inc.

and Symbolic, there is Grammar. We are on the grammatical level when we begin with the "problem of the intrinsic," as reflected in the attempt to characterize the substance of a work. We are faced with *grammatical* problems when we would consider a given work of art "in itself," in what I believe the scholastics might have called its *aseitas,* or "by-itselfness." Considered "intrinsically," the work is said to embody certain "principles." And these principles are said to reside in the division of the work into its parts, and in the relation of these parts to one another and to the whole.

Even though a work of art were to last but a few moments, being destroyed almost immediately after its production, during its brief physical duration you might deal with it *sub specie aeternitatis,* in terms of timelessness. This you could do by considering solely the relation of its parts to one another and to the whole. And you would thereby be thinking in terms of the "eternal" or "timeless" since the relations prevailing among the parts just are. Each part *is* in a certain relation to the others; and all the parts *are* in certain relations to the whole. You would thus be concerned with a work in terms of its *being*—and being is by definition an "eternal now." (Recall that the Aristotelian word for substance is *ousia,* being. Anything capable of consideration by itself, *kath auto,* would be a substance in this sense: as a man, a tree, a stone.) "Beings" may come and go; but insofar as you treat of something in terms of its *being* (in contrast, for instance, with treatment of it in terms of its genesis), by the sheer technicality of the treatment you are working in terms of the eternal—outside the category of time. (It may possess a kind of "internal time," in the sense that, if it is a work of literature or music, some of its parts may precede others. But such order can be discussed in terms of purely structural relationships. And time in this sense is not the kind of time we have in mind when we consider the work in terms of personality, or class, or epoch, etc.)

In sum, when you consider a thing just as it *is,* with the *being* of one part involved in the *being* of its other parts, and with all the parts derived from the being of the whole considered as a generating principle, there is nothing but a "present tense" involved here, or better, a "tenselessness," even though the thing thus dealt with arises in time and passes with time.

In Aristotle, such a concept of substance or being (*ousia*) was carried to its full metaphysical limits. For he abided by the logic of his terminology to the extent of concluding that the world itself was not created, but was eternal. Every vocabulary has its limits, imposed by the internal logic of its terms; and Aristotle, as a superior thinker, carried his own vocabulary to its limits. And though individual beings came and went, he held that their *genera* (their family identities that contain the principles of their being, as the principles of an equilateral triangle reside in the class of such triangles) had existed and would exist forever.

But, though in Aristotle every individual stone or tree or man, or any other thing capable of treatment as a separate entity, was a being, I think we should be wrong in saying that he treated beings simply in terms of their *individuality*. Rather, he located an individual thing's principle of being in its identity as a member of a *tribe* (his word *genos*, or genus, being originally a word of strong familistic connotations, with the same root as our words "generate" and "generation"). It was the types, or kinds, or classes, or families of natural beings that continued permanently. Hence the intrinsic principles of a being were not unique, but were variations of principles common to the whole family, or genus, of such beings. The internal principle of motivation, the "entelechy" (or "that which contains its own aim") was the incentive of the thing to attain the kind of perfection proper to the kind of thing it was (a stone's kind of perfection thus being quite different from a tree's, or a man's).

Aquinas in his borrowing from Aristotle retained the Aristotelian stress upon being. But the Christian acceptance of Genesis made it impossible for Aquinas to retain the ultimate implications of this key term. For him, as a Christian, the most important fact about the nature of the world was that we might call a *genetic*, or "historical," or "temporal," fact: its derivation from a divine Creator. Thus the *substance* of things was determined not solely by their nature as beings in themselves; it also involved their place, or grounding, as *creatures* of God in a *creation* of God. And by giving the Aristotelian concept of the genus this "ancestral" emphasis, he engrafted an "extrinsic" principle of substance. Men's abilities and habits were said to be "intrinsic" principles of action—the "extrinsic" motives were God and the Devil.[1]

Spinoza, taking the Aristotelian notion that a being, or substance, is to be considered "in itself" (*id quod per se concipitur*), went on to observe that nothing less than the totality of all that exists can meet this requirement. For any single object in the universe must be "defined" (limited, determined, negated) by the things that surround it. Only when considering the universe as a whole, and in considering the principles of the relations of the universe's parts to this universal whole, would we really be dealing with an "intrinsic" motivation. And when dealing with such individual things as a tree, a man, a stone (which are merely *parts* of the universe), we should have to consider their nature as grounded in a wider context, rather than simply as individuals embodying principles of their own. As Locke was to point out later, though we use the word "substance" to designate properties within a thing, etymologically the word means that which supports or grounds a thing (in brief, not something *inside* it but something *outside* it). And when the most "intrinsic" statement we can make about a thing is a statement not about it in itself but about its place as part of the whole world, have we not just about reversed the meanings of the words "intrinsic" and "extrinsic"?

Paradoxically, the Spinozistic advice to see things *sub specie aeternitatis* was really a splendid introduction into philosophies that would see things in the terms of history. Spinoza, to be sure, considered the universe in terms of *being;* he proposed to

---

[1] You will note the beginning of an ambiguity here. For an ancestral God is not wholly "extrinsic." A creature who was descended from God and whose substance was grounded in the creative act of God would somehow bear this qualification "within." The logical completion of such thinking, however, would lead to pantheism, as the substance of God would be "within" his creation—and in Aquinas God is expressly classed as an "extrinsic" principle of motivation. From the sociological point of view, we may note that in proportion as the notion of an "extrinsic" God attained its institutional counterpart in the formalistic externalization of religion, the Protestant pietistic stress upon God as a principle "from within" came by reaction to the fore. And at the time when this change was taking place, the meanings of two very strategic terms in philosophy changed places. The terms "subjective" and "objective" (bearing upon the "inner" and the "outer") reversed their meanings; medieval philosophers had called the "objective" what modern philosophers call "subjective" and vice versa.

treat of the parts in terms of this eternal whole; and when considering *historical* sequence, he proposed to consider it in terms of *logical* sequence (here using one of the profoundest puns in all thought, as one event in history is said to "follow" another the way the conclusion of a syllogism "follows" from the premises). But to treat individuals in terms of a much more inclusive whole is certainly not to consider them "eternally" in the Aristotelian sense, which required that they be treated "in themselves." As soon as you begin treating things in terms of a surrounding context (and a naturalistic context at that) you have laid the way for their treatment temporally, in terms of history. At every important point in Spinoza's doctrines, he had a compensation for such a movement. His history was equated with a timeless logic; his nature was equated with God. But when you equate two terms, either can replace the other, which is to say that the equating of two terms prepares the way for eliminating one of them. Hence, Spinoza's equating of naturalistic history and pantheistic being could be developed into a doctrine of naturalistic history pure and simple by merely dropping the theological side of the equation. (Spinoza himself made seminal contributions to the study of religion from the *historicist* point of view.)

In proportion as theological geneticism developed into a purely secular historicism, the notion of a thing's intrinsic substance dissolved into the out-and-out extrinsic, until now many philosophers of science would formally abolish the category of substance. Aquinas had balanced intrinsic and extrinsic motivations by saying that, though God moved all beings, he moved each according to its nature. But modern science is *par excellence* the approach "from without" (the "scenic," "environmentalist," or "situational" approach). It is interested not in what men "are," for instance, "in themselves," but in what respects men are to be treated as animals, in what respects they are to be treated as vegetables, in what respects as minerals, as electro-physical impulses capable of conditioning by material manipulations, as creatures of food, or climate, or geography, etc. Thus, typically, the papers recently reported of a "gerontologist" who was making investigations designed to increase longevity by increasing the "intrinsic resistance" of the body to the processes that make for old age; and he proposed to do this by dosage of the body with various sorts of chemicals. We are not in a position to know what are his chances of success. But we may raise doubts about his terms. Could such extrinsic agencies as chemical dosage properly be expected to *increase* the body's intrinsic resistance? Insofar as it was effective, wouldn't it rather gain its effects by *decreasing* intrinsic resistance (somewhat as we keep warm "scientifically" not by methods that increase our intrinsic resistance to cold, but by improved modes of heating that decrease our resistance to cold).

Indeed, the question as to what a thing is "in itself" is not a scientific question at all (in the purely empiricist sense of the term science), but a philosophical or metaphysical one. Recently, for instance, there appeared a very intelligent book by a contemporary psychiatrist, Dr. Andras Angyal, entitled *Foundations for a Science of Personality.* But opening it, one finds the entire first half of this project for a "science" of personality constructed about the relationships between "organism" and "environment," two terms that in their very nature *dissolve* the concept of personality by *reducing* it to nonpersonal terms. Strictly speaking, the expression "science of personality" is a contradiction in terms, a perspective by incongruity." For "personality" (derived from a word referring to a man's role) is a "dramatist" concept, and as such involves philosophical or metaphysical notions of human identity. But a "science" of personality would be evolved by translating matters of personality into terms wholly outside the personal (as the biologistic terms "organism" and "environment" are outside the personal). I do not say that there cannot be a "science" of the personality, for Dr. Angyal's valuable book goes a long way towards showing that there can be. (Or at least it shows that there can be a "scientific terminology" of the personality.) I am trying simply to suggest that such a science will be totally "extrinsic" in its approach, not aiming to consider the philosophic problem of what the personality is "in itself," but perfectly at home in a vocabulary that simply dissolves the person into a non-person.

One will quickly realize why we wanted to approach the three essays[2] thus circuitously as we turn now to Mr. Crane's

[2] This article was written as comment on three essays (by the "Neo-Aristotelians," R. S. Crane, Norman Maclean, and Elder Olson) originally

"Prefatory Note," built about his opposition to the method he calls "Coleridgean." In the Coleridgean method, Mr. Crane says, one begins by expounding some general philosophic or metaphysical or psychological frame. Next one treats poetry in general as a representative aspect of this frame. And finally one treats specific poems as individual instances of vessels of poetry. The Coleridgean critic thus employs what we might call a process of narrowing-down. For he begins with the terms that apply to much broader fields of reference than to poetry alone; these are paired with contrary terms (such as "subjective and objective," or "extension and intension"); then other terms, more specific in reference, are added (I think Mr. Ransom's "structure and texture" pair would be an example); and this process is repeated "until, by a series of descending proportions, a transition is effected between the universality of the 'principles' and the particularity of the texts."

The poem would thus not be explained in itself, but "as a kind of emblem or exemplar of principles broader in their relevance than poems or any given kind of poems." The conclusions of such inquiry could be related to the texts "only as universal forms or platonic ideas are related to the particulars in the world which are their more or less adequate reflection." There might even be no need to consider the poem as a whole, since representative passages or lines can be also treated as vessels of the abstract qualities which the critic would discover in the particular work. Hence, "Coleridgean" critics are given to talk about "poetry" rather than about "poems"—and they may like to cite passages that can serve as "touchstones" of the qualities they would select as "poetic."

Messrs, Maclean and Olson, on the other hand, "represent a radical departure" from this tradition:

> They are interested in lyrics not as exemplars but as objects; they insist on approaching them as poems of a distinctive kind rather than as receptacles of poetry. . . . The appreciation they wish to make possible is one of which the object is not a universal form or value reflected in the poem but the poem itself in its wholeness and particularly as a structure of mutually appropriate parts.

published in *The University Review*. Mr. Maclean's was constructed about the analysis of a sonnet by Wordsworth, Mr. Olson's about the analysis of one of the Yeats "Byzantium" poems; and Mr. Crane contributed a general statement on the theory and method exemplified by the two analyses.

To attain this "theoretical grasp of the parts of lyrics and of the principles of their unification," Mr. Crane says, we must confine ourselves to "an inductive study of lyrics pursued apart from any a priori assumptions about the nature of poetry in general." And after many more such essays, on many more poems, we may begin to see "what an inductive poetics of the lyric is likely to be." It is a necessary part of Mr. Crane's position, taken in dialectical opposition to the "Coleridgean," that he adopt this excessive stress upon the *inductive*.

If you consider philosophic or critical terminologies as languages, however (languages from which we derive kinds of observation in accordance with the nature of the terms featured in the given philosophic idiom), you find reason to question his claims in advance. For the critic does not by any means begin his observations "from scratch," but has a more or less systematically organized set of terms by which to distinguish and characterize the elements of the poem he would observe. In this sense, one's observations will not be purely "inductive," even though they derive important modifications from the observing of the given poem. They will also in part (and in particular as to their grammar, or form) be deduced or derived from the nature of the language or terminology which the critic employs. Such languages are developed prior to the individual observation (though one may adopt the well known philosophic subterfuge: "Let us begin simply by considering this object in front of us, just as it is").

If there were only some few "true" things to be said about a poem's structure, and if men of various sorts readily made these same observations independently of one another, one might be justified in considering these observations a matter of "induction." But since so many valid things are to be said, a given vocabulary coaches us to look for certain kinds of things rather than others—and this coaching of observations is a deductive process, insofar as one approaches the poem with a well-formed analytic terminology prior to the given analysis, and derives observations from the nature of this terminology. Hypothetically, one might be perceptive or imaginative enough to transcend any vocabulary, as one might hypothetically add enough "epicycles" and other qualifications to the Ptolemaic system of astronomy to make it do the work now done by the modern system of astro-physics. But under conditions of ordinary experience, such a transcending of vocabulary is decidedly limited. Ordinarily, we see somewhat beyond the limits of our favorite terms— but the bulk of our critical perceptions are but particular applications of these terms. The terms are like "principles," and the particular observations are like the judicial casuistry involved in the application of principles to cases that are always in some respects unique.

Some terminologies contain much richer modes of observation than others. And the "dramatist" nature of the Aristotelian vocabulary could be expected to provide the observer with very rich modes indeed. But one cannot be purely "inductive" in his observation of poems when making these observations through the instrumentality of so highly developed a philosophic language. One owes too much to the language. However, if Mr. Crane admitted that his "inductive" method also contained strongly "deductive" elements, he would have to relinquish the symmetry of his own dramatizing, got by pitting his position in dialetical opposition to the "Coleridgean" mode of derivation. When considered in a linguistic, or terministic, perspective (the perspective in which we would consider "dramatism"), the apparent distinctness between "inductive" and "deductive" modes of observation and derivation here ceases to exist. Indeed, insofar as the writers do abide by their pretensions, and begin with each analysis anew, their interpretation of the principles by which a given poem is organized is mere "prophecy after the event," which is not a very exacting kind of "induction." Induction must also use generalizations which, in effect, prophesy *before* the event. It should not be merely a casuistry ready to rationalize any case after the case has occurred (a temptation to which Aristotelianism has been prone in the past). It must also risk statements as to *what to expect*, and *why*. Otherwise, such criticism becomes merely a disguised variant of impressionism, a kind of improvisation wherein the critic simply translates the unique imaginative sequence of the poem into a correspondingly unique conceptual equivalent.

As for the two long analytic essays by Messrs. Maclean and Olson, I should have to quote or paraphrase nearly every paragraph to convey how ably and discerningly they carry out their project. But as one cannot do justice to a poem in paraphrase, but must follow it from line to line, and from word to word, in its unique order, so these exegetes analyze their poems with a particularity that must be read in its particularity to be appreciated. However, in the course of their analysis, they make generalizations about their method and their conclusions —and we can consider these.

Mr. Maclean takes as his opponent specifically a critic who had based his discussion of a Wordsworth sonnet upon a theory about its reference to the poet's illegitimate daughter. Against this somewhat sorry position, Mr. Maclean says of his own:

> As the unity of a poem arises from the facts that it is divisible into parts and that these parts are harmoniously related, so the obligations resting upon this kind of criticism are twofold: to discover the parts of a poem and to render an account of their relationships.

He convincingly divides the sonnet into three parts, and considers their relation to the whole, in producing a "spiritual and religious translation of the evening." And he does well in making us realize the steps by which this translation progresses, as in his remarks on "the completeness with which the beauty and serenity of the Nun have been transferred to the immensity of the evening."[3]

At this point I must introduce some reference to the line of thought developed in my Grammar. In my analysis of the drama, I try to show how the quality of the scene contains the quality of the act that is enacted on that scene. (Most obvious example: the Shakespearean use of storm or darkness as setting for a sinister bit of action. Hardy's use of background as a

---

[3] I quote the sonnet herewith:

> It is a beauteous evening, calm and free,
> The holy time is quiet as a Nun
> Breathless with adoration; the broad sun
> Is sinking down in its tranquillity;
> The gentleness of heaven broods o'er the Sea:
> Listen! the mighty Being is awake,
> And doth with his eternal motion make
> A sound like thunder—everlastingly.
> Dear Child! dear Girl! that walkest with me here,
> If thou appear untouched by solemn thought,
> Thy nature is not therefore less divine:
> Thou liest in Abraham's bosom all the year;
> And worshipp'st at the Temple's inner shrine,
> God being with thee when we know it not.

source of motivation is an obvious instance of this scene-act ratio in the novel.) This is a "grammatical" principle of much wider application than the drama (hence, open to Mr. Crane's charge of "Coleridgean"). For in the various mythological, theological, metaphysical, and scientific theories of motivation the character we attribute to human action changes according to the character we attribute to the universal scene in which human acts take place. (Contrast, for instance the quality of human acts when placed against a background of struggles among the gods, and the quality of human acts in a behaviorist's background of mechanism and reflexes.) In considering the lyric, where there is no action but where there may be reference to persons (agents), we find that this same relationship may apply between scene and agent. Indeed, it is this scene-agent identification that makes it possible for the poet to convey states of mind (psychological processes) by the use of corresponding scenic imagery. "Dramatistically," therefore, one is invited to observe that this particular sonnet is constructed quite neatly about this scene-agent ratio. The octave establishes the quality of the scene; then at the beginning of the sestet, we turn to the agent ("Dear Child! dear Girl!"); and we find the quality of the agent so imbued with the divine quality of the scene containing this agent, that she can possess this quality even without knowing it, by the simple fact of having it as her ground.

Also, I would hold that a "dramatistic" placement of the lyric is to be arrived at "deductively" in this sense: one approaches the lyric from the category of *action*, which Aristotle considers the primary element of the drama. And then by dialectic coaching one looks for a form that will have as its primary element the moment of *stasis*, or *rest*. We are admonished, however, to note that there are two concepts of "rest," often confused because we may apply the same word to both. There is rest as the sheer cessation of motion (in the sense that a rolling ball comes to rest); and there is rest as the end of action (end as finish or end as aim), the kind of rest that Aristotle conceived as the *primum mobile* of the world, the ground of motion and action both. It is proper for the physical sciences, we would grant, to treat experience non-dramatically, in terms of motion, but things in the realm of the social or human require treatment in terms of action or drama. Or rather, though things in the realm of the human *may* be treated in terms of motion, the result will be statements not about the intrinsic, but about the extrinsic (as per our remarks on an "incongruous" science of the personality).

A treatment of the lyric in terms of action would not by any means require us merely to look for analogies from the drama. On the contrary, the *state of arrest* in which we would situate the essence of the lyric is not analogous to dramatic action at all, but is the dialectical counterpart of action. Consider as an illustration the fourteen Stations of the Cross: The concern with them in the totality of their progression would be dramatic. But the pause at any one of them, and the contemplation and deepening appreciation of its poignancy, in itself, would be lyric.

A typical Wordsworthian sonnet brings out this methodological aspect of the lyric (its special aptitude for conveying a *state* of mind, for erecting a moment into a universe) by selecting such themes as in themselves explicitly refer to the arrest, the pause, the hush. However, this lyric state is to be understood in terms of action, inasmuch as it is to be understood as a state that sums up an action in the form of an attitude.

Thus approached, an attitude is ambiguous in this sense: It may be either an incipient act or the substitute for an act. An attitude of sympathy is incipiently an act, for instance, in that it is the proper emotional preparation for a sympathetic act; or it may be the substitute for an act in that the sympathetic person can let the intent do service for the deed (precisely through doing nothing, one may feel more sympathetic than the person whose mood may be partially distracted by the conditions of action). In either case, an attitude is a state of emotion, or a moment of stasis, in which an act is arrested, summed up, made permanent and total, as with the Grecian Urn which in its summational quality Keats calls a "fair Attitude."[4]

We have here a cluster of closely related words: action, rest (designated in the sonnet by such synonyms as "calm," "quiet," "tranquillity," "gentleness"), motion, attitude or potential action. Mr. Maclean says something much to our purposes here, in his gloss on the word "free" in the first line: "It is a strange

---

[4] Wordsworth's formula, "emotion recollected in tranquillity," could be translated into our terms as "a state of emotion conveyed as a moment of stasis."

word when coupled with 'beauteous' and 'calm.' As endowing the evening with the power to act, it seems at variance with the beauty of tranquillity." The comment enables us to discern that in "free" we find obliquely a reference to potential action. However, our thoughts on the relation between action and the rest that is the end of action would lead us to hold that there is nothing "strange" about this usage. Who would be more "tranquil" than the wholly "free"? For his complete freedom would so thoroughly contain the potentialities of action that there would be no problem to disturb the state of rest.

Nearly every particular observation that Mr. Maclean makes about the sonnet, I could salute and zestfully, if he but gave it the pointedness that would derive from an explicit recognition of the "dramatistic" element in his vocabulary. Thus I would hold that an explicit concern with the scene-agent ratio provides a central statement about the grammatical principles involved in the structure of the poem. Or Mr. Maclean cites a passage from "Lines Composed Above Tintern Abbey":

> . . . that serene and blessed mood
> In which the affectations gently lead us on,—
> Until, the breath of this corporeal frame
> And even the motion of our human blood
> Almost suspended, we are laid asleep
> In body, and become a living soul:
> While with an eye made quiet by the power
> Of harmony, and the deep power of joy,
> We see into the life of things.

And here by the use of an explicitly dramatist perspective we would distinguish between a level of bodily motion ("the motion of our human blood") and a level of mental or spiritual action ("a living soul"). The "power of harmony" here would be another synonym for the rest of "potential action." And the state of arrest is said to be attained when the level of mental action transcends the level of bodily motion. (The "Ode on a Grecian Urn" is constructed about a similar transcendence. Progressively through the stanzas we can watch the poet's fever split into two parts: a bodily passion and a mental action. But in the "Ode" it is a state of agitation that is arrested, to be transformed into its transcendent counterpart.)

It is to be regretted that none of these three writers, in stressing the importance of an analysis which considers the relations of parts to whole, makes any mention of the fact that in Aristotle's treatment of tragedy, there are *two* versions of this relationship. In Chapter 6, Aristotle writes:

> There are six parts consequently of every tragedy, as a whole (that is) of such or such quality, *viz.* a Fable or Plot, Characters, Diction, Thought, Spectacle, and Melody.

But in Chapter 12, he writes:

> The parts of Tragedy to be treated as formative elements in the whole were mentioned in a previous Chapter. From the point of view, however, of its quantity, i.e., the separate sections into which it is divided, a tragedy has the following parts: Prologue, Episode, Exode, and a choral portion, distinguished into Parode and Stasimon.

In any event, it is notable that both these treatments of part-whole relationships apply not only to single tragedies but to tragedies as a *class*. Yet Mr. Maclean says, in conclusion to his article: "To explain the poem . . . in terms of its particular beginning is to explain as exactly as possible its uniqueness, and to distinguish it from other poems by Wordsworth that treat much the same 'theme.' " And likewise Mr. Olson will end his article on a similar remark to the effect that "great art . . . is always in the last analysis *sui generis.*" There is, of course, a sense in which every work is unique, since its particular combination of details is never repeated. But is the emphasis upon this fact feasible if one would develop an "Aristotelian" poetics of the lyric, treating lyrics as a class? And a mere concern with one lyric, then another lyric, then another would not yield the kind of observations needed to treat of lyrics as a class. For to treat lyrics as a class, one must examine individual lyrics from the standpoint of their generic attributes. And to do this, one must have terminological prepossessions, prior to the analysis, even before one can select a poem that he considers representative of the lyric. At least, one must have negative or tentative touchstones that enable him roughly to differentiate lyrics as a class from such classes as epic, drama, epigram, etc.

One does not place a form in isolation. The placement of a given form involves the corresponding placement of other forms. Thus *a vocabulary wider in reference than the orbit of the given form is needed for the classifying of that form.* Though the authors would presumably get immunity from such objections by presenting their analyses as mere *preparations* for a poetics of the lyric, we would object that observations confined in their reference to the unique are not classificatory at all.[5]

The point is made still clearer by considering another citation from Mr. Olson:

> The scrutiny of particular poems would thus be the beginning of the critical enterprise; but the principles eventually reached, as disclosed by analysis, would not be rules governing the operations involved in the construction of any further poem, nor would the enumeration of poetic parts and poetic devices suffer extension beyond those objects to which analysis had been turned. . . . Poetic questions would be concerning the poetic structure of a particular work . . . [and] would terminate in a discovery of the parts of a work and of the interrelations through which the parts are parts of a whole.

Now, if the principles of a specific work were so defined that the definition would not apply to "any further poem," would not this also mean that the definition would not apply to any *other* poem? In brief, would not this conception of the relation between parts and whole be so particularized as to make statements about the lyric as a *genus* impossible? And could a critic, aiming at analyses that meet these particularized requirements, go beyond the merely statistical to the generic unless at the same time he happened to be taking some other kind of step not expressly signalized? Surely it is ironic to find Aristotle, who

[5] Mr. Crane reminds us of Coleridge's distinction between "poetry" and "poem," in the *Biographia Literaria.* But perhaps he and his colleagues have been victimized by the "Coleridgean" here: perhaps the distinction between "poetry" and "poem" is not enough. "Poetry" itself may have two different meanings. We may use it as one member of such dialectical pairs as "poetry and science," "poetry and mathematics," "poetry and anarchism," "poetry and politics," "poetry and morals," etc. Or we may use it as a term for poems in a *generic* sense (as Aristotle in his *Poetics* treats of part-whole relationships not by treating of tragedies one by one, in their uniqueness, but generically). So we may need three terms rather than two here: a term for "poetry" (as member of a dialectical pair), and a term for "poem" (this poem, that poem, the next poem), and a term for "poems" (as a class, with corresponding terms for classes and sub-classes).

was so long admired and resented as the Prince of Deducers, now serving as Prince of Inducers.

As a matter of fact, there are many passages in Mr. Olson's essay where he profits by going beyond his principle of uniqueness. For he launches into generalizations about the lyric generically that are not at all confined to the particular poem he is analyzing (Yeats's "Sailing to Byzantium," of which by the way he makes what I think is a really superb analysis). These place the lyric as a class with relation to other classes. When he says, for instance, that tragedy, epic, and comedy are "dynamic, for they imitate change," whereas "the kind we have been scrutinizing is static," his concern here with stasis profits by dramatistic reference.

His discussion of the poem itself is thoroughly dramatistic in its choice of vocabulary, being built about distinctions between "action" and "passion," explicitly recognizing the theme as a problem of "regeneration," and treating the whole series of transformations from stanza to stanza as a "dialectic" wherein character is determined "not by its share in an action, but by its role in a drama, not of action, but of thought." Yet, surprisingly, this highly developed vocabulary is employed quite as though it had been forced upon the critic purely by inspection of the given poem—and we are warned against an attempt to find in the lyric "some analogue of plot in the drama and epic." However, imagery, like attitude, has the quality of "incipient action"—and in noting how, in a given poem, it undergoes a series of developments from ambiguous potentiality to clear fulfillment, we should be considering it "dramatistically" without thereby treating it merely as the analogue of dramatic plot.

And let us cite two other statements that are thoroughly *generic*, and as such are derived not from mere observation of the single poem but from the nature of the "dramatist" vocabulary:

There can be no plot because there can be no incidents; the "events" in a lyric poem are never incidents as such, connected by necessity or probability, but devices for making poetic statements. . . .

Since there is no action, there is no agent, that is, *character*, in the sense in which there are differentiated agents in the drama; rather, the character in the sense in which character may be said to exist here is almost completely universalized. . . .[6]

What, then, is the upshot of our fluctuancy between agreement and disagreement? It is not merely that we would have

[6] "Universalized" is a good word here. The poetic "I" that is the ground of a lyric fills the whole universe of discourse.

Mr. Olson's distinction between the dramatic "act" and the lyric "event" opens up interesting possibilities. In the *Philosophy of Literary Form* I had used a similar distinction, but with a quite different application. But by combining Mr. Olson's application with my own, I believe I come a bit closer to glimpsing why the lyric is a better fit with the scientific than the dramatic is. The steps are as follows (first quoting from my summary of the dramatistic perspective, *op. cit.*):

> We have the drama and the scene of the drama. The drama is enacted against a background. . . . The description of the scene is the role of the physical sciences; the description of the drama is the role of the social sciences. . . . The physical sciences are a calculus of events; the social sciences are a calculus of acts. And human affairs being dramatic, the discussion of human affairs becomes dramatic criticism, with more to be learned from study of tropes than from a study of tropisms. . . . The error of the social sciences has usually resided in the attempt to appropriate the scenic calculus for a charting of the act.

Now science, as we have observed in the present paper, is "scenic." And since it speaks in terms of motion rather than in terms of action, the typical scientific vocabulary is non-dramatic.

Recall next Yvor Winters' notion of "Pseudo-Reference," one kind of which is "reference to a non-existent plot." As an instance of "pseudo-reference," he cites from "Gerontion":

> To be eaten, to be divided, to be drunk
> Among whispers; by Mr. Silvero
> With caressing hands, at Limoges
> Who walked all night in the next room;
> By Hakagawa, bowing among the Titians;
> By Madame de Tornquist, in the dark room
> Shifting the candles; Fräulein von Kulp
> Who turned in the hall, one hand on the door.

On this Mr. Winters comments:

> Each of these persons is denoted in the performance of an act, and each act, save possibly that of Hakagawa, implies an anterior situation, is a link in a chain of action; even that of Hakagawa implies an anterior and unexplained personality. Yet we have no hint of the nature of the history implied. A feeling is claimed by the poet, the motivation, or meaning, of which is withheld, and of which in all likelihood he has no clearer notion than his readers can have.

In this form which Mr. Winters is considering, do we not see a "watershed moment," the very point at which dramatic "actions" are undergoing a trans-

these authors ply their trade under the trade-name of "dramatism" rather than "Aristotle." Mr. Crane gives us a choice between the poem as "exemplar" and the poem as "object"—and as though these alternatives had exhausted the field, he discusses no other. But if we begin by explicitly recognizing the dramatistic nature of the vocabulary, then looking at our pentad (the terms Act, Scene, Agent, Agency, Purpose), we may ask ourselves: "What about the poem considered as an *act?*" Thus, when Mr. Crane says that the poem is to be considered "as a product of purposive activity on the part of its author," we would agree with him, only more intensely than he would want us to.

The treatment of the poem as act would not, by any means, require us to slight the nature of the poem as object. For a poem is a *constitutive* act—and after the act of its composition by a poet who had acted in a particular temporal scene, it survives as an objective structure, capable of being examined in itself, in temporal scenes quite different from the scene of its composition, and by agents quite different from the agent who originally enacted it. The enactment thus remaining as a constitution, we can inquire into the principles by which this constitution is organized.

The poem, as an object, is to be considered in terms of its nature as "finished." That is, it is to be considered in terms of "perfection," as per the stressing of part-whole relationships. These men have done criticism a great service in helping to reaffirm this aspect of criticism, particularly at a time when the state of the sciences has offered so many extrinsic approaches to

formation into lyric "events"? Indeed, this would be the way of translating the concept of pseudo-reference into our present terms.

By reason of correspondences between the "objective" and the "subjective" (or what we have called the scene-agent ratio) these "events" (which are more like "scenes" than "acts") convey attitudes, or states of mind, through the use of "objective imagery." The "events" here are "moody," quite as though they were such attitude-purveying imagery as storms, sunsets, or bird sounds. In their nature as imagery, as "scenic," they invite us to *feel* as the situation *is*.

From the standpoint of science, the content of a scene is "knowledge." And knowledge is a *state*. Hence, scientific events and lyric events are both received in the psychological form of *states*. A whole set of such relations would be: science is to the lyric as the impersonal is to the personal, as materialism is to idealism, as scene is to agent, as knowledge is to knower, as the epistemological is to the psychological. (In the "dramatistic" perspective, the primary category is not the epistemological-psychological one of *knowing*, but that of acting.)

poetry, which can be considered as the "exemplar" of political exigencies, neurosis, physique, diet, climate, cultural movements, economic classifications, etc. But consideration of it as an act surviving as a constitution would also enable one to consider its intrinsic relations.

The dramatistic perspective, if I may refer to my *Philosophy of Literary Form*, points equally towards a concern with "internal structure" and towards a concern with "act-scene relationships." "Words are aspects of a much wider communicative context, most of which is not verbal at all. Yet words also have a nature peculiarly their own. And when discussing them as modes of action, we must consider *both* this nature as words in themselves *and* the nature they get from the non-verbal scenes that support their acts." But while proposing to consider words "as acts upon a scene," I held that the approach to literature in terms of "linguistic, or symbolic, or literary action" could avoid the excesses of the purely environmental schools "which are usually so eager to trace the relationships between act and scene that they neglect to trace the structure of the act itself."

The explicit treatment of the poem as an act, however, would remind us that it is not enough to consider it solely in terms of its "perfection," or "finishedness," since this conventionalized restriction of our inquiry could not possibly tell us all the important things about its substance. This seems to be particularly the case with the study of lyrics—for often, to grasp the full import of the terms employed in one poem, we must see how these terms are qualified by their use in other poems. That is, the individual lyrics are not to be considered solely as isolated acts, but also as stages or stations of a more comprehensive act. And statements about this more comprehensive act are also statements about the *intrinsic* nature of the enactment in the single poem. I began by speaking of the three fields: Grammar, Rhetoric, and Symbolic. It is perhaps only in the third of these categories that modern criticism has something vitally new to offer the student of literature. And it would be a pity indeed if a dogmatic or formalistic preference for an earlier method interfered with the progress of such an inquiry, which promises greatly to increase our knowledge of poetic substance in particular and of human motivation in general. (Nor would it be the first time that the great name of Aristotle had served to stifle fresh inquiry.)

The concern with Symbolic has already been developed to a point where we can see that, as regards the analysis of literary texts at least, it can be more empirical in its methods than is possible to most studies in the human realm. Yet in trying to abide by the neo-Aristotelian ideals for the compartmentalizing of inquiry, one would simply be taking on many encumbrances that interfered with the development of methods proper to the nature of the subject-matter.[7]

---

[7] To complete the placement of these critics, perhaps we should also have considered the part that the Scotist stress upon the "thisness" (*haeccëitas*) of a thing might have had in shaping their aims. They seem to be encountering in their way what Duns Scotus encountered in his, when he contended that the step from genus to species should be completed by a step from species to individual. And their concern to define the lyric as a *kind* while placing stress upon the unique generating principles of *particular* lyrics seems similarly on the road to nominalism. Or should we say rather that, having encountered the nominalist stress by way of modern empirical science, they would translate it back into scholastic terms?

And always on the look-out for secular analogues to theological doctrine, perhaps we should note that the stress upon the individual poem as *sui generis*, coupled with a search for the principle of the lyric as a *kind*, has somewhat the pattern of Aquinas' doctrine of angels, each of which in his view is both a genus and an individual at the same time. The search for the intrinsic, demanding in its logical completion a complete divorce of relations with contextual impurities, would seem to require in the end such a view of "pure" or "separate" forms subsisting without admixture of "matter." That is, the subsistence of the poem must be discussed without reference to any individuating principle drawn from some extrinsic source, which would function as "matter" in being *scenic* to the poem as act.

X

FRANCIS FERGUSSON

On Certain Technical Concepts

The few technical concepts used in this study are to be understood in relation to the plays themselves, which qualify them
and give them their meaning. The medium and the forms of
drama are so protean, and have been used in so many ways, that
it is impossible to devise a technical vocabulary and system of
notation comparable to that of music, for example. But there
are a few terms I have used throughout the book which may
suggest a general and analogical notion of the dramatic art; and
it may be useful to indicate where I got them and how I
understand them abstractly.

Aristotle made the most ambitious effort to describe the
nature of the dramatic art and the concepts described below are
derived in one way or another from the *Poetics*. My purpose,
however, is not to invoke Aristotle's authority (if it still exists),
nor to tackle once more the vexed question of what he really
meant, but to assist the reader to understand the concepts
themselves as I use them.

PLOT AND ACTION

The distinction between plot and action is fundamental, but
it is very difficult to make in general terms. I have pointed it out
explicitly in most of the plays studied, but the actions and the
plots of these plays are all different. Aristotle does not explain
the distinction, but in the first nine chapters of the *Poetics*,
where he is concerned with tragedy in itself, and before he
studies its purpose, or distinguishes the kinds of tragedies, he
seems to me to assume it. I have collected a few passages which I
think cannot be understood unless this distinction is admitted.
The translation is Butcher's, and the page references are to the

Reprinted from *The Idea of a Theatre* (Princeton, N.J.: Princeton University
Press, 1949), pp. 229–40, by permission of the author and the publisher. Copyright 1949 by Princeton University Press.

fourth edition of his *Aristotle's Theory of Poetry and Fine Art*.

"The plot is the imitation of the action—for by plot I here mean the arrangement of the incidents. . . . But most important of all is the structure of the incidents. For Tragedy is an imitation, not of men, but of an action and of life, and life consists in action, and its end is a mode of action, not a quality."—p. 25.

"The plot, then, is the first principle and as it were the soul of a tragedy."—p. 27.

"Unity of plot does not, as some persons think, consist in the unity of the hero. For infinitely various are the incidents in one man's life which cannot be reduced to unity. . . . But Homer . . . seems to have happily discerned the truth. . . . He made the *Odyssey*, and likewise the *Iliad*, to center round an action that in our sense of the word is one. As therefore, in the other imitative arts, the imitation is one when the object imitated is one, so the plot, being an imitation of an action, must imitate one action and that a whole."—p. 33.

"It clearly follows that the poet or 'maker' should be the maker of plots rather than of verses; since he is a poet because he imitates, and what he imitates are actions."—p. 37.

Aristotle offers a general definition of plot—the arrangement, or synthesis, of the incidents—but he offers no definition of action. I have already recorded my view that "action" is an analogical concept and that it can therefore only be understood with reference to particular actions. In this study the word refers to the action of which the play is an imitation; to the mimetic acts of the dramatist—plot-making, characterization, and speech—whereby he makes the play; and to the mimetic acts of the performers who reproduce, in the medium of their own beings, individual or characterized versions of the action the author had in mind. Thus the whole book is a study of action in some of its many modes; and at this point I propose to let the instances stand in place of a general definition. If the reader wishes to consider the difficulty of a univocal definition of this term, he is invited to read the symposium entitled "What is Action?" held in 1938 by the British Aristotelian Society. Professors Macmurray, Franks and Ewing read papers; they all saw the distinction between action and the events in which it is manifested; and they all agreed upon the fundamental importance of the concept. But they did not produce a definition which would help us much. It is interesting to note that none of them mentioned the art of imitating action.

If action cannot be abstractly defined, of what use is the concept in the study of the dramatic arts? It is to be used to indicate the direction which an analysis of a play should take. It points to the object which the dramatist is trying to show us, and we must in some sense grasp that if we are to understand his complex art: plotting, characterization, versification, thought, and their coherence. For this purpose practical rules may be devised, notably that of the Moscow Art Theater. They say that the action of a character or a play must be indicated by an infinitive phrase, e.g., in the play *Oedipus,* "to find the culprit." This device does not amount to a definition but it leads the performer to the particular action which the author intended. Thus whether one is interested in the arts of the dramatist or the arts of the performer, the distinction between plot and action is essential.

Two Aspects of the Plot: Form and Purpose

In the remarks quoted above, tragedy is considered as a species of art, and the plot is described as its first principle—its "soul," on the analogy of the soul of the living creature as the form of its body: in other words, as formal cause. But the purpose, or final cause, of tragedy is to produce a certain effect upon the audience; and the plot may be studied from this point of view also. In any given tragedy (if it is good) action, form, and purpose are one; yet the conceptual distinctions may be made; and for criticism and technical analysis they are very important.

Most of Aristotle's discussion of plot is concerned with its purpose, or final cause. He is showing how the dramatist produces the desired effect upon the audience. This is the part of the *Poetics* which has attracted most attention: the playwrights have gone to Aristotle in search of recipes for moving, diverting, or instructing their audiences. But Aristotle has a particular audience in mind, that of Athens in his day; and he assumes the "idea of a theater" which that audience assumed. For this reason it is a mistake to try to take his recipes literally, as the theorists of Racine's time tended to do. Moreover, Aristotle described the purpose of tragedy (its effect upon the audience) in at least two ways, which imply two views of what the audience expected or would accept.

The first of these is the famous formula of purgation:

"Tragedy is an imitation not only of a complete action, but of events inspiring fear or pity."—p. 37.

"Tragedy, then, is an imitation of an action . . . through pity and fear effecting the proper purgation of these emotions."—p. 23.

I do not wish to join the discussion of this formula, or to attempt to limit its fertility, beyond pointing out that the aim of purgation, however understood, is certainly different from the aim of diversion which our commercial theater assumes. It seems to be connected with the ritual origin of tragedy, and with the "ritual expectancy" which the audience must still to some degree have had in Aristotle's time. Mr. George Thomson, in his very interesting book, *Aeschylus and Athens*, points out this connection, and interprets it according to a curious combination of Freud and Marx: "The actor who spoke the part composed for him by the poet was descended from the poet-actor; and the poet-actor, who spoke the words which he had been inspired to compose, was descended through the leader of the dithyramb from the priest at the head of the *Thiasos*, who, since the god had entered his body, *was* the god."[2]

Mr. Thomson's Freudian-Marxian interpretation (which I do not quote) seems to me unsatisfactory, but the connection which he affirms between the purgative function of tragedy and the ritual basis of that theater is unmistakably there. Tragedy, in this view, celebrates the mystery of human nature and destiny with the health of the soul in view.

But Aristotle also describes the purpose of tragedy in far more rationalistic terms, for instance in the following diagnosis:

"It is not the function of the poet to relate what has happened, but what may happen—what is possible according to the law of probability or necessity. . . . Poetry, therefore, is more philosophical and a higher thing than history: for poetry tends to express the universal, history the particular."—p. 35.

In this passage it is assumed that the audience is enlightened, skeptical, and in need of reasons, satisfactions for the mind; the faith in ritual order, and in the revelatory and purgative proper-

---

[2] *Aeschylus and Athens* (London: Lawrence and Wisaart, 1946), chapter xix, p. 382.

ties of the ritual is not here in question—though Aristotle apparently feels no contradiction between the two versions of the tragic poet's purpose. Perhaps we must conclude that, at the mysterious moment when tragedy was formed, the audience had a free use of the reason without having lost the habits of feeling, and the modes of awareness, associated with the ancient tribal religion. However that may be, this second and more rationalistic view of the purpose of tragedy and the function of the plot is more acceptable than the first view in periods like ours when no guide except abstract reason is generally accepted. The notion of poetry as expressing the universal underlies the ideal theater of Racine, as well as the opposite, but equally ideal, theater of Wagner.

But what is probable or necessary? What is abstractly true? Aristotle, in the *Poetics*, is not worried about these questions as contemporary poets are, because he was describing a drama which in fact was accepted by its audience as sufficiently probable or necessary, and as expressing the universal. When Aristotle then proceeds to give his recipes for various kinds of recognition scenes, or for making a good man, a woman, a slave, or a king, he is simply analyzing and comparing techniques and attitudes which worked in actual practice, more or less well. From this distance it appears that they worked because of the whole complex culture of that time and place. That is why they will not work in the same way for us. In short, though it is still true that the purpose of any play is to have some effect upon the audience, and to mean something to it, Aristotle's analysis of the nature of this effect and this meaning cannot be directly applied to subsequent forms of drama. His detailed analysis of plot applies directly only to the tragedy he knew.

The question then arises, how we are to understand the plot; does this notion have any general validity at all?

The architects of the well-made plays have their answer to this question. They developed their very general lore of the plot by reducing the whole conception of drama to an empirically determined least common denominator. Sarcey committed himself to the view that the one constant purpose of drama was to hold an audience for two hours; hence the art of plot-making is the art of making an exciting arrangement of incidents with carefully controlled and mounting suspense. On this view, the action, its primary form (plot in Aristotle's first sense), the nature of the pleasure intended, and the meaning of the play need not be considered at all in our conception of the dramatic art. They are dismissed as subjective, mere matters of personal taste, or of passing fashions, incidental to the one constant purpose. Many playwrights of talent or genius have proved that the principles of the well-made play work; but they have also proved that they assume all the aspects of a drama which Sarcey refused to consider in his general definition: i.e., a certain very reduced view of human action, of the kind of pleasure best calculated to hold a crowd, and of the kind of meaning which anyone at any time is willing to attribute to a picture of human life. In other words, it has turned out in practice that the principles of the well-made play define, not all drama, but a very limited form of drama; and when an Ibsen or a Shaw tries to use them for his deeper purposes, there is a contradiction between this superficial form and the action which the author is trying to imitate.

The "well-made-play"-doctrine of the plot is as empirical as Aristotle's: it generalizes the techniques of the playwrights of the time, and takes the audience which they excited and diverted as determining the final cause of all drama. But Aristotle has a better philosophy and a better drama to study; and his doctrine of the plot is valuable precisely because it recognizes as essential the elements which Sarcey rejected as subjective. In the masterpieces of Greek tragedy which Aristotle examined, the action, the first form of the action, its ritual meaning, and its abstract intelligibility, were one; but Aristotle, in accordance with his careful principles, starts with those aspects of tragedy which make it what it is: first the species and then the actual individual tragedies, with their particular purposes and their particular appeal to the audience.

The most general definition of tragedy (which applies to all drama) is "the imitation of an action." And the most general definition of the plot is "the first principle and as it were the soul of the tragedy"; and this applies to all plots. After that comes the question of the playwright's purpose in the particular work, which depends upon the idea of the theater which the audience accepts or can be made to accept.

Though the distinctions between action and plot, and between the plot as the "soul of the tragedy" and the plot as the means of reaching the audience, seem to be in the *Poetics*, it is not clear that these distinctions were as important to Aristotle as they must be to us, if we wish to use his principles for the analysis of subsequent forms of drama and for understanding the ritual origins of Greek tragedy itself. Aristotle lacks our gloomy sense of the contingency of all cultural forms; he does not try to take account of the shifting perspectives of history as modern inquirers do. He explains that tragedy developed out of ritual, but he does not see (as the Cambridge Classical Anthropologists do) that the very existence of that tragedy depended upon the ritual order of that culture. He did not have the *Purgatorio* to read, and so could not imagine its sublimed Aristotelianism, its imitation of action in many modes, completely freed from the cultural forms of the Greek City. He did not forsee the ideal theaters of modern times, which seek some sort of substitute for a traditional cultural order. And for that reason, the parts of the *Poetics* in which he studies the effect of drama upon its audience are of limited value for other forms of drama. But his most general descriptions of the art of drama, and the principles of his investigation, are still the best we have and may be used with caution to bring out the analogies between various forms of drama in the varying theaters which the culture provided.

The Notion of Analogy

In this study I have used the term *analogy* again and again, hoping that the meaning would be reasonably clear in the context. But "analogy" is a very slippery concept. It has a disconcerting way of meaning all things to all men. Perhaps it is desirable to explain where I got it and, if not define it, describe the use I wish to make of it.

Thomas Aquinas distinguishes between univocity, equivocation, and analogy, for example in his discussion of terms applied to God, in *Selected Writings*, ed. by Father D'Arcy, pp. 148–153. Father Penido's book, *De L'Analogie*, is an extended study of this notion, chiefly as it is used by St. Thomas. He shows that the term itself is an analogical, and not a univocal concept; and he distinguishes so many kinds of analogy that one might well be afraid to use the term at all. But he also offers the following general description which I think is useful: "D'une manière très générale, toute analogie suppose deux conditions ontologiques: 1° une pluralité réelle d'êtres, et donc entre ces êtres une diversité essentielle—le Monisme est l'ennemi-né de l'Analogie; 2° au sein de cette multiplicité, de cette inégalité, une certaine unité." It is in that sense that I consider the plays I have studied as analogous: actually they are all different, each with its own action and its own form; yet they have "a certain unity" in that they may all be regarded as imitations of actions.

Father Penido offers a more extended list of the bases of what he calles true analogy, as follows: "Bases ontologiques de proportionalité-propre: une perfection doit exister objèctivement, qui réponde aux trois conditions suivantes: 1° participation intrinsèque en chaque analogué; 2° selon des modes essentiellement divers et gradués; 3° tels cependant que rien en eux ne soit extrinsèque à la perfection analogique où ils s'unissent." This seems to me to apply to the relationships between the elements in realist drama of all kinds, that of Ibsen or Chekhov as well as that of Sophocles or Shakespeare. The "objective perfection" is the action of the play as a whole, which "participates" in the parts of the composition—plot, characters, diction, and so forth, each regarded as "real" in itself and, in our acquaintance with the play, as prior to its unity or objective perfection.

This formula does not apply to the structure of the "ideal" dramas of Racine or Wagner, for in them the unity—reason or passion—is assumed as it were a priori, and the process of composition is felt, not as a succession of acts of imitation, but as a deduction from the one idea—i.e., as demonstration or expression. And the parts of the composition are taken, not as real in themselves, but as corollaries or illustrations of the central idea. Thus the dramas of Racine and Wagner are not only different from each other: in the "univocal sense of form" which they share they are different kinds of composition from all realist drama. In order to see any analogies between them, one must recur to the most general definition of drama and consider demonstration and expression themselves as forms of action, close imitations of their respective single objects.

Thus the notion of analogy which I am using is derived from Thomist realism. But Aquinas, and after him Father Penido, use this idea for the purposes of metaphysics and epistemology and I wish to use it merely for the formal analysis of drama.

They are investigating Being, and the nature of our knowledge of Being; while my investigation is confined to the make-believe world of the imitation of action. In what sense is the Oedipus of Sophocles' play, with his mask and buskin, his versified speech, and his legendary background, real? Or Mrs. Alving, with her photographic surfaces? For my purposes it is unnecessary to inquire. In both cases the dramatist makes-believe their reality, while Racine and Wagner, in their different ways, use the characters and the other elements rather for metaphorical purposes; and "La métaphore ne rapproche pas des natures, mais simplement des éffèts," as Father Penido writes.

Though I make no attempt to study the epistemological, metaphysical, and theological questions, I do not deny for a moment that they "bristle" (Henry James's favorite word) whenever one attempts to study various forms of drama. Sophocles must have believed in the objective reality of the human situation which the tragic theater enabled him to mirror and celebrate. Dante must have believed that Being, Act Itself, dictated the form and content of his great fiction, for he writes, in explanation of his *dolce stil nuovo:*

> Io mi son un che, quando
> amor mi spira, noto, ed a quel modo
> che ditta dentro, vo significando.[3]

And I suppose that we shall not have a comparable form of the imitation of action unless a comparable sense of the reality of the human situation should again become available. But in the meantime, we may hope to get some light—if not upon what drama may be in our time, at least upon what it has been at its best—by studying the modes of awareness, and the structural principles, of the realist masters who worked with analogical relationships.

Father Penido points out that an analogical concept is not, like a univocal concept, completely abstracted. The many small actions in *Oedipus* are not related to a single idea but to a single action, that of the play as a whole. That is why one cannot get the coherence of the play at all unless one makes-believe its

---

[3] "I am one who, when Love inspires me, take note, and go setting it forth after the fashion which he dictates within me."—*Purgatorio* XXIV.

characters and events. That is what I mean by saying that it appeals primarily to the histrionic sensibility, just as a musical composition (in spite of its mathematical theory and abstract notation) can only be perceived by the ear. The concept of analogy (like that of action) is useful, not in making an abstractly intelligible scheme of the art of drama, or of a particular play, but in directing our attention to the relationships between concrete elements. And these elements—actions in various modes—we must perceive directly, "before predication."

THE HISTRIONIC SENSIBILITY: THE MIMETIC PERCEPTION OF ACTION

"Poetry in general seems to have sprung from two causes, each of them lying deep in our nature. . . . Imitation is one instinct of our nature. Next there is the instinct for harmony and rhythm."

—Aristotle's *Poetics*

"The histrionic sensibility" is another phrase which I have used so frequently that it has acquired an almost technical meaning: the dramatic art is based upon this form of perception as music is based upon the ear. The trained ear perceives and discriminates sounds; the histrionic sensibility (which may also be trained) perceives and discriminates actions. Neither form of perception can be defined apart from experience but only indicated in various instances of its use. Perhaps it will help the reader to understand what I mean by the histrionic sensibility if I indicate a few of these instances.

Kittens, in their play, seem to be using something like our histrionic sensibility. They directly perceive each other's actions: stalking an imagined quarry; the bluff and formal defiance which precedes a fight; flight in terror; the sudden indifference which ends the play. Their perception of each other's actions is itself mimetic, a sympathetic response of the whole psyche, and may be expressed more or less completely and immediately in bodily changes, postures, and movements. The soul of the cat is the form of its body; but to some degree the soul is actual in different ways at different moments, depending upon what the cat believes, or makes-believe its situation to be; and to some degree the body instantly assumes these varied forms. When kittens perceive and imitate the action of grown cats, the histrionic sensibility is being used for educational, moral, or (by analogy) religious purposes: to explore the potentialities of the cat nature and the dimensions of the world in which the cat finds itself. When the kittens are only playing, their perception and imitation of action resembles art: they seem to enjoy something like the pleasure of the contemplation of form; and the actions of hunting or defiance, more rhythmic and harmonious than those of real hunting or fighting, approach the ceremonial or artistic disinterestedness of the hunting-dance or the war-dance.

Human nature has vaster potentialities for good or evil than cat-nature and our situation is far wider, more complex, and more unmanageable. But we also use the histrionic sensibility for education in many forms, as well as for the purposes of the dramatic art. When learning athletic skills we get as much from our direct sense of the instructor's action—the focus of his being upon the ball to be caught or the bar to be cleared—as we do from diagrams and verbal explanations. Spastics are trained histrionically—they are taught to concentrate, not upon the fork and the muscles being used, but upon the action of food-getting itself; and this focus of the psyche if repeated often enough gradually makes the proper neural and muscular patterns. It would appear that the same principle applies—the same appeal to the histrionic sensibility is made—when the skill to be communicated is not a physical skill at all. Good teachers, even of theoretical sciences, or of the arts of word and concept, teach by example: they reveal directly to the student the peculiar focus of psychic being, the kind of concentration, which their discipline requires. Hence the empirical wisdom of the apprentice-system, as it prevails in laboratories, studios, and schools of philosophy. *The Spiritual Exercises* of Ignatius Loyola would seem to be far removed from the play of kittens; yet their purpose is to reveal, through the techniques of make-believe, the potentialities of human nature and the realities of the human situation, as Loyola understood them. When he explains to the devout how to make present to their feelings and imaginations as well as their reason, scenes from the life of Christ, he sketches a technique like that which the Moscow Art Theater used to train actors. His immediate purpose is similar: to reveal a scene significant on many levels, and a mode of action capable of evoking a mimetic response of the whole being.

Because the histrionic sensibility is a basic, or primary, or primitive virtue of the human mind, it is difficult to describe in other terms; and it can only be cultivated by practice. For this reason there is little literature about it except drama itself, though from time to time a lore is developed, a traditional askesis, based upon a particular use of it for educational or therapeutic or moral purposes like those I mentioned. When the theater is cultivated, a lore of the art of acting is developed; and a few connoisseurs of the histrionic sensibility and of the art of acting have tried to write down their observations. Shakespeare's plays are full of obiter dicta on the acting art. Coquelin to some extent rationalized his own subtle practice as an actor. Henry James, a great admirer of Coqueline and of the French theater, became a connoisseur. And he has very revealing things to say about the actor's perception and imitation of action which he compares with his own as he practiced it in the different medium of the novel.

The technique of the Moscow Art Theater (which is cultivated here and there in this country by students of Moscow actors and directors) is a conscious and often highly developed method of training actors. Its purpose is to teach the actor to perceive and imitate *action* so that he can play accurately the roles which dramatists of all kinds have written. The actor must learn to free his mind, his feelings, and his imagination as far as possible, both from the clichés of his own time and from the special limitations of his own personality. He must make his own inner being "an instrument capable of playing any tune," as it is often put. To this end he practices the recall of sensory impressions (those of washing or shaving, for instance). He learns to make-believe situations, emotionally charged human relationships, and to respond freely within the imagined situation. This is as much as to say that he learns a certain kind of concentration, closely akin to that recommended by Loyola for a different purpose. When skilled actors improvise a playlet upon an imagined situation, they respond freely to each other's actions and words within it yet never violate its basic donnés. Thus the technique is intended to free the psyche, and then control it, for the purposes of playing; and the training of the body and voice, which is often supposed to be the only training an actor can receive, is merely ancillary. But it is necessary to emphasize the fact that a technique of acting, even so fundamental a one as this, merely leads to the literature of drama, just as the performer's technique of the violinist leads to the literature of the violin, where the possibilities of the instrument are explored.

The notion of action and the imitation of action is the connecting link between the art of the dramatist and the interpretive art of the actor. I cannot discover whether Stanislavksy and Nemirovitch-Dantchenko got their concept of action from Aristotle or not. Perhaps they merely rediscovered it empirically through a close study of the psychic content of many roles. In their system it is a technical-empirical notion, a convenient rule of thumb, which the actor needs in his study of the role he is to play: when he has discovered the "main action" and the many smaller actions of his character and can indicate them by an infinitive phrase, he knows what he has to reproduce in his stage-life. Because of their limited purposes, the masters of the Moscow technique did not explore the general possibilities of "action" as Aristotle did—it is one of the key notions in Aristotelian philosophies of Act and Potency, Form and Matter. But wherever they got this notion, the Moscow Art Theater's lore of action has, potentially, great value. It provides a kind of bridge between theory and practice; points to the pre-conceptual basis of the dramatic art; and offers a means of access to masterpieces of the tradition which our contemporary mental habits obscure.

I am aware that most contemporary theory—whether of art or of knowledge or of psychology—leaves no room for the notion of action or the imitation of action. Probably it is the primitive realism of this concept which is unacceptable, both to those who wish to reduce all knowledge to "facts" and abstract concepts, and to those who try to maintain the absoluteness of art.

The objections of the semanticists to Aristotle's epistemology with its basis in the *nous*, or "apperceptive intelligence," are not very convincing but they represent an important and stubborn contemporary habit of mind. Aristotle is not as *inaverti* as they think; "what he has that they haven't got" is not naïve credulity but a recognition that we are aware of things and people "before predication," as he puts it. The histrionic sensibility, the perception of action, is such a primitive and direct awareness.

Contemporary theories of art which omit or reject the notion of the imitation of action are more disquieting than pseudo-scientific theories because of the insight they give us into the actual work of artists in our time. They remind us how difficult it is—after three hundred years of rationalism and idealism, with the traditional modes of behavior lost or discredited—to see any action but our own. Eliot, for instance, probably the most accomplished poet alive, does not seem to find the Aristotelian formula useful or valid. Thus he suggests that the aim of the poet is to find objective equivalents for his feeling. The phrase "objective equivalent" seems to support Eliot's announced classicism. Yet it refers, not to the vision of the poet, but to the poem he is making; and it implies that it is only a *feeling* that the poet has to convey. Thus the formula is closer to the romantic notion of art as the expression of feeling or passion than to the doctrine of imitation. The emphasis on the poem and its form, to the exclusion of what it represents, recognizes only one of the instincts which Aristotle thought were the roots of poetry in general, the "instinct for harmony and rhythm." Perhaps this emphasis on the distinguishing feature of art—what separates it from other perceptions of action—is necessary in order to reaffirm the existence of art. Perhaps it is poor strategy for a poet at the moment of composition to worry about "truth" in any sense except truth to his feeling. And it may be that in our bewildered age the poet has only a pathetic inspiration; and that if he does not cling to the uniqueness of the mantic passion he is in danger of having nothing left to work with. "Poetry," says Aristotle, as though to recognize the limitations of his own theory, "implies either a happy gift of nature or a strain of madness. In the one case a man can take the mould of any character; in the other he is lifted out of his proper self." Such considerations remind us of the mystery of the creative act in any art; of our dependence upon the masters, and of their dependence upon the surrounding culture.

Yet the notion of drama as imitation of action is both possible for us and very valuable. We do actually in some sense perceive the shifting life of the psyche directly, before all predication: before we reach the concepts of ethics or psychology; even before imitating it in the medium of words or musical sounds. When we directly perceive the action which the artist intends, we can understand the objectivity of his vision, however he arrived at it; and thence the form of his art itself. And only on this basis can one grasp the analogies between acting and playwrighting, between various forms of drama, and between drama and other arts.

XI

REUBEN A. BROWER

The Heresy of Plot

It does not take a historian to see that the spirit of the mid-twentieth century is reactionary—whatever meaning, favorable or unfavorable, we attach to that adjective. The tendencies in the great world are obvious; a minor sign in the minor world of literary criticism is that Aristotle is again in fashion, which is in turn a sign of a desire to move away from the critical principles and techniques characteristic of the past twenty-five or thirty years. The temper of the time is "either-or"; and the critic, like the liberal in politics, is asked to be either for or against Aristotle or Arnold or the nineteenth century or somebody or something. A strayed explicator who comes into a conference on the *Poetics* and modern criticism is puzzled, especially if he has read Aristotle and found on reflection that he must be both a New Critic and an Aristotelian. Without assuming the role of a Jeremiah, he feels he should hold up a warning hand—a kid-gloved hand, of course—to fellow readers who are about to take Aristotle as their guide. Before embracing critical principles of the fourth century B.C. or of the nineteenth century, it is well to consider what we are embracing. In our eagerness to correct excesses of recent criticism, we may sacrifice important gains in awareness and method, and forget, as Mr. Ransom suggests, that "a linguistic revolution" separates the twentieth century from the nineteenth and earlier centuries. Shakespearean criticism offers a good example of the difficulties of the new reaction: we may read Bradley with a more tolerant eye than we did twenty years ago, but are we therefore to unlearn what we have learned from Stoll and Knights and Empson?[1]

Reprinted from *English Institute Essays, 1952* (New York: Columbia University Press, 1952), pp. 44–69, by permission of the author and the publisher. Copyright 1952 by Columbia University Press.

[1] In *The Structure of Complex Words* (New Directions, 1951), Empson is much concerned with the problem of combining "pattern" and "character"

On the present occasion it would be easy to produce a caricature of an Aristotelian critic and draw the appropriate moral. But to be just to Aristotle, to face the obscurities of his text, to acknowledge his points of weakness and strength is another matter. If we want to learn from him, we must translate his concepts to our purposes, eliminating if possible the liabilities. Radical translation is needed not only because the *Poetics* is written in Greek but also because Aristotle is talking much of the time from the writer's point of view, a fact that has often proved troublesome to critics, more especially since the Renaissance. As modern literature gained its distinctive character, and as readers were compelled to adjust their sights to both Sophocles and Shakespeare, the problem of "turning Aristotle's statements around" and making them relevant was staggering. Mild critical schizophrenia resulted; the Aristotelian Dryden of the Preface to *Troilus and Cressida* is hardly recognizable in the genial appreciator of Shakespeare and Chaucer.

With the passage of time, the difficulties have increased. A contemporary reader who asks himself whether the *Poetics* has any relevance to his interpretation of a poem or play or novel will sympathize with Dryden. The Great Amphibium who can breathe the lucid air of the *Poetics* and swim in the deceptive currents of the *Seven Types of Ambiguity* has yet to be born. While waiting—we can try to retranslate Aristotle and indicate the kind of practice that hopefully might bridge the two worlds of critical activity.

But why concern ourselves with Aristotle? Because he is the clearest and most influential exemplar of a position. He stands for the familiar principle that literature offers a representation of human life and that the basic order of a work is the arrangement of successive "actions." Aristotle will not let us forget that literature, if literature at all, is dramatic.

But what is our own position? In reading Aristotle nothing is easier to forget than where we are. The standard translators and commentators on the *Poetics* are firmly planted in the nineteenth century, a world in which plots were certainly plots; and less conservative interpreters, the ritualists, though they wrote in the earlier decades of this century, show more than a trace of

approaches to Shakespearean drama. The interesting chapter "Honest in *Othello*" represents a move toward Bradley, a protest against the view that "coherence of character is not needed in poetic drama, only coherence of metaphor and so on."

nineteenth-century nostalgia for primitive and simply unified societies in a happy, happy past. The romanticism of Murray's translations and his interest in ritual are not unconnected. But I am thinking of a critical reader aware that he is functioning here and now, a reader who has undergone the critical revolution imitated by Eliot and Richards in the twenties and early thirties. This revolution, particularly in the analysis of the text that it popularized, might be described as a reaction of "Cambridge" against the Oxford of Bradley and Pater.

The mark of the reader-critic bred in the "Cantabrigian" climate is a consciousness that he is a reader, that the experience of literature is a complicated event in response to words on a page—hence his realization that he can describe the event only by quotation and continual reference to the language of the work being interpreted. But the kind of analysis accompanying quotation is important and more characteristic. The prinicple, or the intellectual bias, that determines the analysis is a renewed awareness of the multiple meanings of words and of the abstract character of all language, in particular the language of literary criticism. Our critical reader is sensitive to the fact that when he speaks of a work as "tragic," or when he refers to a "character," he has gone through a process of selecting and relating one sort of item from the great range of items of experience symbolized and generated by a writer's words.

Although he employs many old and new critical abstractions, his effort is directed toward discovering the felt order of a particular literary event. He knows that he cannot communicate the order directly or "render" it adequately by descriptive gestures, though of course he uses every expressive resource at his command. He aims rather to delineate the verbal arrangements that control and shape the total ordered response.

That it is difficult for such a reader to assimilate Aristotle is comically obvious. But the ghost of Aristotle, or of something very like Aristotle, keeps haunting him. How, without sacrificing valuable principles of linguistic and aesthetic analysis, is he to deal with dramatic structure in anything like Aristotle's sense of the term? How can a mind that is positivist in bent have any commerce with even a reformed Platonist? To focus on a point where the *Poetics* seems at once most compelling and most alien to our critical reader, how can he think of action in an Aristotelian sense without falling into the "heresy of plot"? He is haunted by another fear which may seem paradoxical, that he may slip via this heresy into the "religion of ritual." But that error belongs to another paper.

What do we mean by the melodramatic phrase "heresy of plot"? Nothing very sensational; it is the notion that in a poem or a play or a novel there is an order of events that may be thought of in complete isolation from other structures and that "somehow" exists independent of the language of the work. So described, the idea is revolting; no self-respecting contemporary critic is guilty of this. Crude hypostatizing of plot and separation of plot from expression is a nineteenth-century error, left behind with character sketches and the well-made play. But is this quite true? It is difficult to catch a modern literary critic in the act of "talking plot"; but we can still find ample evidence of the heresy in numerous contemporary hand-books on interpreting drama. There are generalized discussions of rising and falling action, of plot as logical sequence of incidents; the point of view of the writer-builder is often confused with the reader's, and so forth. More significant is the silence that eddies about these discussions and the eager loquaciousness when the subject of verse drama appears. As Eliot has observed: "It is unfortunate when they [people] are repelled by verse, but can also be deplorable when they are attracted by it—if that means they are prepared to enjoy the play and the language of the play as two separate things." Though the student is warned that they must not be separated, the warning comes late after pages of talk in which they have been separated in practice.

It is not my business to decide whether Aristotle is guilty of this gross heresy, but to use the questions it raises in order to define his position on dramatic structure and its relation to *lexis*, or expression. Can we translate Aristotle's statements in terms meaningful to a present-day reader and make them relevant to interpretation? We begin with the baffling term *praxis*, "action" in the most general sense, as in "tragedy is a representation not of human beings, but of action and life" (1450a 16, 17).[2]

---

[2] The line references are to *The Poetics of Aristotle*, ed. by S. H. Butcher, 4th ed., London, 1907. Except where otherwise noted, quotations in English from the *Poetics* are taken from Butcher's translation. In a few instances small changes, usually no more than a word or two, have been made. The other editions most frequently consulted were: *Aristotle on the Art of Poetry*, ed. by Ingram Bywater, Oxford, 1909; *Aristoteles Poetik*, ed. by Alfred Gudeman, Berlin and Leipzig, 1934; Lane Cooper, *Aristotle on the Art of Poetry*, rev. ed., Ithaca, N.Y., 1947.

The last two terms are probably synonymous; *praxis*, as Cornford notes, is sometimes the Greek word for "experience." Readers of the *Ethics* will agree that for Aristotle "life" must be activity, human behavior, and must include inner conscious, as well as overt bodily, action.

When Aristotle talks of *praxis* in a particular sense, definition becomes harder. As examples of "one action," that is, a single, unified action (1451a 16–36; 1459a 17–1459b 7), he cites the *Iliad* and the *Odyssey*, poems that have the narrative variety of novels. But Aristotle does not say what this "one action" is. He notes that unlike the *Cypria* the Homeric epics offer matter for only one, or at the most two, tragedies, which leaves us where we were. If we say that the action of the *Iliad* is the "wrath of Achilles," that of the *Odyssey*, "Odysseus' trying to get home," what is the meaning of "action" common to these two very different abstractions?

We turn with relief to *mythos*, or plot, a term that has pleasantly concrete attributes: here is something we can get our teeth into "literally," as undergraduates say. There is the solid body of the biologist and the equally solid "body" of the work of art, whether painting or poem. The plot of a tragedy is a "putting together, a composition of parts"; and the parts are "incidents," or *pragmata* (1450a 15; 1450b 22–35). As long as "dramatic incident" is used for bodily movements on the stage, the illusion of the objective concrete plot is easily maintained. But with *pragmata* in the sense of the "other kinds of dramatic action," the mind of the playwright enters; and the comparisons with enormously large and extremely small organisms suggest a kind of intellectual "seeing" of the whole by both poet and spectator.

What is seen, the incidents so easily assumed, is not defined. If Aristotle uses *logos* as equal to *mythos*, we have examples of plots and incidents in the generalized "stories" (*logoi*) of the *Iphigenia at Tauris* and the *Odyssey*. But these two scenarios do not help us much in defining an incident. We say, "something that one of the agents does or suffers." But if we look at Aristotle's examples—and they are of the sort we all give—we find extraordinarily different kinds of statement: "A young girl is sacrificed; sometime later her brother arrives"; or, "A man is away from his own country for many years; he is jealously watched over by Poseidon and yet alone, quite on his own." An element of the plot may be the simplest sort of physical event: "Someone arrives." Or it may be a complicated set of relationships between agents, implying distinct attitudes; or it may be a total impression of a situation. If we refer either outline to the works, we become even less sure of exact definitions of plot or incident. More than half of Aristotle's Iphigenia story consists of statements of events that Euripides recounts in the prologue; they are included in the plot, in spite of the fact that they seem to be "outside the drama." The remarks about Odysseus's isolation and his relations to Poseidon hardly correspond to discrete segments of narrative or even to happenings; they represent complicated abstractions based on grouping and comparison of narrative facts and on inferences as to their meaning.

In addition to plot as an arrangement of incidents, there is also in the *Poetics* quite a different definition of plot, as Mr. Fergusson has pointed out. But it, too, depends on the organic analogy and is even more purely "Aristotelian," the plot being compared to the *arche*, or soul, of a tragedy (1450a 37, 38). The analogy is almost overpoweringly suggestive;[3] the soul in relation to the body, is much more than the formal cause; it is also the efficient and the final cause. By comparison, the plot is "the origin of movement" in a play, and also "what determines its essential nature." "Essential nature" must mean intelligible order or form, but the exact philosophical meaning of Aristotle's terms cannot be pressed here or elsewhere in the *Poetics*. The point of the metaphor lies in its exaggeration, in the insistence on "plot" as the most important ordering principle in a work of literature. This broad sense of the word is clearer from the curious analogy that follows: "Character holds second place. A similar fact is seen in painting. The most beautiful colours, laid on without order, will not give as much pleasure as the chalk outline of a human figure." The stress of the comparison is on "without order" and "outline of a figure." "Plot" must be an ordered sequence of expressions (the chalk lines) that build up in the reader's consciousness a recognizable pattern of human behavior. Here, as we shall see, is a conception of plot that may be useful to a modern reader.[4]

[3] See S. H. Butcher, *Aristotle's Theory of Poetry and Fine Art*, 3d ed., London, 1902, pp. 345, 346.

[4] Aristotle does not here or in his remarks on the pleasures of recognition reduce the pleasure of art to recognition of likeness. He is defining the pleasure

But in the ease with which Aristotle elsewhere separates the pleasures of recognizing likeness from the medium that projects it, there is a glimpse of the heresy with which we began. In most of the *Poetics* the body-structure analogy is very much in evidence; and by a paradoxical law of critical economy, as the plot and incidents become more material, the words, the cells that compose them, oddly disappear. But the too, too solid flesh rarely melts. It may be said that Aristotle was too Greek, too aware of poetry as a craft of words, to think of literary structure apart from the words that "make" it. He was certainly free from any taint of the nineteenth-century heresy of spirit, of poetry as a nonliterary essence. It is also clear from his initial discussion of media that he is mainly concerned with mimesis through language (*mimesis en logois*). But from the order of importance in which Aristotle lists media, it appears that *lexis* (diction, style, or expression) is to him of minor importance.

We ask whether Aristotle in fact talks of the plot as existing and producing its effect independent of language, or if not, how he does describe the relationship between the two. We must not get into the solemn position of accusing Aristotle of using abstractions; but one sign of critical health is the degree of discomfort shown by a critic while using his machinery. And it must be admitted that Aristotle is extremely comfortable in classifying plots, their elements, and types. His units of analysis, we should note, are not verbal, but dramatic, that is, stage actions or reported actions; and he cites examples. But by citing the *Oedipus* too often, abstract model and example tend to become identical. In reading the *Poetics*, who comes very close to the felt particular moments of the *Oedipus* or the *Iphigenia?* Who could, in the seminar shorthand of this curious Greek, which no translator would dare to imitate? Only in discussing recognitions does Aristotle refer more exactly to speeches. But he does not quote from most of the texts, not from the *Odyssey*, or the *Iphigenia*, or the *Oedipus*, or the *Choephori*. In the last example, it is the syllogism that interests him, not dramatic speech.

Perhaps the silence about language is only a matter of attention; but there are two points at which Aristotle seems to go out

---

that comes from viewing likenesses; the other pleasures have other sources, in execution, coloring, and so forth (1448b 15–19).

of his way to eliminate the medium. The first comes in a discussion of "spectacle" (1453b 3–8):

For the plot ought to be constructed in such a way that anyone, by merely hearing an account of the incidents and without seeing them, will be filled with horror and pity at what occurs. That is how any-one hearing the story of Oedipus would be affected. To rely on spectacular means is less artistic.[5]

Though "hearing" implies words of some sort, Aristotle shows little or no concern about them.[6] Any telling will do that keeps the order of incidents (whatever we mean by an incident). The mere chain of events, if heard, will produce tragic pity and fear. If we translate "anyone hearing the story of *The Oedipus*" (Sophocles's play), then Aristotle shows an even greater indifference to the telling. The test of his statement is to compare the *Oedipus* of Seneca: the generalized story of the *Oedipus Rex* is there, but it does not work. Although several Sophoclean scenes are followed closely, the swiftness and anger and dread so constantly underlined in the speeches of the Greek play have disappeared. Though there are, as Robert Frost says, "re-tellable stories," retelling is something more than "arrang-ing incidents."

The other passage (1456b 2–8) is more obscure; Butcher's version preserves some of its ambiguities.

Now, it is evident that the dramatic incidents must be treated from the same points of view as the dramatic speeches, when the object is to evoke the sense of pity, fear, importance, or probability. The only difference is, that the incidents should speak for themselves without verbal exposition; while the effects aimed at in speech should be produced by the speaker, and as a result of the speech. For what were the business of a speaker, if the thought were revealed quite apart from what he says?

With that triumphant question in our ears, we can hardly suppose that Aristotle could for long think of a plot as working its effect apart from special handling of words. But the ambi-guity is the familiar one: what are "the incidents" that "speak for themselves without verbal exposition," or explanation? If

---

[5] Translation from *Aristotle*, Philip Wheelwright (New York, 1951), p. 307.

[6] Bywater confidently explains (*ad. loc.*) that "As the poet is an imitative artist in language, a *mimetes en logo* . . . it follows that the poetic effect has to be produced by language, and not by means other than language."

they are overt stage movements[7] of the actors, the meaning is perhaps clear enough. But as soon as we think of writing a play—which is what Aristotle is talking about—the haziness of his account is evident: he has nothing[8] to say about how actions get into the play and how they are made to produce the effects he insists on as necessary.

In discussing the plot Aristotle is on the whole indifferent to the verbal medium; at his best he implies that it exists; at his worst he lapses into talk about the direct effect of incident. But these may be local defects of Aristotle's method of dividing and conquering the field he is studying. Perhaps we shall find what we want in his treatment of *lexis*, a term as hard to define as *praxis*. It means in the most general sense "expression through language" (1450b 14, 15),[9] probably as Bywater says, "expression of whatever is in the mind" of the characters. The so-called inner life of a character being made up of the "ethical element" and the "intellectual and affective elements," *lexis* is mainly a medium for expressing them. As usual, plot is lost sight of; there is some reference to character and thought, none to action. In the more detailed account of *lexis* the term is limited to the choice of words conventionally appropriate to tragedy, epic, and iambic poetry. In this culinary account of style as combining foreign and ornamental and current and metaphorical words, and so forth, there are only two or three points where Aristotle refers to the connection between words and what is being expressed or indicates that a change in a word changes the experience of the listener.

In the *Rhetoric* we find a more refined account of the relation between words and the structures of thought, emotion,

[7] In the fifth century, when the author was director or working with the director, he could work out a completely nonverbal "rhetoric of action," as Bywater calls it. But Bywater's phrase and Aristotle's term are ambiguous and include all the countless kinds of action that may be expressed.

[8] This is all the more strange since he has just been insisting that "speech" produces all the various kinds of "thought," or we might say "psychic life," of the agents: "proof and refutation; the excitation of feelings, such as pity, fear, anger, and the like; the suggestion of importance or its opposite" (1456a 36—1456b 2). He then moves on, in our passage, to say that the "dramatic incidents" must be made to produce similar effects. The same types of thought must be conveyed through the poet's handling of incidents. Aristotle is no less dark than Butcher; the passage has been translated in various ways.

[9] In 1460b 11 *lexis* is expression of the poet's whole mimetic act.

character, and narrative. Discussion of diction is as limited as in the *Poetics*, the object being to show speakers how to satisfy current Attic standards; but Aristotle has another and more generous standard of propriety, essentially a dramatic one (*Rhetoric*, III. 7). A speaker must use language in a way to project the role he has assumed. He must use words appropriate to what he feels or wants his hearers to feel; he must select idioms that will delineate a certain "disposition" (*hexis*) and so convey the impression, let us say, of a farmer or of an educated man. Such advice could serve as a basis for critical interpretation of dramatic speech.

In both treatises it is what Aristotle does not say that is disturbing. His omissions in discussing metaphor and rhythm and sound are well known; they result in part from overemphasis on the logical and dramatic structure of a speech or a poem. The golden sentences about metaphor seem to open extensive vistas: ". . . the greatest thing by far is to have a command of metaphor. This alone cannot be imparted by another; it is the mark of genius, for to make good metaphors implies an eye for resemblances" (1459a 5–9). But what follows? We are told that metaphors are best suited to iambic verse, that is, to the dialogue of tragedy. In the *Rhetoric* Aristotle stresses the value of metaphor in producing a sense of actuality (*energeia*), of having things "before your eyes" (*Rhetoric*, III. 10). But the figure is regarded in general as a local expressive device, a way of surprising and pleasing an audience. There is no thought of any larger unifying function of metaphor. Similarly, rhythm and musical sound (*harmonia*) are only incidental embellishments; there is no suggestion that the order of argument or plot may be subtly modified by sound pattern. In general, the scant treatment of metaphor and sound is reflected in the slight attention given to the chorus in Greek tragedy. The *Poetics* does not offer much support for replacing analysis in terms of plot by analysis in terms of ritual sequence.[10] The attitude expressed in the *Rhetoric* toward the finer arts of language offers equally cold comfort to explica-

---

[10] But Jane Harrison, the *manga mater* of the ritualists, has said that if we want to grasp the relation between dramatic art and ritual "it is essential we should understand . . . the chorus, strangest and most beautiful of all" the surviving ritual forms in Greek drama. J. E. Harrison, *Ancient Art and Ritual*, New York and London, 1913, p. 122.

tors: "All such arts are fanciful and meant to charm the hearer. Nobody uses fine language when teaching geometry."[11] (*Rhetoric*, III. 1.) The suspicion arises that this excellent geometrician did not know what poetry was; in other words, his "art of poetry," *mimesis en logois*, excludes much that we feel essential.

It may now seem more than generous to return to our original questions: What can a contemporary critical reader "do" with the Aristotelian account of dramatic structure? And how can he translate it to his advantage?

He begins by accepting the Greek prejudice that literature is "of"[12] human action and life. With plot as a composition of incidents, our critic will not have much to do, though he grants that the notion has a limited usefulness for a playwright. Ibsen's often quoted account of how he composed *The Wild Duck* seems to be a good example: "I have just completed a play in five acts—that is to say, the rough draft of it; now comes the elaboration, the more energetic individualisation of the persons and their mode of expression." But this statement hardly represents what Ibsen did when he wrote the play, as Archer's comparison of the draft and the final text shows. The sentence emerging in the mind and arriving on the page must have borne a total freight of incident and speaking tone and symbolic implication, all of them, in James's phrase, "intimately associated parts of one general effort of expression." Although an abstract structure of incidents may be present to the writer planning his play or novel, only plot "written" concerns the library critic.

In plot as *arche*, as "origin of movement" and "intelligible order," he can find an idea adaptable to his purposes. For the writer it is what Elizabeth Bowen means by plot as "the knowing of destination." Aristotle makes the shift to the reader's point of view with his analogy of "the chalk outline," the perceived order that we take as standing for a human figure. In terms of reading experience, plot is one of the orders that we apprehend in our response to a writer's words, the order of meanings that we take as "of" a man living. It is a sequence of ordered meanings going toward a destination; plot includes

[11] Roberts, *op. cit.*

[12] For definition of this "of" (*mimesis*) see Philip Wheelwright's paper in this series.

movement. For this definition "dramatic sequence" is a more appropriate term.

How do we translate "dramatic sequence" in relation to our reading of a poem, play, or novel? We start from Aristotle's reminder that personality in literature is expressed by a selection of words and idioms, and we remember that our term is analytical, a way of directing attention to one abstracted aspect of literary experience. In referring to dramatic structure, we think first of meanings and uses of language that compose a distinct speaking voice; we hear someone speaking in a role, if only the role of "poet." We hear the voice as speaking to "someone" and infer various relationships between the fictional speaker and the auditor. We describe the total of their relationships as a "situation." The slightest shift in tone brings a shift in relation, and drama begins with this movement.

> Had we but world enough and time,
> This coyness, lady, were no crime.

The intimate companionship of lover and mistress in "we" is finely altered by "lady," with its note of detached, ironic decorum. The situation in the second line is not the same as in the first—an example of a small-scale dramatic sequence. By "dramatic structure" (or design) we mean one of these inferred sequences of changing human relationships. "Human," because the relations and changes belong to the distinct impersonation evoked by the words.

This definition may be "blown up" and made sufficiently complex to fit a play by Shakespeare or a novel by James, though the interrelations become innumerable and the changes correspondingly large in scale. In longer works we usually come on points of major change, often with a "recognition" in a derived Aristotelian sense. We have Elizabeth in *Pride and Prejudice* saying, "Until this moment, I never knew myself," or Oedipus, "All comes true now!" or Antony, "I am so lated in the world that I Have lost my way forever." We accept the implication of Aristotle's remark that tragedy is not possible without plot; no rendering of life will affect us much that does not give us a sense of movement and of reaching points of radical readjustment in relationships. But we wear the peripatetic robe with a difference; the contrast between our definitions and Aristotle's appears in the analysis indicated, in what we "do" with them. At this point someone is saying with an earlier dramatic critic, "Bless thee, Aristotle! Thou art translated!"

We may follow Quince a step further: "To show our simple skill That is the true beginning of our end." We began with the aim of indicating a kind of translation and practice that might bridge the gap between the Aristotelian position and that of contemporary critical readers. While adopting a disinfected definition of plot, we are still thinking of the reader as exposed to the totality of the language of a poem or play and as responding to the "total connotations" of words. We see in this whole structures as potent and as "real" as the dramatic: designs in image, metaphor, and irony. We remember also that the different sorts of connotation are the connotations of the same words. In the glow of imaginative experience, there is no immediately felt distinction between a "plot" meaning and a metaphorical one; to the cool eye of analysis a single key word may be seen as the focus for several distinguishable designs—metaphorical, ironic, and rhythmic. When we return to our reading, we may feel at the edge of consciousness a double action of drama and metaphor or of drama and irony, or of drama and rhythm.

We experience this double or even triple action most keenly at an "Aristotelian" moment when the dramatic sequence reaches a point of decisive change. Let me try to interpret one of these moments, keeping in mind the language that shapes and projects it: the point in Act V of *The Tempest*,[13] when Prospero describes the behavior of the king and his courtiers as they return from madness to sanity. Shakespeare has been preparing for this readjustment by a movement both dramatic and metaphorical. The play has been moving from a scene of tempest toward a promise of "calm seas, auspicious gales," through a series of punishments or trials toward a series of reconciliations and restorations. Although as Dr. Johnson would say there is a "concatenation of events" running through Prospero's "project" and though the play has a curiously exact time schedule, there is often little connection in time or logic between dialogues or bits of action. To be sure, Shakespeare has the Elizabethan conventions "on his side," but the freedom of

[13] The following analysis is adapted from the writer's essay "The Tempest" in *The Fields of Light*, Oxford University Press, Inc., New York, c. 1951.

his dramatic composition in *The Tempest* never seems merely conventional or capricious, because the connection through analogy is so energetic and pervasive. Recurrent analogies—of sea and tempest, noise and music, sleep and dream, of earth and air, freedom and slavery, usurpation and sovereignty—are linked through the key mataphor of "sea-change" into a single metaphorical design expressive of metamorphosis, or magical transformation. Shakespeare is continually "prodding" us—often in ways of which we are barely conscious—to relate the passing dialogue to other dialogues by a "super-design" of metaphor.

If we now read Prospero's words announcing the great changes that are taking place, we shall see many references back to the metaphorical preparation for this moment. We shall also realize that various dramatic lines and various lines of analogy converge almost simultaneously.

> A solemn air and the best comforter
> To an unsettled fancy, cure thy brains,
> Now useless, boil'd within thy skull! There stand,
> For you are spell-stopp'd.
> Holy Gonzalo, honourable man,
> Mine eyes, even sociable to the show of thine,
> Fall fellowly drops. The charm dissolves apace;
> And as the morning steals upon the night,
> Melting the darkness, so their rising senses
> Begin to chase the ignorant fumes that mantle
> Their clearer reason.—O good Gonzalo!
> My true preserver, and a loyal sir
> To him thou follow'st, I will pay thy graces
> Home, both in word and deed.—Most cruelly
> Didst thou, Alonso, use me and my daughter:
> Thy brother was a furtherer in the act;—
> Thou'rt pinch'd for 't now, Sebastian.—Flesh and blood,
> You, brother mine, that entertain'd ambition,
> Expell'd remorse and nature; who, with Sebastian,—
> Whose inward pinches therefore are most strong,—
> Would here have kill'd your king; I do forgive thee,
> Unnatural though thou art!—Their understanding
> Begins to swell, and the approaching tide
> Will shortly fill the reasonable shores
> That now lie foul and muddy. Not one of them
> That yet looks on me, or would know me.—Ariel,

> Fetch me the hat and rapier in my cell:—[*Exit Ariel.*]
> I will discase me, and myself present,
> As I was sometime Milan.—Quickly, spirit;
> Thou shalt ere long be free.

If this is a climactic moment, what is happening dramatically? The "men of sin," like Ferdinand, have come to the end of trials which began with the storm and continued through various "distractions." Now, as Prospero explains, they are undergoing a moral, as well as a mental, regeneration; they are "pinch'd" with remorse and are being forgiven. In a few moments, "Th' affliction of Alonso's mind amends," he resigns Prospero's dukedom, and "entreats" him to pardon his "wrongs."

But these are the prose facts, the bare bones of the changes in dramatic relationships. We cannot feel the peculiar quality of what is taking place or grasp its meaning apart from the metaphorical language through which it is being expressed. And the expressions acquire their force and precision from the metaphorical preparation glanced at earlier. The courtiers' senses are restored by "an airy charm," by magic similar to that worked by Ariel and his spirits. The allusions to "heavenly music" and "solemn air," in contrast to the "rough magic" that Prospero has abjured, remind us that these changes will be musically harmonious, like the songs of Ariel, not noisy and confused like the storm sent to punish these men and reveal their "monstrous" guilt. Toward the end of the speech, the imagery recalls the tempest metaphor, but it is altered so as to express the mental and moral changes that are taking place. The return of understanding is like an "approaching tide" that covers the evidence of a storm (both "foul" and "muddy" have storm associations from earlier occurrences).

The metaphor that best expresses this "clearing" is the one for which the preparation has been most complete.

> The charm dissolves apace;
> And as the morning steals upon the night,
> Melting the darkness, so their rising senses
> Begin to chase the ignorant fumes that mantle
> Their clearer reason.

"Dissolving" and "melting" and "fumes" take us back at once to the grand transformations of the masque and "the cloud-capp'd towers" speech, to earlier cloud-changes both serious and comic; and they take us back further to the association of clouds with magical tempests, inner storms, and clearing weather. We read of the moral and psychological changes with a present sense of these analogies. They are qualified for us as a dream-like dissolution of tempest clouds, as events in the "insubstantial" region where reality and unreality merge.

It is through such links that Shakespeare concentrates at this dramatic moment the fullest meaning of his key metaphor. There is, of course, no separation in the reader's experience between dramatic fact and metaphorical qualification. The images that recur take us back to felt qualities, but to felt qualities embedded in particular dramatic contexts. "Melting," for example, carries us to the supernatural dissolution of "spirits . . . melted into air, into thin air"; but it also reminds us of the masque pageantry and of Prospero's calming of Ferdinand's fears. We hear Prospero's soothing and mysterious voice in both the earlier and the later uses of the word. The dramatic links and the analogical links are experienced at once; metaphorical design and dramatic design are perfectly integrated.

"Metamorphosis" is the key metaphor to the drama, but not the key metaphor to a detachable design of decorative analogies. Through the echoes in Prospero's speech of various lines of analogy, Shakespeare makes us feel each shift in dramatic relationships as a magical transformation, whether it is the courtiers' return to sanity, or Prospero's restoration to his dukedom, or Ariel's flight into perpetual summer. While all the "slaves" and "prisoners" are being freed and all the "sovereigns" are being restored, the sense of magical change is never lost. The union of drama and metaphor is nowhere more complete than in *The Tempest*.

That is to say, the composition of *The Tempest* is "poetic" in a sense that revives the central Aristotelian meaning of *poietike*, and that extends and adjusts its implications to fit contemporary views of the reading experience and of the relation between structure and language. The poetic art of literature, *mimesis en logois*, is for Aristotle primarily a rendering of human behavior in terms of dramatic sequence, the medium of language being assumed, but often overlooked. A typical contemporary definition of poetic art might run: "an exploitation of the resources of words," or "creation through words of orders of meaning and sound." The aim of this paper has been to take a step toward harmonizing these two sorts of definition, both of them useful, both inadequate. The kind of definition and practice we want may be illustrated from the single word "dissolves" in Prospero's speech. We note first that the word bears the weight of certain limited dramatic relationships: the voice heard in the faintly Latinate, elevated "dissolves" has the objectivity and remoteness characteristic of Prospero. He observes with detachment and without anger. "Dissolves" reminds us that his vengeance is coming to an end; that the courtiers are moving out of their trance and recognizing their guilt. (The word also gives us a cue as to the actors' movements and facial expression.) It is heard in an even iambic rhythm, "The charm dissolves apace," and in the balanced rhetorical pattern of a classical simile, "as . . . so." Prospero's stance in relation to himself and the others is further modified by the steadiness and intellectual "command" of this speech and verse movement. And the analogies with earlier dissolvings and clouds are bringing in all their qualifications, sensuous and philosophic. The Aristotelian sense of "poetic" directs us to the salient dramatic relations and to their place in the movement of the play, and to the total human experience rendered by *The Tempest*. The modern sense of "poetic" directs us to a fuller perception of the variety of meaning and design and to the close interaction of meanings, the fine qualification of one kind of design by another. All structural links, large and small, from an obvious change in narrative fact to a phrasal echo, are perceived in the resonances of particular words.

The Aristotelian emphasis seems, perhaps, the right one now; twenty-five years ago the emphasis on the word seemed equally right. Both are right enough for literature and for criticism in the long run. But an adequate theory cannot be summoned on demand. We may doubt whether the growth of critical intelligence comes by direct steps from theory to practice; it comes rather from feeling our way and fitting our theories to what we must say at our moment in history if we are not to become tools of our machines. The redefinition of plot as dramatic sequence perceived in the progress of meanings is a sample of the kind of adjustment needed—an account of literature that will do justice to its dramatic character without falling into an Aristotelian separation of plot and character from diction. An adjustment by theory or practice that does not face the liabilities and the obscurities of Aristotle's position (or of any similar position) will not be worth much, even for a short run. That is my excuse for spending so much time in translating and evaluating Aristotle's statements: it is hard to say exactly what we are trying to adjust to. If the result has been sufficiently grim, my success may have been greater than I am inclined to suppose.

XII

ELDER OLSON

The Poetic Method of Aristotle: Its Powers and Limitations

No especial recognition [writes A. E. Taylor] is given in Aristotle's own classification to the Philosophy of Art. Modern students of Aristotle have tried to fill in the omission by adding artistic creation to contemplation as a third fundamental form of mental activity, and thus making a threefold division of Philosophy into Theoretical, Practical, and Productive. The object of this is to find a place in the classification for Aristotle's famous *Poetics* and his *Rhetoric*. But the admission of the third division of Science has no warrant in the text of Aristotle, nor are the *Poetics* and *Rhetoric*, properly speaking, a contribution to Philosophy. They are intended as collections of practical rules for the composition of a pamphlet or a tragedy, not as a critical examination of the canons of literary taste."[1]

The problems touched upon in the passage just cited are important, for they involve the entire scheme of the Aristotelian sciences and the role of poetics within that scheme, and even raise the question whether the treatise on poetics is of philosophical character. They bear directly, therefore, on the whole matter of Aristotle's poetic method; and they illustrate not merely how questions of the powers and limitations of a method are dependent upon interpretation of the method but also how that interpretation, in turn, is dependent upon our interpretation of the larger scheme. With all respect to A. E. Taylor, I should like to look into these problems a little. I shall do so by considering (1) what knowledge, especially scientific knowledge, meant for Aristotle; (2) how, consequently, the

Reprinted from *English Institute Essays, 1952* (New York: Columbia University Press, 1952), pp. 70–94, by permission of the author and the publisher. Copyright 1952 by Columbia University Press.

[1] A. E. Taylor, *Aristotle*, London, n.d., p. 19. See also pp. 88–90.

subject of an art would be handled by him; (3) how all these considerations affect the structure of the *Poetics;* (4) the consequent powers and limitations of his poetic method.

For Aristotle, all animals are capable of knowledge in some sense; the character of that knowledge, however, varies according to the object of knowledge, the nature of what is known, the faculties involved, and the end of the knowledge. Thus, all animals have at least one sense, that of touch, which tells them about the tangible,[2] and those with more senses have additional channels of information.[3] But the knowledge provided by sensation is of the fact alone, and is instantial only;[4] that is, it is knowledge, let us say, that this particular flame is hot, but not that flame generally is hot or why flame is hot. Some animals have memory, and so can supplement present sensation by past sensations; and man, moreover, is capable not merely of supplementing present sensation by past but also of so unifying memory that several memories of the same thing have a single effect; this capacity Aristotle calls *empeiria,* experience. Experience is also knowledge of a kind, and is similar to art and science; but art and science are, strictly speaking, produced out of experience, rather than identical with it. For experience is knowledge of individuals, while art and science are knowledge of universals, and although in reference to action and production (the sphere of which is the individual) men of experience alone succeed better than those who have theory without experience, experience provides knowledge of the fact, but not of the cause of the fact, whereas artistic and scientific knowledge is of the cause.[5]

But scientific knowledge is not constituted simply by knowledge of universal and cause. Sensation, which gives particular information, is not scientific, but neither is intuition; if reference of individual to universal were all, intuition would be scientific knowledge, induction would be the solitary scientific process, and science would consist of scientific principles only. We moderns tend to classify the sciences as inductive or deduc-

[2] *De anima*, iii. 12. 434b 13–15. In order to avoid multiplying references I shall merely give the first that comes to mind, except when there is a special point in doing otherwise.

[3] *Analytica posteriora*, i. 18. 81a 36.

[4] *Physica*, i. 5. 189a 7, *Met*. i. 1. 981b 10 ff.

[5] *Metaphysica*, i. 1. 980a 21–981 b9; *An. post*. i. 13. 22 ff.; 31. 87b 27 ff.

tive; Aristotle thought that all sciences are both, in the sense that principles achieved through induction are utilized to demonstrate, through causal reasoning, the inherence of attributes in a subject.[6] Hence, for him scientific knowledge is a matter neither of mere generality nor of mere specificity, but is knowledge of cause as appropriate to (or, we might say, as commensurate or simultaneous with) the inherence of attribute in subject.[7] For example, the figure ABC has its internal angles equal to a straight angle; it has this attribute, not *qua* this individual triangle of wood or *qua* plane figure or *qua* isosceles triangle, but simply *qua* triangle, and the cause is the appropriate cause of the inherence of this attribute in the subject (triangle), in which it inheres primarily.[8] On this conception, the subject matter of a science is neither determined by a subject simply, nor by an attribute or group of attributes simply, but by a subject as possessing certain attributes which inhere in it primarily. Thus, for Aristotle science is not single and all-comprehending; there are several different sciences, according to the inherence of different attributes in different subjects through different causes, and these sciences must necessarily differ in their principles.[9]

In a very general sense the methods of these sciences will be the same, for all will depend upon principles intuitively derived from experience of particulars, and all will be concerned with proof, via cause, of the inherence of attributes in a subject;[10] but more specifically their methods will differ, for as subjects differ, attributes and proofs of their inherence will differ:[11] not all causes will be relevant,[12] not all definitions will be constructed in the same way,[13] directions of proof will differ,[14] principles will differ in number and accuracy,[15] demonstration will be inappropriate to inexact subject matters concerned with probabilities,[16] probable reasoning will be inappropriate to exact subject matters concerned with necessary attributes,[17] and so forth. Again, not all questions relating to a given object are

[6] *Loc. cit.*; see also *Phys.* i. 1. 184a 9 ff., *An. post.* i. 1. 71a ff.; ii. 19.
[7] *An. post.* i. 13. 15 ff.   [8] *Ibid.*, i. 9. 76a 3 ff.
[9] *Ibid.*, i. 9. 75b 37 ff.; i. 10. 76a 37 ff.; i. 28. 87a 38 ff.
[10] *Ibid.*, ii. 19. 100b 1–18.   [11] *Ibid.*, i. 32. 88a 17–88b 29.
[12] *De an.* i. 1. 403a 25–403b 17.   [13] *Phys.* ii. 2.
[14] *Met.* vii. 7. 1032a 25; *Phys.* ii. 9. 200a 15.   [15] *An. post.* i. 27.
[16] *Nicomachean ethics.* i. 3. 1094b 23–27.   [17] 1094b 28.

relevant to the science of that object, but only those which relate to that object as falling under a single universal. For example, not all questions relating to geometrical figures are geometrical questions, but only those which form premises for the theorems of geometry or its subaltern sciences, such as optics.[18] A single object, let us say, poetry, can fall under a whole variety of sciences, but not all questions raised concerning it are "poetical"; some will be metaphysical, some ethical, some political, and so forth. Distinguished as the sciences are in this general scheme, they have also a basic communion, for all are connected through the common axioms of demonstration and the common disciplines such as dialectic.[19]

We have, thus, a body of sciences distinct from each other in subject matter, problems, and methods, but still interconnected. Aristotle divides the sciences into three groups, the theoretical, the practical, and the productive, or "poetic," sciences; he not only makes this division explicitly a number of times (although Taylor has strangely failed to find warrant for it),[20] but makes many correlative distinctions, such as the numerous ones between "knowing," "doing," and "making,"[21] and as a matter of fact the very foundations of his method demand this primary distinction.[22]

The theoretical sciences—metaphysics, mathematics, and physics—differ as they may in certain respects from each other, are alike in that they involve necessary propositions and have knowledge as their end. In the practical sciences of ethics and politics, knowledge is subordinate to action—one knows what virtue is in order to act virtuously[23]—and in the productive sciences, which are the arts, whether useful or fine, the end is neither knowledge nor action, but the product to be produced. As the practical sciences are less exact than the theoretical, so the productive are less exact than the practical; for sciences are

[18] *An. post.* i. 7. 75a 37–75b 20; i. 12. 77a 40 ff.

[19] *Ibid.*, i. 11. 77a 26 ff.

[20] *E.g.*, *Met.* i. 1. 982a 1; vi. 1. 1025b 21, 1025b 26; ix, 2. 1046b 3.

[21] *Nic. eth.* vi. 4. 1140a 1; also 3. 1139b–4. 1140a 24.

[22] Since art is distinct from theoretical science (*ibid.*, vi. 3) and since making and acting are different (1140a 16), and since these distinctions go back radically to the distinction of the sciences in terms of causes, which in turn rests on the subject-attribute-cause formulation of scientific knowledge, the very pivot of the Aristotelian philosophy.

[23] *Ibid.*, i. 3. 1095a 5.

more exact as they involve fewer elements[24] and are less dependent upon other sciences[25]—thus, arithmetic is more exact than geometry—whereas the practical sciences derive many propositions from the theoretical, and in turn the productive derive propositions from both theoretical and practical sciences.

The *Poetics* is so sharply determined in its problems and method by the fact that it is a treatise of productive science that we may well occupy ourselves briefly with some considerations concerning the scope and structure of such science. In the first place, is scientific knowledge of poetry possible? Not, we must answer, if it is a matter of the accidental or the incidental. There is no science of the accidental for Aristotle:[26] science is concerned only with what happens always or for the most part, with what is necessary or probable;[27] hence, to ask whether a science is possible is to ask whether some subject can be found in which attributes inhere, and that not accidentally. Hence, poetic science cannot center in the artist or the producer; for, although art has a natural basis in man, nature does not produce art, and artistic activity is not a necessary attribute of man. Again, the activity itself cannot serve as the subject, for it does not contain its principle in itself; it is for the sake of the product and is determined by the product. The distinction between doing and making is precisely that in doing the activity contains its own end (Happiness, the end of virtue, is an activity and not a quality for Aristotle), whereas in making the end is a product produced over and above the activity—that is, the productive action is for the sake of the product. The ethical and political sciences are possible because ethical and political activities contain as principles their own ends; but a science of artistic capacity or activity, apart from consideration of the product, is not. We are left, thus, with the product itself as a possible subject.

Moreover, according to Aristotle all art is concerned with coming into being, that is,

with contriving and considering how something may come into being which is capable of either being or not being and whose origin is in the maker, not in the thing made; for art is concerned neither

---

[24] *An. post.* i. 27. 87a 33.   [25] *Met.* i. 2. 982a 25 ff.
[26] *Ibid.*, vi. 2. 1026b 24–1027a 28.   [27] *Met.* vi. 2. 1027a 20–21.

with things that are or come into being by necessity nor with things that do so in accordance with nature, since these latter have their origin in themselves.[28]

What is made by the artist is neither the form nor the matter, but the *synolon*, the *concretum*. For instance, the sculptor makes neither the marble which is his material nor the human form which he gives it, but the statue, which is the human form imposed upon marble; and the ironworker makes neither the iron nor the spherical form, but the iron sphere, a *concretum* of form and matter.[29] In art a form in the mind of the artist is imposed upon his medium, to produce the artistic composite;[30] and the productive process may be divided into two parts, which are, as it were, of contrary direction. The first proceeds from the form to be produced to the first thing which can be produced; this is reasoning. The second proceeds from the first thing which can be produced to the form itself; this is making.[31] or example, if a shoe is to be produced—a certain kind of composite—then parts must be stitched or nailed together; but first there must be the requisite parts, and these will have to be cut and prepared, and so forth to the first thing that can be done. All this is reasoning; but the process from the terminus of the reasoning to the final production of the form is making. Now, art according to Aristotle is a state concerned with making, involving a true course of reasoning; and it is precisely this reasoning universalized, the rationale of art or production, which is in a sense scientific knowledge of the productive kind; the reasoning part, that is, not the making part; for the latter is not knowledge, but production in accordance with knowledge, and it depends rather upon skill and experience. By "course of reasoning" Aristotle means, naturally, not the psychological processes of the individual artist, for these are incidental to the individual and cannot be formulated, but the course that would be followed in correct, true, and appropriate reasoning about making a given product. Since the arts propose not productions merely but also productions excellent of their kind—for example, the sculptor seeks to make not merely a statue but also a good statue—such reasoning will have to include not merely the

[28] *Nic. eth.* vi. 4. 1040a 10–16 (Oxford tr.).
[29] *Met.* vii. 8. 1033a 23–1033b 11.
[30] 7. 1032a 32.   [31] 1032b 15 ff.

"nature" of the thing intended but its "excellence" as well.[32]

The scope of any productive science, therefore, is the rational part of production centering in, and indeed based upon, the nature of the product; and the structure of such science may be described as hypothetical regressive reasoning, taking for its starting-point, or principle, the artistic whole which is to be produced and proceeding through the various parts of the various kinds to be assembled.[33] The reasoning is hypothetical because it is based upon hypotheses: If such and such a work, which is a whole, is to be produced, then such and such parts must be assembled in such and such a way; and if the work is to have excellence as a whole, then the parts must be of such and such a kind and quality. The reasoning is regressive because it works backward from the whole, which is to exist, to the parts which must have existence previous to that of the whole. Since the reasoning is based upon a definition of a certain whole as its principle and since that definition must be arrived at in some fashion, any productive science must consist of two main parts: inductive reasoning toward its principle, and deductive reasoning from its principle.[34] One part must make possible the formulation of the whole; the other must determine the parts according to that formulation.

On examination, the *Poetics* clearly follows this general pattern. Chapters i–v are concerned with establishing the definition of tragedy, which is given in chapter vi; chapters vi–xxii resolve tragedy into its proper parts; chapters xxiii–xxiv offer a treatment of epic based upon that of tragedy; and the final chapters conclude with critical problems relative to both forms.

The definition on which everything centers, thus, is no mere statement of the meaning of a term or name, as we ordinarily think of definition nowadays;[35] it is a statement of the nature of a whole produced by a certain art; and it is introduced, not merely to clarify meanings a little but much more importantly, to serve as the principle of the art and hence as the basis of all reasoning. And because it is a definition of a thing produced by art, it must differ sharply from a mathematical or physical

[32] *Poetics*, i. 1447a 10: ἐὶ μέλλει καλῶς ἕξειν ἡ ποίησις.

[33] *De partibus animalium*, i. 1. 639b 24 ff.; *De generatione et corruptione*, ii· 11. 337b 14 ff.

[34] *Supra*, n. 6.   [35] *An. post.* ii. 10. 93b 28–94a 3.

definition. Mathematical definitions treat of forms as abstracted from matter and hence do not include the matter,[36] I do not, for instance, include "brazen" or "wooden" or anything of the sort in my definition of sphere or cube. Physical definitions—dealing with natural things—must include matter;[37] for physical things are composites of matter and form; hence physical terms, as Aristotle repeatedly reminds us, are like the term "snub"—for "snub" involves not merely nose or merely concavity, but both—a nose (matter) which is concave (form).[38] The things of art—also composites—must also be defined through matter and form. But natural things have a natural matter and are in a natural genus, whereas artifical things are not; hence, while natural things are defined by a two-part definition consisting of genus (matter) and difference (form), artificial things must be defined by enumeration and differentiation of the various causes which make them what they are. These will still group themselves into two parts, matter and form: the one part will state what has been organized as matter; the other will state the working or effect or power (*dynamis*) which is their form. For, as Aristotle says, things must be defined through their working or power;[39] thus, a definition of a hand as a certain organization of bones, veins, and tissues would be incomplete, for it would leave out manual power, which is the form of the hand and the end to which these elements are organized, and such a definition would fit a dead hand as well, although a dead hand is really a hand in name only.[40]

The argument leading to the definition may be stated as follows. Assuming that certain arts are imitative (and this is strictly assumed, not proven, for it is not a proposition which belongs to poetics, but to some other science), specific forms of these arts must be specific forms of imitation. To imitate implies a matter or medium (means) in which one imitates, some form (object) which one imitates, and a certain way (manner) in which one imitates. Thus, considered as imitation, every imitation must involve means, object, and manner, and therefore imitations must differ as they involve different means, objects, or manners. Hence, in chapter i Aristotle differentiates a certain

---

[36] *Met.* vii. 10.   [37] *Phys.* ii. 2.
[38] 194a 4–6.   [39] *Pol.* i. 2. 1253a 24.
[40] See, *e.g.*, *Met.* vii. 10. 1035b 25; *Meteorologica*, iv. 12. 389b 26.

body of arts which involve related media (words, rhythm, tune) according to specific differences of the media involved; in chapter ii, according to objects imitated; and in chapter iii, according to the manners of imitation. As he shows,[41] no one of these lines of differentiation is sufficient to discriminate a given art; according to manner alone, comedy and tragedy are indifferentiable; according to object alone, epic would be indifferentiable from tragedy; while according to the means alone, the imitative poet is not distinguishable from the scientist who writes verse treatises. All three lines of differentiation must therefore be used simultaneously; no one is peculiar, but all three collectively are peculiar, to a given art.[42] These lines of differentiation are in fact causes, in the technical sense in which Aristotle speaks of causes as the answers we give when we are asked "Why is this thing what it is?"[43] For if we are asked, let us say, "why is this thing a tragedy?" we respond, "because it is in a certain medium, because it imitates a certain object, and because it does this in a certain manner."

Yet this causal account is still incomplete; for, to continue the example, tragedy is not really owing to these differentiations, although if they did not exist, tragedy would not.[44] A saw, for instance, does not exist simply because of its metal, or because of the saw-maker, or because of a certain shape, although without these the saw would not exist. These are conditions of its existence, and necessary ones; but it exists primarily because it has a certain function, sawing. And the existence of tragedy results primarily from its effect or power; these other things are for the sake of that. Compare the case of the saw just mentioned. Why is a saw such as it is? To effect cutting in a certain way; and if so, a certain shape and material are required, and an artisan must compound them. This fourth, or final, cause must be found for the various arts under consideration; chapters iv–v are devoted to it. Since for Aristotle what each thing is when fully developed is its nature, and since the nature of each thing is its end and is best and self-sufficient,[45] he achieves the final

[41] *Manner*, 1448a 25 ff.; *object*, 1448a 7 ff.; *means*, 1447b 17 ff.
[42] *An. post.* ii. 13, esp. 96a 32. See also 96b 15–24, and for important remarks on differentiational procedure, *De part. an.* i. 2–4, and *Met.* vii. 12. On species, see *ibid.*, x. 8.
[43] *Phys.* ii. 3; ii. 7; *Met.* v. 2; vii. 17; *De part. an.* i. 1. 639b 12 ff.
[44] *Phys.* ii. 9. 200a 5–200b 10.   [45] *Politica*, i. 2. 1252b 32 ff.

cause by recounting the origin and development of poetry. This is a history in terms of the successive final causes which imitative poetry has had; each phase involves a different final cause, and in each that cause is shown as governing the other elements of poetry.

Thus, in the first phase, human instinct for imitation for the sake of the pleasure and knowledge derived from imitation, whether we ourselves imitate or merely observe imitations, is the originating cause; and since man has also an instinct for tune and rhythm, it is natural that imitation in words, melody, and rhythm should result.[46] But instinct is perfectly uniform and consequently cannot account for variation in poetry; and in the second phase, in which poetry diversifies, as poets imitate either noble or ignoble actions and characters, the cause of the diversification lies in the moral nature of the imitator himself.[47] In the third phase, forms desirable in themselves are developed; here we have art proper.[48] Poetry thus passes through phases in which its functions, or final causes, are instinctive, ethical, and artistic. In the first, moreover, the means is developed;[49] in the second, objects of imitation are differentiated, and the means is adjusted to these;[50] in the third, manner is developed, and, art forms such as comedy and tragedy having now come into being, these are improved and perfected by alterations and accommodations of their parts.[51] Taylor, among many others, has said that Aristotle's theory of *katharsis* was intended to answer Plato's charges against poetry;[52] but it is much more accurate to observe that Plato never conceives of poetry as developing into this third phase and that Aristotle's proper answer lies here: it is one thing to imitate the low and vicious through inclinations of one's character; quite another to imitate them for artistic purposes.

The causal account now complete, Aristotle "collects," as he says,[53] the four causes into the famous definition. The specific problem is now to discover what parts, of what kind and number, are requisite for a whole of the sort just defined. If tragedy is dramatic in manner, there must be spectacle; if the means are as described, there must be diction and music; and if

---

[46] *Poet.* 4. 1448b 4–24.   [47] 1448b 25.   [48] 1449a 5 ff.
[49] 1448b 24.   [50] 1448b 26–32.   [51] 1449b 10–31.
[52] *Aristotle*, pp. 88–90.   [53] ἀπολαβόντες.

the object imitated is an action of a certain kind (*spoudaios*, or serious), there must be plot and hence (since action is discriminated in terms of character and thought) character and thought also. But a whole, for Aristotle, does not simply have a certain number of parts but has them in a certain ordering; one part will be determined by another until the principal part is reached, which determines all.[54] Consequently, to determine this ordering he establishes the relative importance of the parts, arguing that plot is the principal part, the "soul" of tragedy; and one may observe in passing that those who attack this view have never answered the arguments here and, perhaps, have never quite conceived of plot itself as it is here conceived.

If tragedy is a whole, and if plot is its primary part, and if a whole has its characteristics according to its primary part, plot must be investigated; for if that is not whole and entire and beautiful, the tragedy also will not be. Aristotle's treatment of plot is governed by three primary considerations: that it, too, is a whole, and a whole of a certain kind; that it is to be a beautiful whole; and that it is to have a certain effect or function. Plot is a whole of the sort that has beginning, middle, and end; has its parts complete and ordered; is not only of some magnitude, but of a magnitude such that it is beautiful; has a certain unity, in this instance a unity achieved by conjunction; and is continuous. Moreover, since actions, as continuities, are simple or complex according as they are or are not differentiable into distinctive parts, plot also must be simple or complex, the latter kind having as its parts reversal, discovery, or both. These matters, resulting from the specification of metaphysical doctrines of "whole," "part," and so forth to the case of plot, occupy chapters vii–xi. But plot is not merely to be whole and beautiful, but is to have a particular effect or power (upon the emotions); the true form of the tragic plot, thus, is precisely to have this effect; hence, Aristotle examines the nature of the tragic protagonist and the tragic deed, which are the conditions of the tragic effect (chapters xiii–xiv). Development of these conditions brings the treatment of plot as principal part to a close, and the remaining parts are discussed in the order of their importance. Finally, since tragedy includes the parts of epic, epic can be dealt with in terms of its similarities or dissimilarities

[54] *Met.* v. 26, esp. 1024a 1 ff.

to tragedy, and the two forms can be compared, and critical questions organized and resolved.

The method of the *Poetics*, thus, is precisely the method of productive science or art as Aristotle conceives it, and as such determined by the entire body of the philosophy of which it is a part. The degree of this dependency can be seen in the fact that, as Aristotle brought all his doctrines of method to bear on the subject matter of poetry, it was necessary, in the foregoing analysis to explain his procedure by reference to most of his extant works. A more thorough-going analysis would, I believe, establish that dependency more clearly and fully, in proportion as it clarified Aristotle's procedure; conversely, apart from such consideration of the philosophy as a whole, not merely the argument of the *Poetics* but even the doctrines, indeed, even individual concepts, such as those of imitation, plot, and *katharsis*, become unintelligible.

In order to illustrate this last point, as well as to exhibit some further aspects of Aristotle's method, let me briefly consider the case of plot. If I may be bold enough to say what I really think, I shall say that Aristotle's conception of plot is unique in the history of criticism and that in the innumerable discussions of "plot" from his day to our own, his conception is never again attached to the term *mythos* or any of its synonyms, such as *fabula, argumentum, argumento, favola, fable,* fable, plot, *Handlung,* and the like.

Critical discussions of "plot" since Aristotle have turned, I think, on several different conceptions. First, "plot" sometimes has the meaning of the material, whether historical or legendary, which is given poetic treatment; in this sense the various Oedipuses and Fausts are said to have the same plot. Again, "plot" often means a tissue of metaphorical or exemplary events or actions used as vehicle for didactic statement. Thus, we have all heard of the "plot" of *The Faerie Queene* and the "plot" of Richardson's *Pamela*, although the former is really sustained allegorical metaphor and the latter a series of *exempla;* and in ages when poetry is conceived of as didactic only—for example, in the greater part of the medieval period—this meaning becomes the principal, if not the exclusive, one. Again, "plot" has meant the sequence of events simply, without regard to the moral agencies involved in the actions; this is the sense in which you tell the "plot" of a movie, and in this sense *Romeo and*

Juliet and "Pyramus and Thisbe" (in *A Midsummer Night's Dream*) are said to have the same general plot, although one is serious and the other comic travesty. Again, "plot" can mean such events as are narrated, or as are represented upon the stage; this is the sense, I think, in which most European critics of the sixteenth and seventeenth centuries employed the term. Finally, there is "plot" in the sense of a string of occasions invented, *ficelle*-fashion, for the manifestation of character and thought and even the use of special diction. This is the conception which critics entertain when they speak of plot as a mere spine, skeleton, or armature, something as arbitrary as the string upon which we string beads.[55] I submit that these conceptions of plot are not equivalent to Aristotle's, that they stem from conceptions of poetry very different from Aristotle's, and that, even if plot should appear as important in any of them, it would hardly be in the sense in which Aristotle thought of plot as important.

For Aristotle was not concerned with everything which we should call poetry, and also he was concerned with some things that we should no longer call poetry. It will not do even to say that he was concerned with tragedy, epic, and comedy, for the significance of these terms has altered since his day. He thought of epic as the *Iliad* and the *Odyssey* and whatever had the same form—not as the sort of epic that Aratus and Nicander were to produce; of tragedy as poetry similar to the *Oedipus* of Sophocles, not to the *Oedipus* of Seneca or *The White Devil*. While he says repeatedly that the arts imitate nature, he means that the causes and productive processes of artificial objects resemble those which nature would have evolved had the products been natural and not artificial; he does not mean that all artificial objects are imitations in the sense in which he thinks tragedy is an imitation.[56]

In brief: he had observed that certain kinds of art had developed to a stage at which they were produced and appreciated for their own sake; that these forms happened to be (he uses the verb *tuxanousi*) imitative of human actions, in the sense that they simulated human actions, and that not simply, but human

[55] See, *e.g.*, Ortega y Gasset, *Notes on the Novel* (pub. together with *The Dehumanization of Art* Princeton, 1948), pp. 65, 82, 87–88.
[56] *Phys.* ii. 8. 199a 8–19. Note Aristotle's careful statement at *Poet.* 1447a 13–16.

actions of different kinds, as serious or ludicrous, affecting us differently according to such differences of kind. The point is not that everything which has been or might be called poetry imitates human action, but that certain forms of poetry undoubtedly do; and it is these that he is discussing. Now, if actions are serious or ludicrous according to the degree in which they involve happiness or misery, and if happiness and misery are functions of the moral characters of the persons involved, the imitative action, or plot, cannot consist of events simply, or actions simply, but of activity of a certain moral quality, such that it produces a particular emotional effect; that is, the kind of action includes the kind of moral choice made, just as the moral choice includes the kind of reasoning and moral principles upon which the choice is made. Plot, therefore, in such imitative forms, is a system of morally differentiated activities or actions; as such, it is undubitably the primary part of such constructions, since it actualizes and completes and gives form to all the other parts, which are related to it as matter to form. But it is primary only in this conception of it, and only in this conception of poetry; and these conceptions are in turn dependent upon the whole body of the Aristotelian philosophy. To separate them from that philosophy is to lose not merely their scientific justification but their very significance as well.

What, then, are the powers and limitations of Aristotle's poetic method? I think that after a fashion we have been discussing them all along. There are some limitations which are almost invariably brought out—that the *Poetics* is a fragment, that portions of that fragment present certain textural difficulties, that Aristotle could have been cognizant of only very few literary forms and of these only to the degree of development which they had reached by his day, and so forth. I regard these "limitations" as trivial. Any philosophic method which is worthy of the name is not one which produces merely passive results, but one through which we may actively inquire, prove, and know; and if Aristotle offers a genuine philosophic method, anyone truly possessed of that method will be able to supply these deficiencies, real or supposed, with the authority of the master himself, for the authority should derive, not from the person, but from the method.

But there are two other kinds of limitation, much more real

and important, although neither impairs the soundness of method or of doctrine. One stems from the method of the *Poetics* proper, the other from the general method of Aristotle; both originate in the fact that to adopt a given method is to be able to do certain things and not to be able to do certain others. The *Poetics* cannot be viewed, without serious distortion of it, as exhausting all questions pertinent to the arts, or even to all of the poetic arts. Of the problems which confront artist or critic, some are peculiar to the individual work, and, as accidental, are not amenable to scientific treatment. Some relate to the artistic faculty or process, some to the psychology of audiences, some to the social and political functions of art, some to the nature of what is imitated, and so forth; while Aristotle can handle such questions, it cannot be under poetic science, but under some other science or faculty. We can grasp something of these limitations, I think, by reflecting on a single point which I do not remember anyone ever to have made about the *Poetics:* that while the center of everything here is imitation, Aristotle in fact never tells us how to imitate; never tells us how to make likenesses of this or that action, this or that character. He tells us that characters must be likenesses, but never how to give them likeness—as he tells us that actions must be necessary or probable, but not how to make them necessary or probable. In fact he presupposes all such things, as he does the natural capacity, skill, and knowledge of the artist, and they do not enter into the art of poetics as he conceives it, although inevitably they must go into the making of any poem. In the *Poetics* he is concerned only with the nature of the forms at which the artist must aim and the causes of success and failure in terms of these. The treatise is not a treatise of the whole poetic art or craft, but of as much of it as can be scientific knowledge of a kind; indeed, it is only the beginnings and principles even of poetic science, for it must be extended to keep commensurate with the generation and development of new forms. To sum up on this point: from the modern point of view the primary limitation is the scope itself of the *Poetics;* and to see that, you have only to look at the first and last paragraphs of the work, in which Aristotle respectively states and restates his program of problems, and ask yourselves whether these questions exhaust all the possible questions of art.

As for the kind of limitation arising from Aristotle's general method, that is, that of his philosophy itself: I mean by this that he is limited, precisely as every philosopher is limited, by the questions which he raises, by the kind of solution he requires for them, and by the devices of inquiry and proof which he employs; and since, as I have already suggested, such limitations are necessarily inherent in any single philosophy, it is our part to be aware of the limitations and of the powers of any one system. This is a view of which I cannot attempt in a moment or two to persuade you; let me therefore make a few large statements, more in illustration of my meaning than anything else.

Let me say that by this second half of the twentieth century I think that we should have learned a few things about philosophy, and about criticism too, since that is also philosophy. We should have learned, for instance, that every philosophy is limited by the problems which it raises and that every philosophic problem is limited by the terms in which it is couched. We should have learned, after all the labors of logicians, that there are many different ways of making propositions and that there are many senses of the terms "truth" and "falsity." We should have learned, after the many kinds of proofs and demonstrations offered to us, that there *are* many kinds, that there are many kinds of valid logics as there are many valid geometries and algebras; and we should be wise enough to conclude that perhaps there are many valid—I say, "valid"—philosophies. We should be too wise to accept any one philosophy as exhausting the whole of truth, and too wise to conclude that therefore every philosophy is false or that we must make a patchwork of philosophies without consideration of the diverse methods which they entail. We should, in short, be wise enough to consider the diverse valid philosophies only as instruments, all with various powers and limitations, and valuable relatively to the kinds of questions to which they are directed.

The conception of mimetic poetry which underlies the *Poetics* is that in these arts the center and principle of all is human beings doing and experiencing things which are humanly interesting and affecting. For Aristotle that humanity is prime: that happiness or misery, that activity serious or laughable, every other part of the poem must serve so as to set it before us as powerfully and vividly as possible; and every part must be as beautiful in itself as it can be consistently with the whole.

The Poetic Method of Aristotle

Insofar as they permit of scientific treatment, questions proper to the synthesis of such objects are the whole concern of the *Poetics;* as new forms of mimetic art emerge, the theory can be extended to cover them as well—provided that the extension is by one who has sufficient knowledge of and skill in Aristotle's method. In this sense Aristotle can be said to have developed not only a permanently true but also an indefinitely operable poetic method. But we cannot legitimately expect it to solve all problems that might be raised concerning all forms of art; especially not when the questions posed, the answers demanded, and the method postulated are all of an order alien to Aristotle's own.

XIII

BERNARD WEINBERG

From Aristotle to Pseudo-Aristotle

One of the main problems of the Renaissance was the discovery and interpretation of the texts of classical antiquity. In the restricted domain of literary theory, the point of concentration of the problem was the text of Aristotle's *Poetics*. I do not mean that this was the only text expounded, commented on, and argued by the humanists. But Horace's *Ars poetica*, known throughout the Middle Ages, continued to be read essentially as before; what was new in its exegesis was precisely its comparison with the *Poetics*. And Plato's dicta on poetry, commonplace since the fifteenth century, provided for the sixteenth century primarily points of contrast with Aristotle on such issues as the nature of imitation, the divine inspiration of poets, and the moral utility of the literary genres. Longinus attracted little attention. Demetrius became a part of the current of rhetorical (rather than of poetic) discussion.[1] But Aristotle's *Poetics*, beginning in 1548, afforded the center of theoretical activity for several centuries to come.

Before 1498, when Giorgio Valla published his Latin translation, the text of the *Poetics* was practically unknown. The few traces during the Middle Ages,[2] the paraphrase of Averroës,[3] the mention in the letters and treatises of the early humanists, do not really constitute a "knowledge" of the text. Literary discussion and theorizing continued, through these centuries, independently of the *Poetics*, which was known only to a few

Reprinted from Comparative Literature, V (Spring, 1953), pp. 97–104, by permission of the author and the editor. Copyright 1953 by *Comparative Literature*.

[1] See my "Translations and Commentaries of Longinus, *On the Sublime*, to 1600: A Bibliography," *Modern Philology*, XLVII (1950), 145–151, and the companion article on Demetrius, *Philological Quarterly*, XXX (1951), 353–380.

[2] E.g., the partial translation of the *Poetics* into Latin in the Eton College manuscript.

[3] First published in 1481; see Cooper and Gudeman, *A Bibliography of the Poetics of Aristotle* (New Haven, 1928), item 108.

scholars. This was still true, as a matter of fact, until around 1548, in spite of the publication in 1508 of the Greek text and in spite of an increasing number of passing allusions.[4] For example, in Trissino's *Poetica* (Books I to IV), published in 1529,[5] there is only a brief mention of the *Poetics;* but his fifth and sixth books, published posthumously in 1562,[6] lean so heavily upon Aristotle that at times they are merely a translation of the *Poetics.* Trissino died in 1550; between the two parts of his work had appeared Robortello's commentary of 1548, which really marks the beginning of the great influence of Aristotle's text in Europe.

I propose to trace briefly here what happened to Aristotle's theory, beginning in Italy in 1548 and ending in France with the neoclassical theory of the late seventeenth and early eighteenth centuries. Such a narrative has a beginning and ending which are determined not so much by the dates involved as by the nature of the development—a constant change, in a single main direction, of the conception and interpretation of the document. If at the beginning we have the text of Aristotle relatively unencumbered by interpretations, at the end, with the French theorists, we have something only vaguely resembling that text—at the beginning, the theory of Aristotle, at the end that of his latter-day interpreters, the pseudo-Aristotelean theorists of the modern period. If we are to discover by what steps the change took place, we must first seek a statement of the two theories of poetry which constitute the extreme terms of the evolution.

Let us state the contrast briefly thus: Aristotle's *Poetics* is a work which concentrates its attention on the poem itself and asks primarily this question: By what means can a poem of a given kind be made as beautiful as possible, so that it will produce the proper artistic effect? Each part of the answer concerns some part of the poem and proposes a means for integrating that part completely into the total structure of the poem. Since the "proper artistic effect" is to be produced upon a reader or a spectator, Aristotle constantly gives consideration to the relationship between the poem and its audience; but the problem is always to know what characteristics of the poem

[4] *Ibid.*, items 1, 405–18.

[5] *La Poetica di M. Giovan Giorgio Trissino* (Vicenza, 1529).

[6] *La Quinta e la Sesta Divisione della Poetica* (Venetia, 1562).

will produce the desired effect upon an unspecified, general audience, rather than how the specific demands of a minutely characterized audience may be met. In the neoclassical French doctrine (if one may generalize in a single statement for a large number of theorists) the procedure is reversed. One begins with a tight and complete conception of the audience—for Boileau, the French "honnête homme" of Paris or the court in 1674. One asks how this audience feels, what are its tastes and prejudices; one decides the kind of reaction, whether of pleasure or utility, that one wishes to create in this audience. Then, working backwards from the audience to the poem, one inserts into the poem the appropriate parts for "pleasing" the audience or exerting upon it a moral influence. The poem may thus become a collection of disparate parts, since there is no guarantee that the needs or the demands of the audience will have any harmonious interrelationship.

How did these theorists arrive at this doctrine, and how could they possibly conceive of it as being Aristotelean? For the first step, we must go back of the date 1498 to the early Renaissance tradition of textual interpretation, perhaps I should say "habit" of textual interpretation. For it was habitual among the commentators and the scholiasts of this early period to center their erudition and their labor about the isolated pieces or lines or passages of a text. Suppose that the text is Horace. The scholar of the fifteenth century will take the text line for line and embroider around it all that his learning can supply in the way of linguistic illumination, of parallel passages, of examples from ancient or modern literatures. He will tell us, apropos of the phrase "ut pictura poesis," how the two arts are alike, who else compared them, the grammatical implications of the construction, how previous critics had interpreted it.[7] This procedure—which we may call one of fragmentation—will be followed for the whole of the text. Nowhere will there be any effort to state the meaning of the text as a whole. The question is not even raised. Is this an art of poetry in which the activity of the poet is foremost, or in which moral considerations dictate poetic forms, or in which the relationship of poetry to the objects imitated is discussed? The commentator does not show

[7] See, e.g., Q. Horatij Flacci poemata: cum commentarijs eruditissimorum grammaticorum reconditissimis: Antonii Mancinelli, Jodoci Badij Ascensii & Ioannis Britannici . . . (Milan, 1518), fols. cxxxvii–cxxxviii.

any awareness of the existence of these questions. There is no synthesis to correct the fragmentation, no philosophical reading of the text.

In the second place, and as a corollary to the first step, for those who use this method all statements in all texts are of an equal value. Since each one is in a sense torn from its context, it loses its status as a first principle, or as an intermediary statement, or as the final conclusion of a long process of deductive reasoning. The structure of a given document disappears; the form of the forest is lost and only isolated trees remain for contemplation. This is perhaps the most striking characteristic of the commentators of the period; they see no text as a whole, they have no notion of the vast differences among various methods of philosophical organization and exposition. It becomes possible, for example, to wrest a single statement from the *Republic* of Plato and discuss it in comparison with a single statement taken from Aristotle's *Politics*,[8] paying no attention to the fact that the two treatises have different points of departure, proceed by a different method of argumentation, produce different conclusions. Nor is it even necessary that the two works be of the same kind; a statement from a political tract may be perfectly coequal with one drawn from an art of poetry, and the fact that they belong to different arts or different disciplines is unimportant.

It was into such a tradition of fragmentation and of methodological insouciance that the *Poetics* of Aristotle was projected in 1498 and in 1508; and it was in the light of the same tradition that Robortello published the first great commentary on the text in 1548.[9] Robortello does indeed make an effort to see the text of the *Poetics* as a whole; he points out how one argument follows another, what the general sequence of the ideas is, where the transitions occur. But the sequence is not the same as structure, and he is no better than his predecessors in the handling of the ideas. Thus he finds numerous points of contact between Horace and Aristotle, and interprets passages from the *Poetics* as if they came from the *Ars poetica*. And, especially, he relates the text to the large number of rhetorical treatises

[8] Compare, in 1582, the Victorius commentary in *Aristotelis Politicorum Libri Octo* (Basel, 1582), *passim*.

[9] See my "Robortello on the *Poetics*, 1548," in *Critics and Criticism: Ancient and Modern*, ed. R. S. Crane (Chicago, 1952), pp. 319–348.

which had long been the subject of study and elucidation. Both in Horace and in these rhetorics Robortello was in the presence of documents oriented, so to speak, towards the audience—Horace with his concern for the preferences of the Roman gentleman and his desire to please and instruct men of his own time at certain social levels, the rhetorics with their proper end of persuading a specific audience to a specific kind of action. It is not surprising then that this first commentary on the *Poetics* should also be a first step in the direction of a pseudo-Aristotelean theory in which the audience supplies all the criteria and determines the content and form of the poem.

I should hasten to say that Robortello is discreet in his proposals; but there is no doubt about the general tendency. He sees poetry as having two ends, the pleasure and the instruction of the audience (cf. Horace), and he sees this instruction as consisting in the moral betterment of the audience through examples, through striking demonstrations, through the exhortations of innumerable *sententiae*. Pleasure is sometimes an independent end, sometimes a servant of utility. But everywhere separate parts of the poem produce separate effects and serve separate ends; Aristotle's conception of the poem as a totality producing a total artistic impression has already been lost. As a consequence—or as a corollary—the principles of internal organization of the poem, Aristotle's necessity and probability, are transmuted into principles for relating the poem to nature and to the beliefs of the audience. In this way the requirement of "credibility" becomes a dominating consideration for Robortello. The question is no longer: "How is such or such a part integrated into the artistic structure of the poem?" but rather "Will the audience believe that such or such an action or character is true?" This shift is entirely consistent with the general movement away from the poem and towards the demands or the expectations of the audience.

This general movement reaches a kind of culmination, for sixteenth-century Italy, in the commentary of Castelvetro on the *Poetics* (1570).[10] In Castelvetro, the audience is not only the chief consideration, but the character of the audience itself is carefully restricted and described. Robortello had been satisfied with a fairly vague indication of the nature of his audience,

---

[10] See my "Castelvetro's Theory of Poetics," *ibid.*, pp. 349–371.

saying that it was composed of educated and uneducated elements, that the latter were in need of moral instruction, that this instruction could best be achieved through a pleasure composed of admiration and the marvelous. Castelvetro changes the point of view considerably. For him the audience is the low populace exclusively—the "rozza moltitudine"—which has no knowledge, no memory, no imagination, no need or capacity for moral improvement. As a consequence, the only end with respect to this audience is pleasure, the kind of pleasure which comes from the illusion that what one sees is true, although it is extraordinary and marvelous. A poem becomes a kind of history, decorated by unusual episodes, made to order to please the ignorant crowd. Since the crowd has no imagination, it cannot believe that the action takes place elsewhere than on the stage immediately visible (which cannot represent more than one locality) nor that it occupies a time greater than that of the actual representation, which is itself limited by the physical capacities of the audience. Hence the so-called unities of place and of time. Moreover, since space and time are thus limited, the action represented will have to be equally restricted. In this way Castelvetro derives the unity of action—the only one recognized by Aristotle—as an auxiliary of the other two, and as a final consequence of the audience's short imagination. Aesthetic preoccupations have disappeared, and their place has been taken by rhetorical and physical concerns of the lowest order.

Robortello and Castelvetro may serve as epitomes of the development in Italy. Many other documents could be called upon to supply the detail of changes and variants.

When we move on to seventeenth-century France, we find that the same tendencies continue, but that there are several new developments. The point of departure is Castelvetro, but he is made to serve a society and a literary tradition of a distinctly different order. We may use as examples here, for the period around 1637, the remarks of Scudéry and Chapelain on Corneille's *Cid*.[11] In these two texts, what are the main points of discussion? First, moral considerations: Is it proper for Chimène to consent to a marriage with her father's murderer?

[11] Corneille, *Oeuvres complètes*, ed. C. Marty-Laveaux, Vol. XII (Paris, 1862).

Second, questions of truth and probability: Would a Spanish nobleman like Don Diègue have so many men at his command? Would the port of Seville be left unguarded in times of war? Third, matters of decorum: Is it acceptable for a king to play a joke? Fourth, the handling of the unities: Can all these events really have taken place within twenty-four hours? I abbreviate and simplify. It is significant that, although there are some artistic problems raised—such as the usefulness of the role of the Infanta—most of the discussion centers about the audience. But the audience has changed. It has no more imagination than its Italian counterpart; but it has, on the one hand, a fixed and severe moral code from which it admits no departure and, on the other hand, a fund of knowledge and general notions which must not be violated by the poet. It is already a superior audience to that of Castelvetro.

In Corneille's *Discours sur la poésie dramatique* of 1660[12] we find once again continuation of Castelvetro along with notable reversals—continuation in the sense that the audience still supplies most of the criteria and most of the "rules," reversal insofar as the end has changed. Corneille specifically seeks utility in dramatic poetry; or, rather, he seeks various kinds of utility in the different parts of a single poem. So far has he removed his point of view from that of Aristotle that for each of Aristotle's qualitative parts—plot, character, thought, and diction—he finds a separate utility, independent of the others and achieving a separate moral effect upon the audience. The poem becomes an instrument of moral edification in which pleasurable elements are ancillary to the utilitarian ends. The audience remains that of Corneille's own commentators, one which has little in common with the crude masses of Castelvetro.

Boileau, in 1674,[13] in a way returns to the position of the early sixteenth-century critics, since he proposes the Horatian *utile dulci* as the end of poetry. But he goes beyond his immediate predecessors in the restriction of the audience to a very select group of the "upper classes." He has only contempt for the idlers of the Pont-Neuf and for the literary forms susceptible of pleasing them. He disdains the Italians and the Spaniards and the French provincials—all peoples and all classes who do not

[12] *Ibid.*, Vol. I (1862).
[13] In the *Art poétique;* see *Oeuvres complètes*, ed. Ch. Gidel, Vol. II (Paris, 1872).

belong to "the court and the town" of his own day. Boileau's audience not only has fixed moral values, as did that of Corneille, but it also possesses a vast store of knowledge and of expectations which must be respected; it knows thoroughly the rules of the poetic art, has absolute ideas about decorum and behavior, is possessed of solid historical notions. It has, in addition, a refined taste which would reject excess of any kind. Obviously, a poet writing for such an audience as this will have other preoccupations than those of Castelvetro's poet. He will need to write up to a refined audience rather than down to a vulgar one, and will have to provide utility as well as pleasure. But both poets will take as their point of departure the conception of the particularized audience and will strive to achieve ends specifically related to this audience. Thus both are descendants of Robortello's poet, and follow a method diametrically opposed to that of Aristotle.

The final step in this evolution consists in the replacing of the refined and restricted audience of Boileau by the "man of taste" of the late seventeenth and early eighteenth centuries. In such theories as those of Batteux[14] even the rules disappear, and the poet has recourse only to his own taste for the discovery of means to please his singular audience. All utilitarian aims once again disappear, and the only remaining end is that of a highly sophisticated pleasure on the part of a highly cultivated individual. In a sense, this step is not only the end of the Aristotelean tradition but also the beginning of the Longinian mode. The pseudo-Aristoteleans, for whom utility or pleasure (or both) was achieved by the observance of set rules, give way to the Longinians, for whom the creation of the poet and the contemplation of the reader are matters of a private sensitivity which, for both, has a common meeting place in the masterpieces of the past.

It should not be forgotten that, throughout the long evolution that I have sketched so summarily, the theorists thought of themselves as Aristoteleans and of their theories as going back to the authority of Aristotle. Rarely did they openly dissent (cf. Scaliger[15] and at times Castelvetro), never did they realize that their ideas would be completely unacceptable to a sound Aristotelean. Their failure to realize this may be ascribed to

[14] Abbé Batteux, *Les Beaux Arts réduits à un meme principe* (Paris, 1746).

[15] J.-C. Scaliger, *Poetices* (Lyon, 1561); cf. my "Scaliger versus Aristotle on Poetics," *Modern Philology*, XXXIX (1942), 337–360.

several errors on their part. First, they came to the text of Aristotle with habits of textual interpretation, habits of fragmentation and methodological anarchy, which made it impossible for them to understand this closely constructed and tightly argued document. Second, they read the *Poetics* in the light of a rhetorical tradition which reduced all aspects of literary documents to considerations stemming from the audience. Third, they could not dissociate from their thinking about poetic matters the numerous details of Horace's *Ars poetica*, which they had long known, and they insisted on reading Aristotle as if he were a kind of Ur-Horace. And finally, they tried to "modernize" Aristotle, to adapt him to their own times and their own peoples, in a manner scarcely authorized by the Aristotelean text. The result was one of the strangest misunderstandings of a basic text in the history of ideas, and the formation of that very curious complex of notions which we call the neoclassical doctrine. Need I add that the ultimate result has been some equally astonishing thinking about poetic matters on our own part? We need not look very deeply within our own habits of literary discussion to discover the last influences of these sixteenth-century Italian and seventeenth-century French pseudo-Aristoteleans.

XIV

RICHARD McKEON

Rhetoric and Poetic in the Philosophy of Aristotle

I

Of all the works of Aristotle, the *Rhetoric* and the *Poetics* have been most directly and most persistently influential on modern thought. Certain of his logical doctrines, or at least the devices and principles formulated in his logic, have had a longer continuous history of commentary and discussion; and the spectacular revolution worked in philosophic thought and expression during the thirteenth century under the influence of his newly translated works lent verisimilitude to the later criticism that the Middle Ages had been subjugated to the physics and metaphysics, the ethics and politics of Aristotle. Yet his theories and technical terms contributed as much to the revolt against scholasticism as they did to medieval "Aristotelianism," for the doctrines developed in commentaries on Aristotle and the tenets attributed to him in criticism or defense, were at many points distant from the genius of the Aristotelian philosophy.

The revolt against Aristotelianism was accomplished in each field by use of Aristotelian doctrines, often applied as heterogeneously as the theories and terms they replaced. Aristotle was at meticulous pains to distinguish his use of "forms" from the Platonic and to trace the errors which result in all fields of knowledge from the conception that the forms are "separated." Hellenistic commentators ignored these refinements and treated the Aristotelian philosophy as a Platonism; Cicero accepted this interpretation without comment and made it available to the Western Latin tradition; Augustine gave Christian theology a Platonic formulation into which the interpretation of Aristotle was assimilated; many of the Greek commentators on the Aris-

This essay has been written at the editor's invitation, for inclusion in the present volume.

totelian works were Neo-Platonic in their philosophical orien-
tation. Aristotle's works were unknown in the West, except for
a portion of the *Organon* fixed by Boethius in a context
strongly influenced by Porphyry, Cicero, and Themistius. The
translation of Aristotle's works, beginning in the twelfth century, set problems of interpretation and speculation which were
worked out in a long series of debates, centering on logic in the
twelfth century, on metaphysics and the physical sciences,
including biology, in the thirteenth century, on ethics and
politics in the fourteenth century, until the *Rhetoric* and the
Poetics eventually supplied in the Renaissance not only materials and subject for a doctrinal battle as bitter and as widespread
as any medieval dispute, but also instruments by which to
reform suspected doctrines, branded as Aristotelian, in all the
previous subjects of inquiry.

The influence of Aristotle is difficult to trace in any of the
fields of philosophy in which his inspiration is acknowledged or
opposed. The enthusiastic reformulation of what he thought
and the construction of what he should have said in exposition
of what he thought frequently carry the defense of his doctrines far from the evidence of his text and even into contradiction of his statements, while his distinctions and analyses
sometimes continue influential, though unrecognized and unsus-
pected, in regions and inquiries other than those in which he
first made them. Even those medieval philosophers who professed the greatest admiration for Aristotle were eloquent in
declaring their recognition of his human susceptibility to error.
Since they professed to follow his doctrines only when they
were convinced of their truth and to modify them freely when
they found them erroneous or incomplete, and since the scope
of his discovered "errors" tended to increase during centuries
following the translation of his works into Latin, the numerous
commentaries and questions on Aristotle's scientific and logical
treatises, on his *Metaphysics, Politics* and *Ethics* became more
and more what they had been to some extent from the first,
vehicles by which to express philosophic differences rather than
exegetical and philological exercises.

All doctrines and attitudes, therefore, even those which
Aristotle had attacked and, what were in many instances the
same, those revised or renewed philosophic methods which
were set in operation against his position, were expressed in his

terminology. The basic problems disputed and the fundamental emphases were often points on which Aristotle had been silent or brief, and with the progress of discussion and attack, the doctrines which passed for Aristotelian grew increasingly difficult to find in the works of Aristotle. The logic, which had been made the subject during the Middle Ages of metaphysical dispute concerning the status of universals, was in the sixteenth century to be criticized as concerned with purely verbal manipulations unsuited to the nature of things and unrelated to the processes of thought, and the physics, which had been a source of theory and suggestion concerning the whole scope of the physical world was at last to be branded a remote exploration for occult qualities; in this eclipse of logic and scientific method, the devices of rhetoric were used to increase the cogency of proof, to broaden the scope of inquiry, and to institute a method of discovery. Cicero had pointed out that Aristotle's logic treated both discovery and proof, unlike the Stoic logic which was confined to proof. Medieval commentators on the logic, once the *Topics* was available in translation, recognized that the method of discovery is dialectic. The increasing influence of Plato and Cicero in the transition to the Renaissance assimilated the Aristotelian method of dialectic to the Platonic dialectic of discovery and the Ciceronian rhetoric of discovery. The merging of logic and dialectic and of dialectic and rhetoric produced from historical confusions influential insights in Rudolph Agricola's *De Inventione Dialectica*, in Peter Ramus' works on logic, dialectic, and rhetoric, and in Francis Bacon's use of "proper places" on the analogy of the "common places" of rhetoric to develop the inductive method of the *Novum Organum*.

When the use of logic and dialectic for the interpretation of Scripture and the systematization of theological doctrine was thought inadequate and inappropriate to the document and the truth it expressed, the Old and New Testaments were treated as works of art; and Moses and Paul emerged as poets. Peter Abailard had argued that the method of rhetoric was essential for the proper interpretation of the Bible, and the enlarged method of dialectic can be detected in the use of "topics" in their dialectical rather than rhetorical sense, and in a manner influenced by the Platonic dialectic, in works like Melchior Cano's *De Locis Theologicis* and Philip Melancthon's *Loci*

Communes. Pico della Mirandola based his interpretation of Genesis in the *Heptaplus* on the understanding of Moses as the poet, as the "Idea" of the writer, the exemplar of the prophet, and Erasmus invited John Colet to study Moses and Isaiah as he had studied Paul. The "poetic" interpretation of Scripture, however, used a poetic method borrowed from rhetoric, and the topics had been applied not only to science, theology, law, and political science, but to poetry and literary criticism in works like Andrea Giglio da Fabriano's *Topica Poetica.* Metaphysics was first adulterated with logic and devoted to the discussion of universals and categories, and later analogized to politics, since rational principles and natural laws govern the universe much as an intelligent ruler governs his subjects; when the resultant formulations of problems seemed lost in subtleties that exceeded human powers and ingenuity, questions of being and knowing were treated with a cautious skepticism interrupted by equally cautious analogies to acting, or making, or ruling, and politics and ethics in turn were made realistic and practical by use of the relativistic devices of rhetorical persuasion to maniupulate means without responsibility concerning ends. Mario Nizolius, in his *De Veris Principiis et Vera Ratione Philosophandi contra Pseudophilosophos,* finds the truths by which to combat pseudophilosophers in the principles of grammar and rhetoric, and the politics of Machiavelli and Hobbes is developed by a method which has been influenced by the devices of rhetoric.

The declining fortunes of Aristotle's doctrines coincided with the period of greatest concern to translate his writings precisely, to paraphrase his works, and to determine by philological inquiry the meaning of what he had said. Even the critics of Aristotle are inclined to soften their strictures of his doctrines when he treats problems that parallel their own interests. Rhetoric, in the terms which Aristotle had used, but in an interpretation that owed much to Cicero and Quintilian, became in the Renaissance a discipline applicable to literature, to thought, and to life. It supplied the means by which to interpret poets, the criteria to regulate demonstration, and the technique for scientific inquiry and discovery, political control, and practical application; even as late as the seventeenth century Hobbes, who had little favorable to say about Aristotle's philosophy, thought his *Rhetoric* worth the labor of paraphrase, while he found use in his political philosophy, as Machiavelli had before him, for the distinctions of forensic oratory. The *Poetics* of Aristotle, bolstered in like fashion by reminiscences of Cicero and Horace, was erected into a standard of taste, and even of morality, in which the artist competed with the statesman and philosopher. Rhetoric, which for Aristotle had a limited function, inadequate for the purposes of scientific demonstration and inappropriate as a substitute for politics, was made again to undertake the diversified tasks Roman rhetoricians had set it of proving, instructing, and pleasing, while poetic, which Aristotle seems to have conceived as an inductive study of works of art, was made to yield rules to guide the making of art. The two disciplines tended to merge, moreover, and the familiar analogies, drawn from one or the other—which operated to the discredit or distortion of other portions of the Aristotelian philosophy—served to increase the reputation of their use and value, broadening both until the rules of rhetoric applied to all knowledge and poetic embraced all the works of nature and of man.[1] The grounds in the works of Aristotle which permitted these analogies, at once seminal in the reputation and interpretation of Aristotle, isolate for later students the minimum requirements for the understanding of Aristotle's work and suggest, in general, disquieting lessons concerning the influence of philosophic speculations.

Even the superficial differences between Aristotle's development of rhetoric and poetic and his conception of the other sciences which constitute his philosophy indicate both distinctions which made them independent and analogies which explain their numerous reductions to each other and to other sciences without the necessity of choosing between the alternatives of convicting Aristotle of simple inconsistencies or making the influence of his doctrine a blank mystery. Aristotle reports that reflection on philosophic method and the application of such considerations of method to the treatment of moral ques-

[1] For a succinct statement of some of the complex interrelations set up and exploited in rhetoric, poetic, and related disciplines, cf. J. E. Spingarn, *A History of Literary Criticism in the Renaissance* (New York, 1912), esp. pp. 311 ff. Cf. also Marvin T. Herrick, *The Fusion of Horatian and Aristotelian Literary Criticism* ("Illinois Studies in Language and Literature," Vol. XXXII, No. 1 [Urbana, Ill., 1946]); Bernard Weinberg, *A History of Literary Criticism in the Italian Renaissance*, (2 vols.; Chicago: University of Chicago Press, 1961), especially Part I, chap. iv for the confusion of Horace with Aristotle.

tions were no older than the inquiries of Socrates, but he makes no mention of the pioneer work of Socrates in analyzing rhetoric and the arts. On the contrary, he refers to no previous philosophic inquiries into that subject in the *Rhetoric*, although he does criticize the writers of handbooks for neglecting to treat of arguments and persuasions, thereby missing the essentials of the art;[2] and one might have the impression from his *Poetics* that no previous philosopher had treated the nature and influence of poetry. We know that among his works, now lost, was a *Collection of Handbooks*,[3] in which he seems to have traced the history of rhetoric and to have summarized the characteristics of rhetorical systems. Since that collection doubtless served, like the outlines of the doctrines of his predecessors which are prefaced to so many of his works, as a preliminary sketch of the subject and as indication of problems and plausible speculations, and since he often comments on and occasionally commends scientific doctrines which were not in his opinion developed according to a scientific theory, his effort in collecting and schematizing the "arts" of rhetoric does not stand in contradiction to his contention that none of his predecessors treated rhetoric as an art.

Aristotle's historical interests in poetry seem to have followed the analogy of his historical interests in politics and to have been concerned rather more with the history of the subject of inquiry than with previous theories, for his lost work *On Poets*[4] was probably a fuller account of the history of literature similar to that adumbrated in the early chapters of the *Poetics*. Aristotle had not grown forgetful of Socrates and Plato, or of the Sophists against whom Socrates so frequently developed arguments bearing on art and rhetoric and their relation to virtue and knowledge, for the "Socratic Dialogue" is instanced with the mime as an art-form in the *Poetics*,[5] and both Socrates

---

[2] *Rhetoric* i. 1. 1354ª11: "Now the framers of the current treatises on rhetoric [τὰς τέχνας τῶν λόγων] have constructed but a small part of that art. The modes of persuasion [αἱ πίστεις] are the only properly technical parts of the art; everything else is merely accessory. These writers, however, say nothing about enthymemes, which are the body of persuasion, but deal for the most part with things which are outside the subject."

[3] Diogenes Laertius, v. 24; Cicero, *De Inventione* ii. 2. 6.; *De Oratore* ii. 38. 160.; *Brutus* 12. 46. Cf. E. M. Cope, *An Introduction to Aristotle's Rhetoric* (London, 1867), pp. 50 ff.

[4] Diogenes Laertius v. 22.   [5] 1. 1447ᵇ 11.

and Plato are quoted for examples and precepts of rhetoric.[6] His silence concerning the treatment of rhetoric and poetry in Plato's dialogues, notwithstanding his tendency to criticize Plato on all other subjects, is to be taken rather as a sign that he thought his own departure from previous methods to have been radical to the point of making the example of his predecessors irrelevant to the problems of poetic and rhetoric as he conceived them. According to his organization of philosophy he was able to find many early examples of metaphysical and physical doctrines; speculation on politics and ethics did not, prior to the time of Socrates, take such form as to permit extensive citation or require systematic refutation; and the contemporary interest in philosophic method had yielded only a single relatively undifferentiated dialectical method. In his view, therefore, his own logic had first differentiated scientific demonstration from dialectic and, for that very reason, had made possible for the first time a consideration of the separate methods and functions of art and rhetoric and their relation to the methods of history, sophistic and dialectic.

Socrates treats rhetoric by arguing, against the pretensions of orators in the *Phaedrus*, that the good rhetorician must also be a dialectician and, against the sophists in the *Gorgias*, that rhetoric is a sham art, or rather no art, but experience and use which are substituted for justice.[7] He frequently employs the example of artists and artisans in the arguments Plato records, usually running through a series of analogies such as would connect the poet in turn and in varying respects with the physician, the carpenter, the cobbler, and the shepherd, contrasting art with the irrational, the incalculable, the habitual, and the empirical, but requiring no fixed differences among the arts, nor even between the arts and the sciences. The judgment of poetry attributed to Socrates in the *Republic*, like the later Platonic judgment expressed in the *Laws* (if indeed such differentiation between the two positions is necessary), is based on consideration of educational, practical, and rhetorical effects, and it leads to moral disapproval and political censorship. Like the orator, the poet finds himself in competition with the dialectician and the legislator, and no method or accomplishment is disclosed in

[6] Cf. *Rhetoric* i. 9. 1367^{b}8; ii. 20. 1393^{b}4; 23. 1398^{a}24; iii. 14. 1415^{b}30; i. 15. 1376^{a}10; ii. 23. 1398^{a}15(?); iii. 4. 1406^{b}32, and *passim*.

[7] *Phaedrus* 265 D ff.; *Gorgias* 463 A ff., 501 A.

Plato's analyses of rhetoric or poetry that would seem to Aristotle to involve problems beyond those of dialectic and morals or to require new acknowledgments of Plato's originality or additional criticisms of his errors. Among the independent sciences instituted by Aristotle's philosophic method, on the other hand, rhetorical arguments could be considered as devices of persuasion apart from consideration of truth or falsity of conclusions, accurate or candid presentation of the character and predilections of the speaker, or preferable ends or desires of the auditor, and poetry could be considered in terms of the structure of the poem apart from its tendency to stimulate moral or immoral conduct or to produce pleasure or other passions. Such separate consideration of things or disciplines depends on a philosophic scheme in which related questions can be treated according to their proper principles in their appropriate sciences. As applied to the arts, the accomplishment of Aristotle's philosophic method was the separation of problems involved in the mode of existence of an object produced or of a productive power (which might properly be treated in physics and metaphysics) as well as problems involved in the effects of artificial objects or artistic efforts (as treated in psychology, morals, and politics) or in doctrinal cogency and emotional persuasiveness (as treated in logic and rhetoric) from problems which bear on the traits of an artistic construction consequent simply on its being a work of art. As applied to rhetorical persuasion, the same method permits the recognition that rhetoric is a counterpart, or offshoot, or subdivision of dialectic; that it borrows from sophistic; that it is derivative from ethics; and that it is a sham substitute for politics when it is not made a proper part of politics; and at the same time it permits the examination of the peculiar devices of persuasion apart from consideration of those relations and analogies.

II

To say that Aristotle thought the arts in general, as well as particular arts like rhetoric or poetry, medicine or strategy, to be independent kinds of activity susceptible of independent analysis and to involve kinds of knowledge independent of other arts and of other sciences, theoretic or practical, involves the statement of what might at first seem contradictory requirements. Such separate analysis and statement of the arts is possible only by explicit recognition of the complex interrelations of arts, and actions, and sciences, such that two or more arts may use independent techniques on identical materials to different ends or on different materials to comparable ends, or such that one art may be subordinate to the purposes of another (as military strategy is to statecraft) without compromise or adulteration of its proper purposes and criteria. Even more, art is to be contrasted to science only if the arts are recognized to be in a sense sciences and the sciences to be in a sense arts; practical sciences can be distinguished from productive sciences, and arts can be considered in terms of their functions and their products only if provision is made in another analysis for the fact that art has moral and political consequences and that political processes and moral actions are in their exercise themselves arts; and finally the opposition of art to nature envisages an art which is natural in that it proceeds from natural powers and operates on natural materials as well as a nature whose processes are comparable with those of art and whose products may be supplemented by art.

The distinctions depend on an overlapping classification, such as Aristotle frequently uses, in which the same situation, process, or entity is analyzed successively in terms of different applications of the causes and, in the respects isolated by successive analyses, is without ambiguity or contradiction defined differently and even subject to analysis in different sciences, as, for example, the passions are diversely conceived and used in psychology, ethics, and rhetoric. Aristotle's treatment of the arts is set in four progressively narrowing contexts: (1) they are particular instances of productive or poetic powers (δυνάμεις ποιητικαί) and share characteristics which are coextensive with nature, yet are contrasted to nature as a principle, (2) they are instances of the rational productive powers which are the sources of all human actions, practical and productive, and which as such are contrasted to irrational natural processes, and (3) they are conceived as restricted to those rational productive powers which result in some artificial product apart from the activity itself and are contrasted with moral and political activities. In most arts a further step is then possible in which (4) the particular art is analyzed in the specific subject matter and objects proper to it. The delimitation of the arts, in other words, like the definition of the virtues does not proceed by strict scientific definition through genus and proper differentia, but employs all four causes in progressive delimitation, and an art may

be considered for various purposes in its broader or narrower significations. The four conceptions of art (and the arts are still considered today in what might be viewed as the remnants of these
ways) in the order of their increasing particularity make use in
turn, (1) of the efficient cause, in the sense that art is conceived as a
"power" directed to ends comparable to and yet distinguishable
from natural powers and to that extent analyzable in common with
them by means of their ends, (2) of the formal cause, in the sense
that art is an "actuality" of the mind comparable to and yet distinguishable from other psychic habits and powers and to that
extent analyzable in common with them by means of the process of
their acquisition or the potentiality and matter actualized in them,
(3) of the final cause, in the sense that art is a preconceived purpose
and so comparable to and distinguishable from other stimulations
to action which partake of reason and to that extent analyzable in
common with them by the means they employ and the ends they
achieve, and (4) of the material cause, in the sense that each art is a
class of objects, comparable to and distinguishable from each
other, and so analyzable in common with other arts by the forms
suited to the materials in which they are embodied in the arts.
Some indication of the significance of this range of treatments to
which art is susceptible may be found in the fact that of the two
arts concerning which independent treatises of Aristotle have survived, one, i.e., rhetoric, is defined in the most general of the terms
applied to art as a "power," while the other, i.e., poetic, is defined
in the most particular of those terms as a composite whole (τὸ
σύνολον).[8]

I.

In its broadest context, as related to natural things and as an
efficient cause productive of change, art is at once (like science
and virtue, or in general like any action which participates in
reason, and, at the other extreme, like chance and fortune or in

[8] *Rhetoric* i. 2. 1355ᵇ26; *Poetics* 1. 1447ᵃ16. Differentiation of these levels of
analysis of art, which, it is hoped, are shown in the text which follows to have
been clearly formulated by Aristotle, has the further advantage of at once removing many of the ambiguities and simple confusions laid at the door of
Aristotle and disclosing the reasons why they seemed to his interpreters to be
confusions. Cf. E. M. Cope, *An Introduction to Aristotle's Rhetoric*, pp. 22–23:
"When it is said, as both Plato and Aristotle *do* say, that art implies a knowledge of causes, which as Aristotle tells us again and again is the characteristic
of science or ἐπιστήμη properly understood, it is plain that the distinction between τέχνη and ἐπιστήμη is lost sight of, a confusion, which as I have already
said is by no means uncommon with ancient Greek philosophers;" cf. also
p. 33.

general like any cause whose indefiniteness and multiplicity removes it from the scope of reason) a natural process and at the same time possessed of characteristics opposed to nature and to what naturally happens. The theoretic sciences treat of nature and are themselves constructions due to natural processes and tendencies; the end of science is knowledge of the universal, and yet knowledge and thought are themselves activities of the mind and so subject to scientific explanation.[9] Chance and fortune are irrational and indeterminate, yet they must be reckoned among the causes and as such be treated in the physical sciences.[10] Art is a principle of change like nature, and what is done by art might be accomplished by chance; at the same time art is a kind of knowledge concerned, like science, with the universals and causes, and science insofar as it engages in the construction of demonstrations and theories is a kind of art.

The relation between science and art is not simple but reflects the complexity of identities and differences found in nature and action or ultimately in the metaphysical distinction between actuality and power on which both relations are based. They are not univocal categories applied in the assemblage of genera of things; rather the distinction recurs anew and in numerous applications in the examination of all natural powers, reaching its greatest complexity in the two actualities, corresponding to the possession and the exercise of a power, necessary for the analysis of psychological functions.[11] "Power" in the narrow sense of "power to move or be moved" is grounded in the broader sense of "power to be,"[12] and the power of a thing is therefore relative on the one hand to the actuality or essence of a thing and on the other hand to its actions

---

[9] *Metaphysics* xii. 9. 1074^{b}38: "The answer is that in some cases the knowledge is the object. In the productive sciences (if we disregard the matter) the substance or essence is the object; but in the theoretic sciences the formula (λόγος) or the act of thinking is the object"; cf. *ibid*. 7. 1072^{b}20; and *De Anima* iii. 4. 429^{b}5 and 430^{a}2.

[10] *Physics* ii. 5. 197^{a}8: "It is necessary then that the causes of what comes to pass by fortune be indefinite. . . . To say that fortune is a thing contrary to formula [παράλογον] is correct, for 'formula' [λόγος] applies to things that are always thus or for the most part, whereas fortune applies to a third kind of occurrence. Hence since such causes are indefinite, fortune too is indefinite." Cf. *ibid*. 6. 198^{a}5.

[11] *De Anima* ii. 1. 412^{a}22.

[12] *Metaphysics* ix. 6. 1048^{a}25 ff.; 1. 1045^{b}32.

or motions. Scientific inquiry concerning natural things and natural processes takes account of power either as the sign of a nature or as the cause of an action or of effects external to the nature. On the one hand, physical science is an inquiry into the natures of things: natures, however, are defined by means of their parts or powers, and their powers in turn are known by means of their functions or objects. In this fashion, scientific inquiry into the nature and operations of the soul begins with the appropriate objects of psychic activities, the activities of the soul are determined and defined from their objects, the powers from their activities, until finally the definition or essence of the soul can be constructed by means of its powers (or, as Aristotle also designates them, its "parts"); thereafter inquiry proceeds to the examination of the powers and their activities. The term "power" in this sense is often conjoined with or even used as a synonym of such terms as "form" (μορφή), "species" (εἶδος), "definition" or "reason" (λόγος), or "nature" (φύσις).[13] On the other hand, the physical sciences are concerned with the interrelations of things and the exercise by one object of actions which have effects in other ob-

---

[13] Cf. *De Anima* i. 1. 402ᵇ9: "Further if there are not many souls, but many parts of one soul, which ought we to investigate first, the whole soul or its parts? It is also difficult to determine which of these parts are naturally distinct from one another, and whether the parts [τὰ μόρια] or their functions [τὰ ἔργα] should be investigated first, as, e.g. the process of thinking or the mind that thinks, the process of sensation or the sensitive power, and so on. If the investigation of the functions precedes that of the parts, the further question arises, whether we ought not first to investigate the correlative objects, as, e.g. the sensible object before the power of sense and the intelligible object before the power of the intellect." Cf. the more positive statement of the sequence of inquiry, *ibid.* ii. 4. 415ᵃ14. The use of "power" for or with terms signifying "form" may be illustrated by typical cases: *De Generatione et Corruptione* i. 5. 322ᵃ28: "This, the form [τὸ εἶδος] without matter, is a kind of power, such as a duct, in matter"; *Politics* vii. 1. 1323ᵇ33: "Thus the courage, justice, and wisdom of a state have the same power and form [μορφή] as the qualities which give the individual who possesses them the name of just, wise, or temperate"; *De Anima* ii. 12. 424ᵃ26: "The sense organ would be an extended magnitude, but neither being sensitive nor sense is a magnitude; they are rather a certain ratio [λόγος] and the power of the magnitude"; *De Generatione Animalium* ii. 1. 731ᵇ19: "That the male and the female are the principles of generation has been previously stated, as also what is their power and essence [ὁ λόγος τῆς οὐσίας]"; also *ibid.* 4. 738ᵇ22; *De Sensu* 3. 439ᵃ21: "But the 'translucent,' as we call it, is not something peculiar to air, or water, or any other of the bodies usually called translucent, but is a common nature [φύσις] and power"; *Politics* i. 4. 1254ᵃ13: "Hence we see what is the nature [φύσις] and power of a slave."

jects: the power of a thing is considered, then, not in terms of the nature of which it is a power but in terms of the change which its action causes other things to suffer, and so considered powers are contrasted to natures, since nature is a principle of change internal to the thing, while power is an external principle of change.[14] The arts are instances of such powers.[15]

It is possible, then, to reason from power either back to the nature of which the power is a part and a sign (and such inference would yield information relevant to its definition or essence) or outward to the action in which the power is actualized in external effects (and such inference would yield information concerning the relation between "agent" and "patient," between "making" and "suffering"). Since power involves something which is acted on as well as something which acts, and since action and passion, or making and suffering, usually occur respectively in different things or at least in distinguishable aspects of the same thing, the power of making (ποιεῖν) and suffering (πάσχειν), although one and single in itself, must be divided into two kinds, a "poetic power" (δύναμις ποιητική) in the agent and a "pathetic power" or power of suffering (δύναμις παθητική) in the patient;[16] and indeed that distinction between making and suffering is important enough to be constituted two of the categories in Aristotle's enumeration of ten.[17] In their first occurrences and primary meanings, therefore, "poetic" or productive (ποιητική) and "making" (ποιεῖν) apply to all processes of becoming which originate in an external principle as contrasted to "natural" processes which originate in principles internal to the thing changed. The contrast does not mean that "making" and "suffering" are unnatural processes (although they are often contrary to nature), but rather that, notwithstanding this contrast between making and nature, a poetic or productive power is itself a natural power, differing from nature not in independent fact but in manner and context of analysis and definition. All things that come into being, natures as well as artificial things, are "made," in this

---

[14] *Metaphysics* ix. 1. 1046ᵃ9: "But all powers that conform to the same type are principles, and are called powers in reference to one primary kind of power, which is the principle of change in another thing or in the thing itself *qua* other." *De Caelo* iii. 2. 301ᵇ17: ". . . 'nature' means a principle of movement in the subject itself, while 'power' is a principle of movement in something other than it or in itself *qua* other. . . ."

[15] *Metaphysics* v. 12. 1019ᵃ15; ix. 2. 1046ᵇ2.

[16] *Metaphysics* ix. 1. 1046ᵃ19; v. 15. 1021ᵃ14.

[17] *Categories* 4. 1ᵇ27; *Topics* i. 9. 103ᵇ23.

broadest sense, and the term extends to other changes as well, to all natural actions of one thing on another, physical, biological, psychological, and even intellectual. Things that are "made," therefore, include not only the "artificial things" made by the fine and practical arts and the natural substances made in physical and biological generation, but sense perceptions, phantasms, sensation itself, pleasure, madness, difficulties and problems, turns in the scale of life, the plots and arguments of tragedies, science, definition, syllogism, paralogism, demonstration, and all of the innumerable things subject to the influence of things other than themselves.[18]

Power as efficient cause and productive principle of motion supplies the broad genus which is narrowed to "art" by differentiating two kinds of "powers" and "makings," the rational and the irrational. The distinction between internal and external principles of change is made the differentiation between nature and art, in its broadest sense.[19] The arts are productive (ποιητικαί) powers which

[18] Cf. *De Sensu* 3. 440ᵃ17; *Metaphysics* xi. 6. 1063ᵇ4; *De Partibus Animalium* ii. 3. 650ᵇ4; *Nicomachean Ethics* vii. 6. 1147ᵇ24; 5. 1147ᵃ17; v. 14. 1137ᵇ11; i. 11. 1100ᵇ24; *Poetics* 5. 1449ᵇ8; *Rhetoric* i. 2. 1358ᵃ24; *Topics* ii. 2. 109ᵇ30; *Prior Analytics* i. 8. 30ᵃ10; 15. 34ᵇ9; 25. 42ᵃ22; 27. 43ᵃ24; 28. 44ᵇ26; 6. 28ᵃ23; *Topics* v. 2. 130ᵃ7; *Poetics* 16. 1455ᵃ16. Cf. *Politics* i. 9. 1258ᵃ6: "For, as their enjoyment is in excess, they seek an art of making [ποιητική] the excess of enjoyment; and if they are not able to supply their pleasures by the art of getting wealth, they try to do it through some other cause, using in turn every power [δύναμις] in a manner not in accordance with nature." *Rhetoric* i. 6. 1362ᵃ31: "Things are productive [ποιητικά] of other things in three ways: first, as being healthy produces health; second, as food produces health; and third, as exercise does—i.e. it produces [ποιεῖ] health usually."

[19] *De Partibus Animalium* i. 1. 641ᵇ10: "Moreover it is impossible that any abstraction can form a subject of natural science, since nature makes (ποιεῖ) all things for some end, for as art is in the case of artificial things, so in the case of things themselves there is manifestly some other principle and some cause of this sort, derived like the hot and the cold from the environing universe." *Metaphysics* xii. 3. 1070ᵃ7: "Now art is a principle of movement in something other than the thing moved, nature is a principle in the thing itself (for man begets man), and the other causes are privations of these two." *Ibid.* vii. 8. 1033ᵇ5: "It is clear then that the form also, or whatever we ought to call the shape of the sensible thing, is not generated, nor does generation relate to it, —that is, the essence is not generated, for it is this which is generated in something else by art or by nature or power. But we make (ποιεῖ) a bronze sphere to be. For we make it out of bronze and the sphere; we make the form in this particular matter, and this bronze sphere is." *De Generatione Animalium* ii. 1. 734ᵇ36: ". . . as is likewise the case in those things which are produced by art. Heat and cold make [ποιεῖ] the iron soft and hard, but the movement of tools makes the sword, this movement containing the principle of the art. For

are rational or sciences which are productive (ἐπιστῆμαι ποιητικαί); and art and nature differ, therefore, in the status of the form or reason which enters into their operation: in art it preexists in the mind of the artisan, in nature it is in the constitution alike of that which generates and that which is generated. Nature and natural powers differ from art in the fashion in which form enters into change, but since nature and art are principles of change, this formal difference constitutes a difference between them both as efficient causes or principles of change and as ends or final causes to which change is directed, for irrational powers can accomplish only a single end, while rational powers may be employed to effect either of contrary ends.[20] Since the distinction between art and nature is a distinction between rational and irrational, the same distinction is found between mind and nature and even between the powers of the soul itself. The soul, however, is itself a nature, and its powers should therefore be treated in terms of their functions as well as in terms of their susceptibility to reason. In the *De Anima*, inquiry into the nature and functions of the soul is pursued as part of physical science and the effort is expressly to arrive at "physical definitions";[21] two powers (δυνάμεις) are distinguished according to their characteristic work or function (ἔργον): judgment which is the work of thought and sense, and local motion which is originated by practical thought and appetite.[22] Considered in terms of principles of change and their ends the soul is constituted of natural powers or parts distinguishable from other powers by their ends. The powers of the soul, on the other hand, may be considered as directed to activity in accordance with virtue and rationality, and the classification of powers must then be reformulated, for morality

---

the art is the principle and form of the product, but existing in something else, whereas the movement of nature is in the thing itself, issuing from another nature which contains the form in actuality."

[20] *Metaphysics* ix. 2. 1046ᵃ36: "Since some such principles are present in inanimate things, and others in animate things and in the soul and in the rational [λόγον ἔχον] part of the soul, it is clear that some powers [δυνάμεις] will be non-rational [ἄλογοι], and some will be with reason [μετὰ λόγου]. Therefore all arts and productive sciences [αι ποιητικαὶ ἐπιστῆμαι] are powers, for they are principles of change in another thing or in the artist himself considered as other. And all those with reason are capable each of contrary effects, but one non-rational power is productive of one effect, as the hot is capable only of heating, but the medical art can produce both disease and health"; and *ibid.* 5. 1048ᵃ8. Cf. *De Interpretatione* 13. 22ᵇ36; *Nicomachean Ethics* v. 1. 1129ᵃ13.

[21] *De Anima* i. 1. 403ᵃ25 ff.
[22] *Ibid.* iii. 9. 432ᵃ15 and 10. 433ᵃ13.

and wisdom, though based on natural powers, are determined, not by nature, but by habit or the influence of reason. In the *Nicomachean Ethics*, therefore, the "parts," or "powers," or "natures" of the soul are distinguished into two kinds, one possessed of reason (τὸ λόγον ἔχον), the other irrational (ἄλογον), and both in turn are distinguished by the same criteria into two kinds: the irrational part into one which is purely irrational and one which, though irrational, is responsive to reason, and the rational part into one concerned with variable things and with the direction of the irrational part and one devoted to the contemplation of invariable things.[23] Art and nature are, as a consequence, associated in many likenesses, notwithstanding the differences in the way in which in the one form operates as knowledge from the operation of form in the other as substance or part of substance, and they are set in contrast on all their points of similarity to chance and fortune as causes of change.[24] Art and nature are both adaptations of means to ends in accordance with reason or formulae (λόγοι); they approximate comparable or identical ends by identical processes; art therefore imitates nature and may supplement or complete natural processes when they are imperfect; and finally the ends of both involve con-

---

[23] *Nicomachean Ethics* i. 13. 1102ᵃ27 and 1102ᵇ11 ff.; vi. 1. 1139ᵃ3. The three terms, "part," "power," and "nature" are used as synonyms in these pages (1102ᵇ4, 5, and 13), and it should be observed that the discussion is in terms of the virtues (ἀρεταί) or actuality (ἐνέργεια) of these powers, whereas in the *De Anima* the similar distinctions are made in terms of their ends (cf. iii. 10. 433ᵃ14).

[24] *Metaphysics* vii. 7. 1032ᵃ12: "Of things that come to be some come to be by nature, some by art, some by chance." *De Partibus Animalium* i. 1. 640ᵃ25: "For man is generated from man, and so the generation of the offspring is determined by the characteristics of the parent, as is similarly the case in things which seem to come about by chance and as is also in the case of the products of art. For some things brought about by chance are the same as those produced by art, as, e.g. health. However, a productive cause [τὸ ποιητικόν] similar to its product preexists in the case of art products, such a productive cause as the art of the statuary, for it does not produce by chance. Art indeed is the reason [λόγος] of the work [ἔργον] as it is without the matter, and the situation is much the same with things which take place by fortune, for fortune produces as art does." Thought often takes the place of art in association with nature in opposition to chance and fortune. Thus, *Physics* ii. 5. 196ᵇ21: "Events that are for the sake of something include whatever may be done as a result of thought and of nature"; *ibid.* 6. 198ᵃ5: "And since chance and fortune are causes of results such as might originate from mind or nature as cause, though in fact they are brought about by some accidental cause, and since nothing accidental is prior to what is *per se*, it is clear that no accidental cause can be prior to a cause *per se*. Chance and fortune, therefore, are posterior to mind and nature."

sideration not merely of powers to be actualized but also of goods and beauty in a fashion that brings to mind the close relation which Kant, more strikingly than most philosophers, discerned between the teleology of natural processes and the construction and perception of things of beauty.[25]

2.

Art in this broad sense, as productive or "poetic" science, is comparable with science in much the same fashion as it is compared with nature, for it is a kind of science, yet distinct from theoretic

[25] The causes, and especially the final cause, are seldom far to seek in Aristotle's analogies of art to nature. Thus, *Physics* ii. 8. 199[b]26: "It is absurd to suppose that there is no purpose because we do not observe the mover deliberating. Art, in fact, does not deliberate, and if the ship-building art were in the wood, it would produce the same results by nature. If, therefore, purpose is present in art, it is present also in nature. The best illustration is the doctor doctoring himself: nature is like that." *De Partibus Animalium* i. 1. 639[b]14: "That cause seems to be first which we call final, for it is the reason [λόγος], and the reason is the principle alike in works of art and in works of nature. . . . Now in works of nature the final cause and the beautiful [τὸ καλόν] are still more dominant than in works of art. . . . As with these productions of art, so also with the productions of nature." Since art is a rational power, these points of contrast between art and nature are complemented by comparisons of nature and thought. Cf. *Metaphysics* xi. 8. 1065[a]26: "The final cause is found in things that happen by nature or as a result of thought"; *De Caelo* ii. 9. 291[a]24: "It is as though nature had foreseen the result, that if the motion [sc. of the stars] were other than it is, nothing in our terrestrial region could be the same." *De Anima* ii. 4. 415[b]15: "And it is clear that the soul is the cause in the sense of the final cause. For just as mind acts [ποιεῖ] for the sake of something, so in the same way does nature, and this is its end." Specific analogies of nature to art or of art to nature and specifications of the operations of one by means of the other are frequent in the scientific writings of Aristotle: cf. *Physics* ii. 2. 194[a]21 ff.; *Meteorologica* iv. 12. 390[b]13; *De Partibus Animalium* ii. 9. 654[b]29; *De Generatione Animalium* ii. 6. 743[b]23; iii. 11. 762[a]16; iv. 6. 775[a]20; *Politics* vii. 14. 1333[a]21. This comparison is indicated frequently by the statement that nature operates like an intelligent artisan consistently with reason (εὐλόγως) in that nature chooses, or that nature itself is the end; cf. *Meteorologica* iv. 2. 379[b]25; *De Partibus Animalium* iii. 2. 663[a]32; 4. 665[b]20; iv. 10. 686[a]8; *De Generatione Animalium* i. 23. 731[a]24; ii. 4. 740[a]28; v. 2. 781[b]22. As final cause nature is best; cf. *Politics* i. 2. 1252[b]30: "And therefore since the first communities are natural, so also is every state, for it is the end of those communities, and the nature of a thing is its end. For what each thing is when fully developed, we call its nature, whether it be a man, a horse, or a family. Besides the final cause and end of a thing is best, and self-sufficiency is the end and best." For much the same reason nature is beautiful, as is apparent in the quotations above; cf. *De Partibus Animalium* i. 5. 645[a]4–16, esp. 22: ". . . for in all there is something natural and beautiful. Absence of the fortuitous and adaptation to an end are to be found in the works of nature in the highest degree, and the end constituted or generated by nature is a place of the beautiful."

science. Moreover, as the differentiation of the form of art from that of nature requires consideration of the efficient and final cause, so the formal comparison of art and science involves not only the efficient and final causes of art and science as forms of knowledge but their subject matter or material cause as well. Art is midway between experience and science: like science it is concerned with the universal, but unlike science it is knowledge of becoming rather than of being; it is directed to actions and productions and therefore like experience treats of individuals, although its speculation is of universals, for the artist, unlike the man of experience, knows not only what is the case, but why and the cause.[26] Notwithstanding their differences in both respects, the arts and the sciences are thus associated in their material causes (since they treat universals derived from experience) and their final causes (since all inquiries, arts, and sciences are directed to an end and a good), but in addition they are both accounted for by a single efficient cause, instruction and the use of pre-existent knowledge.[27] In this first

[26] The evolution and derivation of art and science from sense-perception, memory, and experience are identical; cf. *Posterior Analytics* ii. 19. 100[a]3: "So out of sense-perception comes to be what we call memory, and out of frequently repeated memories of the same thing develops experience; for memories many in number constitute a single experience. From experience again, or from every universal established in the soul, the one beside the many which is in all those things one and the same, arises the principle of art and science, of art if it is concerning becoming, of science if it is concerning being." *Metaphysics* i. 1. 980[b]28: "And from memory experience is produced in men; for many memories of the same thing produce the power of a single experience. And experience seems to be almost like science and art, but science and art come to men through experience; for 'experience made art,' as Polus says, and rightly, 'but inexperience luck.' And art arises when from many notions gained from experience one universal judgment concerning like things is produced. . . . For purposes of action experience does not seem to differ from art, and we even see men of experience succeeding more than those who have the rational principle [λόγος] without experience. The reason is that experience is knowledge of individuals, art of universals, and actions and generations are all concerned with individuals. . . . Yet we think that knowledge and understanding belong to art rather than experience, and we suppose artists to be wiser than men of experience, since wisdom in all cases depends rather on knowledge. But this is the case because the former know the cause, while the latter do not, for men of experience know that the thing is so, but do not know why, while the others know the why and the cause." Cf. *Prior Analytics* i. 30. 46[a]3 ff.; *Nicomachean Ethics* x. 10. 1180[b]13 ff.

[27] *Politics* iii. 12. 1282[b]14: "In all sciences and arts the end is a good . . ."; *ibid.* vii. 13. 1331[b]37: "In all arts and sciences both the ends and the means should be in our control"; *De Caelo* iii. 7. 306[a]14: ". . . as though some principles did not require to be criticized from their consequences and particularly

broad sense the "arts" include any inquiry into any subject, for the scientist is to be classified with the artist as productive of his science by discovery or instruction, notwithstanding the contrast between him and the artist in respect of the ends of their respective sciences. As art and nature are associated in the possession or exemplification of a rational principle (λόγος) and so contrasted to chance and the fortuitous, art and science are associated in their common derivation from instruction and their common dependence on a rational principle and so contrasted to the virtues which are acquired by habituation and involve a fixed character rather than explicit knowledge.

Since this double relation of art to science is formal, it is stated best by discriminating the two senses of "form" which are involved. In relation to the things on which it is employed art is the form as well as the principle of change,[28] and in respect of their

from their end. Now the end of productive science [ποιητικὴ ἐπιστήμη] is the work produced [τὸ ἔργον], of natural science the facts [τὸ φαινόμενον] as presented consistently and indubitably to sense-perception." Cf. *Nicomachean Ethics* i. 1. 1094ª1. In their efficient causes the two are so closely associated that "art" or "science" is used indifferently to cover both; cf. *Posterior Analytics* i. 1. 71ª11: "All instruction given or received by way of argument proceeds from preexistent knowledge. This becomes evident upon a survey of all species of instruction. The mathematical sciences and all other speculative arts are acquired in this way. . . ." Cf. "Mathematical arts," *Metaphysics* i. 1. 981ᵇ23; "demonstrative art," *De Sophisticis Elenchis* 9. 170ª30, 31; 11. 172ª28, 29. The similarity of the arts and the sciences with respect to their material cause, moreover, extends beyond their common concern with universals; cf. *Politics* iv. 1. 1288ᵇ10: "In all arts and sciences which embrace the whole of any subject, and do not come into being in a fragmentary way, it is the province of a single art or science to consider all that appertains to a single subject;" *Rhetoric* ii. 10. 1392ª26: "That things which are the object of any kind of science or art are possible and exist or come into existence"; *Metaphysics* xi. 7. 1063ᵇ36: "Every science seeks certain principles and causes for each of the objects of which it is science—e.g. medicine and gymnastics and each of the other sciences, whether productive [ποιητική] or mathematical."

[28] All the words signifying form which were associated with or equated to "power" (cf. above, note 13) are used to define "art," with the exception of "nature" to which art is in these respects being contrasted and analogized. For εἶδος, cf. *De Generatione Animalium* ii. 1. 735ª2: "For art is the principle and form [εἶδος] of that which is generated"; *Metaphysics* vii. 9. 1034ª23: ". . . thus the house produced by reason is produced from a house, for the art is the form . . ."; *ibid.* 7. 1032ª32: ". . . from art proceeds the things of which the form is in the soul of the artist"; *ibid.* 1032ᵇ9: "Then the motion from this point, e.g. the process towards health, is called a making [ποίησις]. Therefore it follows that in a sense health comes from health and houses from house, that which is with matter from that which is without matter, for the

Rhetoric and Poetic in Aristotle

subject matters, art, since it treats of change, is contrasted to science which treats of being and its invariable causes. Abstracted from subject matter, in the second place, art is a method which the scientist must seek, discover, and have (ἔχειν), and science, like every rationally directed pursuit, is an art in the sense of a method possessed and used, indeed each of the sciences has its peculiar method suited to its proper subject matter.[29] As method, art extends

medical art and the building art are the form of health and of the house"; cf. *ibid*. xii. 3. 1070ª13 and 4. 1070ᵇ33. For λόγος cf. *De Partibus Animalium* i. 1. 639ᵇ14: "Art is the reason [λόγος] of the work without the matter"; *ibid*. 639ª14: "For this is the reason [λόγος], and reason is the principle, alike in works of art and in works of nature"; *Metaphysics* xii. 3. 1070ª29: "For the medical art is the reason [λόγος] of health." For μορφή cf. *De Generatione Animalium* ii. 4. 740ᵇ25: "And as the products of art are generated by means of the tools of the artist, or to put it more truly by means of their movement, and this is the activity of the art, and the art is the form [μορφή] of what is made in something else, so is it with the power [δύναμις] of the nutritive soul."

[29] In the *Rhetoric* the artistic or technical method (ἔντεχνος μέθοδος) is contrasted to non-technical means of persuasion which do not belong to rhetoric; cf. *Rhetoric* i. 1. 1355ª4, where the "technical method" is used as a synonym for "rhetoric," and 2. 1355ᵇ35: "Of the modes of persuasion some are non-technical (i.e. are not proper to the art) and some are technical. By non-technical I mean such things as are not supplied by us but are there from the outset, such as witnesses, evidence given under torture, written contracts, and so on. By technical I mean such as are constructed by method and by us. The former has merely to be used, the latter has to be discovered"; cf. *ibid*. 1355ᵇ22. "Every art and method, like every action and pursuit, appears to be directed to some good"; *Nicomachean Ethics* i. 1. 1094ª1. Method (μέθοδος) means both (1) the way of inquiry and procedure in the arts and sciences, and also (2) the discussion according to method and therefore the discipline and doctrine itself or even the treatise in which the doctrine is expounded. In the first sense it is frequently used interchangeably with "way" (ὁδός). Cf. *Prior Analytics* i. 31. 46ª32 where μέθοδος refers back to ὁδός in 30. 46ª3; cf. *ibid*. ii. 1. 53ª2; i. 27. 43ª21; 28. 45ª21, 29. 45ᵇ37; *Posterior Analytics* i. 21. 82ᵇ29, 32; 23. 84ᵇ24. In the latter sense it is used as the equivalent to "subject of investigation" (πραγματεία). Cf. *Physics* viii. 1. 251ª5: "For the perception of truth concerning these things contributes not only to the contemplation of nature [τὴν περὶ φύσεως θεωρίαν] but to the investigation [μέθοδον] of the first principle"; *Metaphysics* xiii. 1. 1076ª8: "We have stated what the substance of sensible things is, first with respect to matter in the treatise [τῇ μεθόδῳ] on physics, later with respect to that which is actual"; *Topics* i. 2. 101ᵇ3: "For dialectic being a mode of inquiry has the way [ὁδόν] to the principles of all inquiries [τῶν μεθόδων]"; *Meteorology* i. 1. 338ª25; *Nicomachean Ethics* i. 7. 1098ª28; *Rhetoric* iii. 10. 1410ª8; *Poetics* 19. 1456ª36. For the discussion of many methods for many sciences each proper to the appropriate inquiry of its science, cf. *De Anima* i. 1. 402ª14; *Topics* i. 6. 102ᵇ39, viii. 12. 162ᵇ8; *De Sophisticis Elenchis* 11. 171ᵇ11; *Metaphysics* i. 2. 983ª23; 3. 984ª28; xiii. 9. 1086ª24; xiv. 3. 1091ª20; *Poetics* 1. 1447ª12, etc. The "manner" or "variety" (τρόπος) of the science or method is

beyond the limitations imposed by subject matter, and there are universal arts, like dialectic and rhetoric, which may be brought to bear on any subject matter and which may even pass over into the particular science if the method is rendered too specific to a subject matter.[30] In this dimension methods are to be distinguished from each other by the principles or convictions (πίστεις) on which they depend or the grounds on which those principles and convictions are established. The characteristics of the related methods may therefore be brought out by schematizing methods in a series of triangles, in which one method, that of inquiry into the results of actions, whether political institutions or art objects, constitutes art, and at the same time all methods are arts.

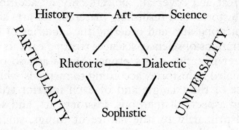

OBJECTIVITY

History ——— Art ——— Science

PARTICULARITY

Rhetoric ——— Dialectic

UNIVERSALITY

Sophistic

In this schematism all methods are universal in the sense that any subject matter may be treated by any of them, but their manner of application and their principles are different. Rhetoric and dialectic have no proper subject matter, but in virtue of the generality of their arguments and of the principles on which those arguments depend, they can be applied indifferently to any subject. While general in their application to all things and all subjects, rhetoric and dialectic base their arguments on the opinions of men. They differ from each other less in the details of the devices which both

---

used, in this sense as the synonym of the method of the science; cf. *Metaphysics* ii. 3. 995ᵃ17; *De Anima* i. 1. 402ᵃ19; *Prior Analytics* i. 31. 46ᵇ36. Finally, the term method is used to signify the treatise in which the results of the inquiry are set forth, as in *Politics* iv. 2. 1289ᵃ26; vi. 2. 1317ᵇ34.

[30] *Rhetoric* i. 1. 1355ᵇ7; 2. 1355ᵇ26. Cf. *ibid.* 1358ᵃ1 ff., where rhetoric is coupled with the dialectical method (διαλεκτική) of syllogisms and other arts (τέχναι) and powers (δυνάμεις) in contrast to sciences determined to particular subject matters; the inquirer who hits upon first principles as his premises makes (ποιεῖ) another science than rhetoric or dialectic.

use for proof and persuasion than in the generality of the opinions to which they appeal: dialectic depends on opinions which are thought to be universal, or common, or expert, or preferable in some other sense, while rhetoric consults the peculiarities of particular men, or groups, or circumstances. Sophistic is part of dialectic and rhetoric in the sense that both dialectic and rhetoric are concerned to differentiate real from apparent proof and persuasion; it differs from them in moral purpose and in its use of words.[31] Sophistic then is more general than other methods, in the sense that it is particularized neither by fixities of argument nor definitions of things, but depends entirely on the manipulation of words and the accidents of association unrestrained by concern to reproduce the opinions of men or to reflect the nature of things. Histories, arts, and sciences, finally, are particularized to the subjects they treat and cover all subjects only by addition, histories completing histories and furnishing materials for arts and sciences, arts supplementing arts and ordering the inquiries of history and the demonstrations of science, sciences treating each its appropriate subject matter in terms of its proper causes and so ordering the things assembled in histories according to methods which are arts.

Each base of the triangle and of each interior triangle indicates related aspects of methods. History, art, and sciences are determined primarily by the nature of things, since habits of thought and modes of expression are adapted in them to the requirements of their proper investigations among things. History as a method of inquiry concerning particular things includes both the collection of information about kinds of things, as, e.g., in the "history of animals," the "history of natures," and the "history of the soul," and the study of processes and actions, particularly those of men, which is in modern usage associated with history.[32] Art, which treats of actions

---

[31] *Rhetoric* i. 1. 1355^{b}15; i. 4. 1359^{b}12; iii. 2. 1404^{b}37; 1405^{b}8; 18. 1419^{a}13; *De Sophisticis Elenchis* 1. 164^{b}27 ff.

[32] *Prior Analytics* i. 30. 46^{a}24: "For if none of the true attributes of things have been omitted in the history, we should be able to discover the proof and demonstrate everything which admits of proof, and to make that clear, whose nature does not admit of proof." *History of Animals* i. 6. 491^{a}10: "Then we must try to discover the causes of these things, for it is thus that the investigation [μέθοδος] is conducted [ποιεῖσθαι] according to nature, once the history of the particulars has been completed, and from them it becomes clear what the subjects and premisses of the demonstration must be." Cf. *De Caelo* iii. 1. 298^{b}32; *De Anima* i. 1. 402^{a}4; *De Generatione Animalium* iii. 8. 757^{b}35 and 758^{a}3 where "historically" based inquiry (ἱστορικῶς) is contrasted to ignorance or

and productions, has a similar double application; it is a method for guiding the processes of action and production and also, in the case of art in the narrow sense, a method of investigating the product.[33] In both history and art there is an externality of thing and idea, for experience of things causes the ideas which constitute history, and the ideas of artist and statesman govern the actions of each in his appropriate subject matter, but in science that externality is removed, and knowledge and the known are identical.[34] The methods of the sciences are concerned with inquiry into being, into natures and changes and into quantitative abstractions. The complete history of any class of things would supply the principles for its scientific treatment, and conversely, correctly established scientific principles would apply to any instance or phenomenon disclosed by the history of such things. The particulars with which art is concerned are artificial things or, more generally, voluntary acts, and therefore the method of art both controls its appropriate history in the construction of art objects and grasps its appropriate causes, since the rules of action and construction attain a universality comparable to the laws of science. The statements of history thus are singulars, while those of poetry partake of the nature of universals, and poetry is therefore more philosophic and graver than history.[35] The methods lying on this base—history, art, and science—touch on existent things in modes which range from the particularity of things "better known to us" to the universality of things "better known in nature," and it indicates the relations involved in Aristotle's frequent appeals to constructive, inductive, and abstractive processes.

Apart from their application to things, methods may be constructed with a view to generality or with a view to the conditions of various possible applications. One of the two remaining bases of the triangle—science, dialectic, and sophistic—consists of methods of attaining and using general

lack of experience (ἀπειρία); *Rhetoric* i. 4. 1359ᵇ32. The term is frequently used in the sense of the history of human actions and in general narrative history of changes; *Rhetoric* i. 4. 1360ᵃ37; iii. 9. 1409ᵃ28; *Poetics* 9. 1451ᵇ3, 6; 23. 1459ᵃ21.

[33] *Poetics* 1. 1447ᵃ12; 19. 1456ᵃ36.
[34] *De Anima* iii. 4. 429ᵇ4 ff.; 7. 431ᵃ1; 431ᵇ16; 8. 431ᵇ20.
[35] *Poetics* 9. 1451ᵇ5.

principles or formulations which may take the place of general principles, and they are differentiated and treated as such in the last three books of the *Organon*.[36] The other base—history, rhetoric, and sophistic—contrariwise, derives its cogency or use from application to particularity: history by treating particular circumstances as its subject, rhetoric by suiting its arguments to the predilections of particular audiences, sophistic by relying on the apparent and genuine implications of particular statements. Within the large triangle, rhetoric, dialectic, and sophistic are related in their common concern with words and statements, and in the purpose of the rhetorician and dialectician to refute the fallacious use of words. Art, rhetoric, and dialectic are related in their common concern with men's thoughts;[37] history, rhetoric, and art in their common concern with men's actions and passions;[38] and finally art, dialectic, and science in their common concern with universals (sophistic being concerned with pseudo-universals, and rhetoric with statements that are probable or true for the most part).[39]

3.

In a broad sense, in which art includes all rational activity, even science, art is contrasted to nature as an efficient cause of change. In a narrower sense, in which art includes questions of practical action, art is contrasted to theoretic science as an activity of the soul. That narrower conception of art is susceptible of further specification in two steps, first by distinguishing ends and so differentiating the arts from the practical sciences, and secondly by distinguishing subject matters and so differentiating the particular arts from each other. The differentiation is progressive and at each stage likenesses as well as differences are involved; consequently the whole classification of the arts and sciences is reduced to confusion and contradiction if a single basis is sought for it, and Aristotle then seems to have confounded, in his distinctions, making with doing, art with

[36] *Posterior Analytics* i. 19. 81ᵇ18; *Topics* i. 1. 100ᵃ25 ff.; *De Sophisticis Elenchis* 2. 165ᵃ38 ff.
[37] *Poetics* 19. 1456ᵃ34; 6. 1450ᵇ4; *Rhetoric* i. 1. 1354ᵃ1; 2. 1356ᵃ30.
[38] *Poetics* 23. 1459ᵃ17; i. 1. 1447ᵃ28; 11. 1452ᵇ11; *Rhetoric* i. 2. 1356ᵃ14; ii. 1. 1378ᵃ19 ff. and in general chapters 2–11.
[39] *Poetics* 9. 1451ᵇ5; *Metaphysics* iv. 2. 1004ᵇ17 ff.; *Rhetoric* i. 2. 1357ᵃ22 ff.

science, and knowledge with nature.[40] Nature, power, and science—productive, theoretic, and practical—are all distinct; yet all powers proceed from nature, and the sciences are kinds of powers so interrelated that the theoretic sciences treat of the materials and faculties from which art proceeds and on which virtue is exercised; the arts are employed in the construction of all things made in accordance with reason, including scientific theories, political organizations, and moral plans; and finally politics pronounces on all permissible pursuits including the cultivation of arts and sciences, and the virtues include the arts and sciences in their number. Much as poetic power, taken in its broad sense as efficient cause, was delimited to "art" by differentiating two forms of power, rational and irrational, so art, taken in its broad sense as productive science, is narrowed to "productive" or "poetic" art by differentiating two varieties of final causes in which human action can be consummated: an object produced by the action or the action itself.[41] That contrast of ends and the correlative contrast of efficient causes constitute the difference between "making" and "doing," "production" and "action," between the productive sciences in the narrow sense and the practical sciences, for the actions per-

[40] Zeller (*Aristotle and the Early Peripatetics* [English translation; London, 1897], I, 180 ff.) summarizes the conclusions of Ritter, Brandis, Teichmüller, and Walter concerning this confusion in which two bases of classification are hopelessly intermingled, a two-fold classification into theoretic and practical sciences, and a threefold classification into theoretic, practical, and poetic. Cf. p. 180: "If we follow out the development of these principles in the Aristotelian system, and seek for that purpose to take a general view of the divisions he adopted, we are met at once with the unfortunate difficulty that, neither in his own writings nor in any trustworthy account of his method, is any satisfactory information on that point to be found"; and p. 184–85: "If, however, we attempt to apply the suggested division to the contents of the Aristotelian books, we run at once into manifold troubles." Cf. O. Hamelin (*Le Système d'Aristote* [Paris, 1920] pp. 81–89) who defends the threefold classification against Zeller, attributing his error to a "heretical" attachment to the primacy of the metaphysical doctrine of the four causes and that of potency and act.

[41] *Nicomachean Ethics* i. 1. 1094ª3: "But a certain difference is apparent among ends, for some are activities, while others are works [ἔργα] apart from the activities that produce them." *Politics* i. 4. 1254ª1: "Instruments so-called are instruments for production [ποιητικά], but a possession is an instrument for action [πρακτικόν]. Thus, something else is derived from the shuttle than only its use, whereas of a garment or of a bed there is only the use. Moreover since making [ποίησις] and doing [πρᾶξις] differ from each other in kind, and since both require instruments, the instruments which they employ must necessarily differ in the same manner."

formed by an agent are traced back to his character, choice, or will, while the products of art originate primarily in knowledge.[42] Art now appears in a third guise and context: as powers first are contrasted to powers, and in that context art is a kind of power; and as rational powers secondly are contrasted in nature and mode of acquisition to irrational powers, and in that context art is a kind of science; so, thirdly, the effects of those processes on the mind and on its future actions are contrasted to those transitory alterations which afford neither training nor habituation, and in that context art is a kind of habit (ἕξις).

Habits may be defined in terms of the two pairs of distinctions thus far employed: it is midway between activity and power, partaking of certain aspects of both, and it is midway between action and suffering. Like power it is a cause of action, but unlike a power a habit is not productive of contrary results; like actuality it is the principle and end of actions, for habits are the result of prior activity as they are in turn the principles from which actions originate.[43] Habits are therefore qualities of

---

[42] Since there are two sources of movement in man, namely, appetite and mind (cf. *De Anima* iii. 10. 433[a]9), the moral problem consists in good part of submitting the appetitive part of the soul to the rational (cf. *Nicomachean Ethics* i. 13. 1102[b]30; iii. 15. 1119[b]15). The problem of art, on the other hand, turns primarily on the application of knowledge to the organization of external materials, and therefore unlike virtue depends on the possession of knowledge and is capable of excellence; cf. *Nicomachean Ethics* ii. 3. 1105[a]27; cf. also *Metaphysics* vi. 1. 1025[b]22: "For the principle of production [τῶν ποιητικῶν] is in the producer—it is either reason or art or some power, while the principle of action is in the doer—viz. will, for that which is done and that which is willed are the same"; and *ibid.* xi. 7. 1064[a]11.

[43] The relation of habit to action and power in the analysis of Aristotle is well illustrated by his inquiry into the nature and cause of imagination, which begins by raising the question whether imagination is a power, habit, or activity (*De Anima* iii. 3. 428[a]1); "habits or powers" are there exemplified in the list, "sensation, opinion, science, understanding." Imagination is eventually defined as a kind of motion, and it is specified that motion makes it possible for its possessor to do (ποιεῖν) and suffer (πάσχειν) many things (*ibid.* 428[b]16). A power or science is related to contrary objects, whereas a habit which is one of two contraries does not produce contrary effects (*Nicomachean Ethics* v. 1129[a]13), and it is a bad error to confuse habits with activities or powers (*Topics* iv. 5. 125[b]15): "Again, consider whether he has reduced 'habit' to 'activity' or 'activity' to 'habit,' as, e.g. reducing 'sensation' to 'motion through the body,' for sensation is a 'habit,' whereas motion is an 'activity.' Similarly, also, if he has called 'memory' 'a habit retentive of a conception,' for memory is never a habit, but rather an activity. They also make a bad mistake who reduce 'habit' to the 'power' that follows habit . . ." Habits are produced from like activities

the agent, contrasted to dispositions which are less stable than habits, and to passions which are the consequences of the activity of an external agent.[44] The prime examples of habit however are the sciences and the virtues.[45] Art, as it was a power and a science in the previous classifications, is in this classification a habit and a virtue. It is a virtue of the rational part of the soul and of the rational part which is concerned with variable things and which is called calculative in contrast to the scientific part by which invariable causes are contemplated.[46] As in the case of all previous correlatives to which art has been contrasted, art is distinct from each of the other intellectual virtues and yet in a sense it is identical with or subordinate to each: it is subordinate, thus, to prudence, the other virtue of the calculative part, particularly in the form of statecraft which regulates arts like other powers exercised in the state, and excellence in art is an instance of wisdom which is the supreme virtue of the scientific part of the soul. By the same token, all the other virtues are arts insofar as they exercise a method of

---

(*Nicomachean Ethics* ii. 1. 1103^b21; 2. 1103^b30); conformity to habit is the end of every activity (*ibid*. iii. 10. 1115^b20); and a single habit may give rise to many activities, whereas a single activity can originate only its single proper habit (*Physics* v. 4. 228^a12). Habit is a kind of activity of the haver and the had, comparable in this respect to action, making, and motion (*Metaphysics* v. 20. 1022^b4), and even a privation may be a habit (*ibid*. 12. 1019^b6), although habit is also the contrary of privation (*Categories* 10. 12^a26); the kinds of good are activities and habits (*Nicomachean Ethics* vii. 13. 1152^b33).

[44] Habit is one of the kinds distinguished under the category of quality; and having is one of the categories as well as one of the so-called post-predicaments (*Categories* 8. 8^b27; 4. 1^b27; 15. 15^b17). All things are either substances or passions, dispositions, habits, or motions of substances (*Physics* ii. 1. 193^a23; *Metaphysics* xi. 3. 1061^a8). Habits may be natural (*Nicomachean Ethics* vii. 13. 1152^b34; 1153^a14); change tends toward nature, while invariable repetition produces a settled habit (*Rhetoric* i. 11. 1371^a26); and one kind of power is the habit of insusceptibility to change (*Metaphysics* ix. 1. 1046^a13; v. 12. 1019^a26). The genus of virtue is found by eliminating among the three things that virtue might be: passions, powers, or habits (*Nicomachean Ethics* ii. 4. 1105^b19), and the attributes of sensible things seem to be exhausted by habits and passions (*De Anima* iii. 8. 432^a6).

[45] *Categories* 8. 8^b29; *Politics* iv. 1. 1288^b17; *Nicomachean Ethics* vi. 3. 1139^b31; *Posterior Analytics* ii. 19. 99^b18, 25, 32; *De Partibus Animalium* i. 1. 639^a2; *Nicomachaen Ethics* ii. 4. 1106^a12; *Physics* vii. 3. 246^a10, 30; *Politics* i. 13. 1259^b25; ii. 6. 1265^a35; *Rhetoric* i. 6. 1362^b13; ii. 12. 1388^b34; iii. 7. 1408^a29. The two habits corresponding to the two parts of the soul, rational and irrational, are referred to as reason and appetite; *Politics* vii. 15. 1334^b17.

[46] *Nicomachean Ethics* vi. 2. 1139^a6.

construction or insofar as they are influenced by the arts or affected by knowledge.

4.

In a fourth and most particular sense, art and making is defined by the materials ordered and formed by means of the particular arts, and in that context arts are contrasted to arts. "Art" may be applied to what is artistic or to works of art, as "nature" is applied to what is according to nature and natural.[47] The terms "poetic" and "making" assume the sense of "poetry," as limited strictly to the art which makes use of words as its material and contrasted to prose as the alternative manner in which words might be used.[48] The enumeration of the arts at the opening of the Poetics is in terms of the concrete objects (τὸ σύνολον) which constitute the art, and so considered the arts are modes of imitation, analyzable like natural things which are also concrete objects, by means of their matter and form as well as by the cause of their generation, and the arts are therefore differentiated and classified in terms of differences in the means, object, and manner of their imitation.[49]

The schematism of the four causes determines a schematism of four senses in which art is treated in the works of Aristotle. Art enters into many interrelations with other things and processes, determining them and being determined by them, and it has many likenesses and many differences from the things which it is like. Art is a power like nature, in its first sense as a cause of change; it is an object like nature in its fourth sense as an object possessed of independent existence and intelligible characteristics. All arts may be analyzed as powers possessed by the artist, but that manner of analysis is particularly well suited to those arts, like dialectic and rhetoric, which have no proper

---

[47] *Physics* ii. 1. 193ª31.

[48] Both ποίησις and ποιητική are used in this strict sense throughout the *Poetics* and the third book of the *Rhetoric*. Cf., for ποίησις, *Poetics* 1. 1447ª10, 14; 1447ᵇ14 (where ποιεῖν is used in the restricted sense of "poetry"); 1447ᵇ26; 4. 1448ᵇ23, 24; 1449ª3, 23; 9. 1451ᵇ6, 10; 22. 1458ª20; 23. 1459ª37; 25. 1461ᵇ10, 11; *Rhetoric* iii. 1. 1404ª28; 2. 1405ª4, 34; 3. 1406ª12; 7. 1408ᵇ19; also *Meteorologica* ii. 3. 357ª26; *Politics* iv. 11. 1296ª20; v. 7. 1306ᵇ39. Cf., for ποιητική, *Poetics* 1. 1447ª8; 4. 1448ᵇ4; 6. 1450ᵇ18; 15. 1454ᵇ16; 17. 1455ª32; 19. 1456ᵇ14, 18; 25. 1460ᵇ14, 15; *Rhetoric* i. 11. 1371ᵇ7; iii. 1. 1403ᵇ25; 2. 1404ᵇ4; also *De Interpretatione* 4. 17ª6. The terms ποιητικῶς, ποιητής and ποίημα are used in the same restricted fashion, while ποιεῖν and τέχνη retain in the context their broader meanings.

[49] *Poetics* 1. 1447ª13.

subject matter, while only the fine arts can be defined and analyzed completely in terms of the characteristics of their products. Art is a kind of knowledge like science, in its second sense, generated from experience and conversant with causes; it is a kind of habit and virtue like prudence and wisdom, in its third sense, possessed of a permanent status consequent on practice and instruction. All arts may be treated in terms of the processes and materials of their generation, and the productive arts may be treated in terms of ends, not only the moral and political ends to which they contribute, but also the esthetic ends which knowledge of the practical and theoretic sciences may be made to serve. Art has, without necessity of confusion, all of these diversified significances: (1) it is a natural faculty or skill which initiates and guides production; (2) it is a psychological stage in education and a method in the development of knowledge; (3) it is, in the moral interpretation, a virtue or habit of the mind, an end of human activity, and an instrument of political action; (4) it is finally a class of objects to be known, judged, and appreciated. Relative to objects, "art" is applied to either the process of generation or the products for contemplation; both depend on knowledge, and as knowledge "art" is applied to the characteristic forms in which its materials may be assembled or the ideal ends which they may be made to serve. Art is a natural power and as such is subject for scientific inquiry, yet it is distinguishable, together with all processes that depend on reason, from natural powers by the possession of a rational form and method. Art is a science and as such involves knowledge and the exercise of reason, yet it is distinguishable, together with the practical arts or sciences, from science in the the sense of theory, since science has only knowledge as its end, while art and the practical sciences are directed to action or the results of action. Art is a virtue and as such a habit of the soul, yet it is distinguishable, like the virtues of the scientific part of the soul, from moral virtue since it is subject to analysis apart from the habits and ability of the individual agent. Art, finally, is a concrete object and as such analyzable in terms of form and matter, but unlike natural objects its form and definition are not determinate or natural but are determined ultimately not only by the potentiality of the artistic material but by the nature of the artist and the susceptibilities of the audience. Art is distinct from nature, and yet a natural power; it is distinct from science, and yet a productive science; it is distinct from virtue, and yet an intellectual virtue; it is distinct from natural objects, and yet a concrete object. Art has greater latitude of choice than morals, since the productions of the artist are not fixed by a natural end as are the actions of a moral agent, and it admits of less determinateness of knowledge than physics since the objects produced by art are not fixed by a natural form and therefore cannot be treated, like natural objects, in strict definition or scientific demonstrations. While art has all four general senses, it is treated most characteristically in the fourth and narrowest sense, for in that sense the arts are distinguished into particular arts composed of distinctive art-objects, and arts are compared and contrasted, as arts, with each other.

The treatment of the arts which results from the application of the four causes to their analysis is more elaborate and complex than the treatment of nature, because form and matter are separable in the arts—indeed separate arts may be concerned, one with the production of a matter, the other with its use—whereas function and end are inseparable from matter in the products of nature.[50] Scientific knowledge, therefore, is based ultimately on substance; physical definitions involve form and matter; and frequently only two of the four causes are distinguishable in nature. Art as knowledge is either identical with the power of the artist, or it is a science concerned with the products of the art. The power of the artist, which is indeterminate, is particularized in his person, situation, and materials, while the definition of the art is generalized from examination of the form and matter of its particular products. All four of the causes are distinguishable in art—indeed they are distinguishable in nature only by the analogy of art—and they enter in some fashion in fixing the matter of any discussion of art. Rhetoric, like medicine and political science, is defined as a power or faculty ($\delta\acute{v}\nu\alpha\mu\iota\varsigma$) while poetic is defined as a concrete object ($\sigma\acute{v}\nu o\lambda o\nu$). When arts are defined as powers, their mode of exercise or their use of rational principles rather than the outcome of their exercise is important, for success in the arts depends on matter and circumstance, and their ends are determined by another art. Arts like rhetoric and dialectic can be defined only in terms of power. When art is defined as concrete objects, the goodness or badness of their form and the success or failure of their devices rather than the rules followed for their construction are important. While the fine

[50] Cf. *Physics* ii. 2. 194ᵃ33.

arts may be considered in terms of the power of the artist or the potentialities of the matter, or in terms of their proper ends or further extraneous ends which they may be made to serve, or in terms of related ideas and methods, they may also be considered in themselves, as esthetic entities and as matter and form. Other arts fall between these two extremes: medicine, like rhetoric, is a power, but it has a proper subject matter; politics, like rhetoric and medicine, is a power and like medicine it has its proper subject matter, but it also embraces and determines the ends of the other arts.

III

Of all the arts there are two, dialectic and rhetoric, which are not confined to any class of subjects, and their treatment therefore is peculiarly dependent on consideration of the power from which they proceed. Since rhetoric is defined in terms of the power or faculty by which rhetorical arguments are perceived, it should be treated apart from consideration of any actual persuasion which it may produce, for art is characterized by its method, not its effects, and it may therefore be unsuccessful because of unfavorable circumstances, even when properly exercised.[51] In this, rhetoric is like medicine and all other arts,

[51] *Rhetoric* i. 1. 1355^{b}7: "It is thus evident that rhetoric is not of one separate class of subjects, but, like dialectic, is of universal application; also that it is useful; and further, that its function [ἔργον] is not so much to persuade, as to find out, in each case, the existing means of persuasion, as is the case also in all the other arts, for it is not the function of medicine to make [ποιῆσαι] the patient healthy, but to contribute as much as possible [ἐνδέχεται] to this, since even those whose return to health is impossible may be properly treated"; *Topics* i. 3. 101^{b}5: "We shall have the method [μέθοδος] perfectly, when we are in a position like that which we occupy in regard to rhetoric and medicine and powers [δυνάμεων] of that kind. This means to do [ποιεῖν] what we choose with the materials available [ἐκ τῶν ἐνδεχομένον]. For the rhetorician will not persuade by every method [τρόπον], nor will the doctor heal, but if he omits none of the available means, we shall say that he has the science [ἐπιστήμη] adequately." Cf. *ibid.* vi. 12. 149^{b}24 for criticism of a definition of rhetoric which depends on success in persuasion, and *De Anima* iii. 9. 433^{a}4 for specification that knowledge alone is insufficient to produce action according to knowledge. Rhetoric and medicine are used as examples to indicate the character of deliberation; *Nicomachean Ethics* iii. 5. 1112^{b}11: "We deliberate not about ends but about means. For a doctor does not deliberate whether he shall heal, nor an orator whether he shall persuade, nor a statesman whether he shall produce [ποιήσει] law and order, nor do the practitioners of any of the other arts deliberate about ends." The pursuit of an end in an art is infinite; it is delimited either by the means available or by the limitation imposed on the end by a

but it is contrasted to those same arts precisely in terms of the subject matter to which their powers and functions apply.[52] The ends of all arts are determined by the most authoritative art and science whose end is in the highest degree a good, the political art in the sphere of practical action and wisdom in general.[53] But the arts are also imitative and they may therefore be treated not merely in terms of the ends sought in what we do but in the characteristics of what is made. The technique of analysis relevant to art and the criteria to be employed in judging it are determined by these various forms under which art may be treated. First, art, though distinct from nature, is none the less a natural power, and as power exercised by the

superior art. This natural limitation of means and end is well illustrated by the "art of getting wealth" (χρηματιστική): it too is a poetic art (i.e., an art of making); it is defined, not in terms of the function of making money (much as the definition of rhetoric in terms of the power of persuading was avoided), but in terms of the power to discover whence wealth may be obtained; when it is made part of economics a limitation is placed on its end and it is a natural art, and as such is to be distinguished from the unnatural art of getting wealth in which no end or limit is imposed. Cf. *Politics* i. 9. 1257ᵇ5: "For this reason the art of getting wealth seems to be concerned chiefly with money, and its function [ἔργον] to be the power of considering whence there will be an abundance of wealth, for it is the art of making [ποιητική] riches and wealth. . . . (23) And the riches from this art of getting wealth are without limit. For just as in the art of medicine there is no limit to the pursuit of health and as in each of the arts there is no limit in the pursuit of their ends (for they aim to accomplish [ποιεῖν] their ends to the uttermost), but the means to the ends are not infinite (for the end in all cases is the limit), so, too, in this art of wealth-getting there is no limit to the end, but the end is riches of this sort and the possession of wealth."

[52] *Rhetoric* i. 2. 1355ᵇ26: "Rhetoric may be defined as the power [δύναμις] of observing in each case the available [τὸ ἐνδεχόμενον] means of persuasion. This is not the function [ἔργον] of any other art. Every other art can instruct or persuade about its own particular subject-matter; for instance, medicine about what is healthy and unhealthy, geometry about the properties of magnitudes, arithmetic about number, and the same is true of the other arts and sciences. But rhetoric we look upon as the power of observing the means of persuasion on almost every subject presented to us; and that is why we say that, in its technical character, it is not concerned with any special or definite class of subjects."

[53] *Politics* iii. 12. 1282ᵇ14; i. 1. 1252ᵃ1; *Nicomachean Ethics* i. 1. 1094ᵃ26; vi. 7. 1141ᵃ20 and esp. 28: "It is evident that wisdom and the political art are not the same, for if habituation concerning things useful to oneself is to be called wisdom, there will be many wisdoms; there will not be one concerning the good of all animals (any more than there is one art of medicine for all existing things), but a different wisdom concerning the good of each species."

artist is subject to strict scientific analysis. Secondly, art, though distinguished from natural powers by the use of reason, is none the less a poetic power, and such powers delimit appropriate fields of activity in which they constitute expertness; this is the reason why in rhetoric Aristotle's chief emphasis is on determining the "body"[54] of that which is essential to the art. Since the deliberation of art bears only on the use of means to achieve ends which are not themselves examined within the art, a third analysis is possible within the art of politics; and art, though not a moral virtue, is none the less a virtue and as such relevant to human happiness. Finally, art, as a mode of imitation, may be considered in terms of the actuality of the art-object as well as in terms of the power of the artist, for two "natural causes" are added to set art, conceived as a rational poetic power, in actual operation, a natural tendency in man to imitate and a natural delight in imitation; and the analysis of the objects of the fine arts therefore has an independence and completeness impossible in other arts which have indeterminate ends, for it turns not merely on powers or habits of artists nor on consideration of the materials susceptible of treatment or the "body" of the art, but it is concerned with examination of the form or the "soul" of poetic production.[55]

IV

The influence of Aristotle on later thought is complex, and any statement of that influence is involved in paradoxes illustrated in alternative interpretations of major shifts in the course of intellectual history as revolts against his outworn authority or as discovery of his forgotten methods. The story that his works were made inaccessible shortly after his death is plausible since there is little or no evidence of their direct influence. After they were rescued from the cellar in the Troad and edited in the first century A.D., only the *Categories* and the *On Interpretation* seem to have been available in Latin translation. The works of Aristotle were unknown in the West from the

[54] *Rhetoric* i. 1. 1354ª15. Since the enthymeme is the "body" of proof, the importance of "places" (τόποι) as "elements" (στοιχεῖα) of the enthymeme is apparent from the analogy to the elements of natural bodies; cf. *ibid*. i. 2. 1358ª35; ii. 22. 1396ᵇ21; 26. 1403ª17.

[55] *Poetics* 6. 1450ª38: plot is the principle and soul of the tragedy; 1450ª22: it is the end of tragedy; 7. 1450ᵇ23: it is the first and most important thing in tragedy.

third century B.C. to the twelfth century A.D., and as soon as they were translated during the twelfth and thirteenth centuries, they were subject to radical new interpretations, adjustments, and refutations. Since the Renaissance, his influence has been accommodated to the formula that the minds of men had been enslaved by his doctrines for two thousand years and that the rebirth of learning had been made possible by liberation from his authority in field after field. The errors consequent on his distinctions are so well-known that the analyses on which they were based and in which they were used have been broken into parts to be rearranged in chronologies of changes in the evolution of his doctrines and his styles: ten categories, four predicables (which became five after Porphyry and six after Avicenna), three figures of the syllogism (which became four after Theophrastus or Galen), four causes (which gave prominence to the final cause), natural and violent motion (which excluded the possibility of action at a distance or inertia), discrete and continuous quantities (which disjoined arithmetic and geometry), and he thought that there are substances and entelechies, and that slavery is natural and that art is imitation.

Yet the influence of Aristotle is not in question because of these paradoxes. On the contrary, the paradoxes provide a sure guide to the nature of his influence, and they suggest the reason for the particular influence of the *Poetics* and the *Rhetoric*. Aristotle was at pains to differentiate terms according to their meanings, and methods according to their subject matters. Philosophers who seek analogies rather than literal distinctions deny the separation because common properties are found in both the distinguished terms, or because one is a variety subordinated to the other. A single method can then be substituted for the plurality of methods.

If physics is concerned with natural motion, scientific generality will be achieved by a scientific method distinct from the method of dialectic, which finds generality in the opinions of men, and the method of sophistic, which encounters generality in the paradoxes of thought and expression. The beginnings of the study of local motion in modern physics derive more directly from the studies of "sophisms" concerning local motion[56] or from studies of propor-

[56] Curtis Wilson, *William Heytesbury, Medieval Logic and the Rise of Mathematical Physics* (Madison, Wis., 1956) is a study of Heytesbury's *Regule*

tions[57] and analogies (two translations of the single word, ἀναλογία) than from Aristotle's study of natural motions and natural places. If poetics is concerned with artificial objects, scientific objectivity will be achieved in the study of the nature and properties of a poem by a poetic method which seeks unity, necessity, and probability in ways distinct from those used in the historical method or the scientific method. The beginnings of the study of occurrences and actions in modern history, literary criticism, and physics depends on no such distinction: they are all poetic, or methods of discovery, but the method of discovery has been assimilated to common-places of rhetorical discovery.[58] Once that transformation has been made, Aristotle's influence and his shortcomings are both easy to understand: the study of the poem as a concrete whole and its classification in kinds determined by the object, means, and manner of imitation must be transformed into the study of the poem as the product of the creative art of the poet and as productive of its proper effects of pleasing, informing, and moving in an audience. Thereafter the vocabulary of Aristotle is readapted to the study of poetry in its circumstances and its influences as they are found in content and style. This redefinition of terms depends on *Rhetoric* rather than *Poetics*. Moreover the relation of form and matter is involved, for the "commonplaces" become themes, that is, matter, rather than

---

Solvendi Sophismata which treats local motion in one of its chapters. The chapter is entitled *De Motu Locali* in the edition of Venice, 1491.

[57] Cf. H. Lamar Crosby, Jr. *Thomas of Bradwardine, His Tractatus de Proportionibus, Its Significance for the Development of Mathematical Physics* (Madison, Wis., 1955).

[58] We have become so unaccustomed to recognize the use of rhetorical commonplaces that the term has taken on pejorative associations which deprive us of a useful instrument in the understanding of the use of concepts in physical theory. Niels Bohr makes a supple and shrewd use of them in "Quantum Physics and Philosophy: Causality and Complementarity," (*Philosophy in Mid-Century*, ed. R. Klibansky [Florence, 1958], I, 308–10): "The significance of physical science for philosophy does not merely lie in the steady increase of our experience of inanimate matter, but above all in the opportunity of testing the foundation and scope of some of our most elementary concepts. . . . A new epoch in physical science was inaugurated, however, by Planck's discovery of the *elementary quantum of action*, which revealed a feature of *wholeness* inherent in atomic processes, going far beyond the ancient idea of the limited divisibility of matter. Indeed, it became clear that the pictorial description of classical physical theories represents an idealization valid only for phenomena in the analysis of which all actions involved are sufficiently large to permit the neglect of the quantum. . . . by the word 'experiment' we can only mean a procedure regarding which we are able to communicate to others what we have done and what we have learnt."

sources of arguments, that is, organizing principles, and the "tropes" become figures of speech rather than modes of thought and being. The long history of the influence of Aristotle has rarely produced an "Aristotelian" dedicated to his diversity of methods, but the same history does suggest that there is a richness of method in his distinctions which might be used to modulate the modern cold war between the two unified methods which have been formed by reducing all methods either to the operationalism of a rhetorical poetics or to the organicism of a dialectical poetics.